La Buena Mesa

THE HIPPOCRENE COOKBOOK LIBRARY

Afghan Food & Cookery
Alps, Cuisines of the
Aprovecho: A Mexican-American Border
  Cookbook
Argentina Cooks!, Exp. Ed.
Austrian Cuisine, Best of, Exp. Ed.
Belarusian Cookbook, The
Bolivian Kitchen, My Mother's
Brazil: A Culinary Journey
Cajun Cuisine, Stir the Pot: The History
  of
Cajun Women, Cooking with
Calabria, Cucina di
Chile, Tasting
China's Fujian Province, Cooking from
Colombian Cooking, Secrets of
Corsican Cuisine
Croatian Cooking, Best of, Exp. Ed.
Czech Cooking, Best of, Exp. Ed.
Danube, All Along The, Exp. Ed.
Egyptian Cuisine and Culture, Nile Style:
English Country Kitchen, The
Estonian Tastes and Traditions
Filipino Food, Fine
Finnish Cooking, Best of
Germany, Spoonfuls of
Greek Cooking, Regional
Haiti, Taste of
Havana Cookbook, Old (Bilingual)
Hungarian Cookbook, Exp. Ed.
India, Flavorful
Indian Spice Kitchen, The, Exp. Ed.
International Dictionary of Gastronomy
Jewish-Iraqi Cuisine, Mama Nazima's
Kerala Kitchen
Laotian Cooking, Simple

Lebanese Cookbook, The
Ligurian Kitchen, A
Lithuanian Cooking, Art of
Malaysia, Flavors of
Middle Eastern Kitchen, The
Naples, My Love for
Nepal, Taste of
New Hampshire: from Farm to Kitchen
New Jersey Cookbook, Farms and Foods
  of the Garden State:
Ohio, Farms and Foods of
Persian Cooking, Art of
Pied Noir Cookbook: French Sephardic
  Cuisine
Piemontese, Cucina: Cooking from Italy's
  Piedmont
Polish Cooking, Best of, Exp. Ed.
Polish Heritage Cookery, Ill. Ed.
Polish Holiday Cookery
Polish Traditions, Old
Portuguese Encounters, Cuisines of
Punjab, Menus and Memories from
Romania, Taste of, Exp. Ed.
Russian Cooking, The Best of
Scottish-Irish Pub and Hearth Cookbook
Sephardic Israeli Cuisine
Sicilian Feasts
Slovenia, Flavors of
South Indian Cooking, Healthy
Trinidad and Tobago, Sweet Hands:
  Island Cooking from
Turkish Cuisine, Taste of
Tuscan Kitchen, Tastes from a
Ukrainian Cuisine, Best of, Exp. Ed.
Uzbek Cooking, Art of
Warsaw Cookbook, Old

La Buena Mesa

The Regional Cooking of Spain

ELIZABETH PARRISH

Hippocrene Books
New York

Interior color photography by Elizabeth Parrish.
Book and jacket design by Wanda España/Wee Design Group.

For more information, address:
HIPPOCRENE BOOKS, INC.
171 Madison Avenue
New York, NY 10016
www.hippocrenebooks.com

Library of Congress Cataloging-in-Publication Data

Parrish, Elizabeth, 1959-
  La buena mesa : the regional cooking of Spain / Elizabeth Parrish.
    p. cm. -- (Hippocrene cookbook library)
  Includes index.
  ISBN-13: 978-0-7818-1255-9 (hardcover)
  ISBN-10: 0-7818-1255-0 (hardcover)
  1. Cooking, Spanish. 2. Cookbooks. I. Title.
  TX723.5.S7P344 2010
  641.5946--dc22
                                        2010034507

Mixed Sources
Product group from well-managed
forests and other controlled sources
www.fsc.org Cert no. SW-COC-002283
FSC © 1996 Forest Stewardship Council

Printed in the United States of America.

For my grandmother, Vicenta Torcida Jiménez, and my mother, Belia Herrera Parrish, both of whom paved the way for me in and out of the kitchen, and for my son, Marc, a budding gourmand and enthusiastic little eater.

Amor fino y buena mesa no quieren prisa.
Neither good love nor good food will be rushed.

—Spanish proverb

CONTENTS

ACKNOWLEDGEMENTS

Throughout the many years that I have lived in Spain, I have always found Spaniards to be inordinately generous when it comes to sharing their cuisine. Were it not for the countless people who have guided and informed me, be it the waiter who explained the house specialty to me, the friend who allowed me to come into the kitchen while dinner's cooking, or the local vendors where I regularly shop, I would never have been able to write this book. I owe them all a debt of gratitude. I would also like to make special mention of the following people:

My editor, Priti Chitnis Gress, for giving me the opportunity to publish in the first place and for expertly guiding me every step of the way.

Barbara Keane-Pigeon, who did much of the copyediting on the manuscript, for her meticulous pen that makes me sit up straight, at least in writing.

Wanda España, for her lyrical design that just wraps around the text.

My good friends, Meg Holmes and Joan Samarra, who proved to be indomitable taste testers for quite a few of the recipes in this book and who on more than one occasion were subjected to strange menu combinations (*cocido* and *sangría*?), all for the greater cause of writing a cookbook.

My mother, Belia Herrera Parrish, sister, Margaret Parrish, and dear friend, Joie Samuelson, for their encouragement and support.

And last, but certainly not least, my son, Marc, for being such a good sport when it comes to trying new recipes.

INTRODUCTION

La buena mesa— literally, the good table—is a Spanish expression synonymous with fine food and drink. It doesn't take long for the visitor to Spain to realize that this is a country of good tables. Spaniards are passionate about eating well and enormously proud of their cuisines. I say "cuisines" because Spain is a fiercely regional country and each region has its own representative cuisine. Spain is made up of no less than nineteen autonomous regions. In case you're wondering or, even worse, have come up with eighteen regions and can't remember the nineteenth, they are *Andalucía, Aragón, Asturias, Cantabria, Castilla-La Mancha, Castilla-León, Cataluña, Ceuta, Comunidad de Madrid, Comunidad Valenciana, Extremadura, Galicia, Islas Baleares, Islas Canarias, La Rioja, Melilla, Murcia, Navarra,* and *País Vasco.* That's a lot of autonomy for a country that is about the size of Texas!

The traditional foods from these different areas have developed over time, influenced by history, climate, terrain, and availability of ingredients. The Iberian Peninsula has been crisscrossed by different groups of people, each leaving indelible culinary prints wherever they have settled, such as the Celts in Galicia or the Moors in Andalusia, to cite two examples. In fact, the Moorish influence on Spanish cooking cannot be underestimated. It's hard to imagine a Spanish kitchen without saffron or Christmas in Spain without marzipan. And what would Spanish cooking be without olive oil, first introduced by the Greeks and Phoenicians? Or tomatoes, potatoes, and peppers brought back from the New World? Over the centuries, Spanish cooks have masterfully brought together the best of these outside influences to create a richly varied cuisine that is uniquely their own.

Spain is not just hot and sunny and the rain definitely doesn't stay mainly in the plain, but in the north. Climates vary across the country and within regions. The same is true of soil and terrain. I live in Tarragona on the Mediterranean coast where snow is such a rare occurrence that when it happens it is remembered as the year in which we had snow on the ground for a few hours. However, just a few hours north, in the Pyrenees, the roads are sometimes blocked in winter due to heavy snowfall. These differences in climate inevitably affect the way people eat. In cold weather, warm, stick-to-your-ribs food is comforting, while lighter, more refreshing dishes have greater appeal when it's hot. The cooler, rainy northern coast of Spain has produced memorable meals-in-a-pot that would be unheard of in a warmer climate, while the south of Spain has given us that lovely liquid salad known as *gazpacho*, perfect when the mercury soars. The Mediterranean coast of Valencia is ideal rice-growing country and home to paellas in all their variety. Wheat fields stretch for miles across the austere Castilian plain where shepherds tending flocks of sheep are not an uncommon sight. It should come as no surprise that roast suckling lamb is the specialty there. Climate and terrain determine what can be grown which, in turn, determines availability of products. It's only natural for people to cook with what they have available to them and therein lies one of the secrets of Spanish cooking: the use of fresh, high-quality ingredients, many locally grown.

Apart from its regional character, I think that it is also possible to view Spanish cuisine from another angle, what I call traditional, avant-garde, and everyday cooking. Spanish chefs such as Juan Mari Arzak or Ferran Adrià have made heads turn with their innovative dishes, many of them based on traditional Spanish recipes. As someone who has eaten in Spain just about every day for quite a few years now, I can tell you that Spaniards don't eat elaborate traditional dishes on a daily basis. Few people have the time or budget to shop for, cook, and eat such emblematic fare seven days a week. This is not to say that these traditional foods or styles of cooking do not influence everyday cooking, because they do. What I mean to say is that instead of eating paella complete with expensive shellfish, one might have chicken and rice with a handful of shrimp or clams thrown in. It's still paella, it's still satisfying, but it's not a dish you would order in a restaurant or prepare for a special meal. What these two seemingly disparate styles of cooking have in common is that they draw heavily on traditional Spanish cuisine and it is this traditional cooking that I wish to reflect.

What I propose is a gastronomical tour of Spain beginning on the Atlantic coast of Galicia, continuing across the north along the Bay of Biscay, turning inland towards the Spanish plains, and then heading east to the Mediterranean Sea with a final stop in Andalusia. From the mainland, we journey to Africa, specifically to Ceuta, Melilla, and the Canary Islands. And lest anyone forget that all of these regions make up what is Spain, a look at dishes that know no region and yet are familiar to everyone: dishes such as Spanish Omelet or Chicken in Garlic Sauce that are common to all of Spain. As with all tours, there will undoubtedly be stops that we will miss. It is not my intention to create a complete catalog of each and every regional specialty, but to give an overview of some of the more emblematic dishes that each region has to offer. As with any journey, there is always the promise of a return trip.

Measuring, Spanish-Style

My maternal grandparents came from the northern coast of Spain, from the city of Santander. My grandmother was a fabulous cook, but like most Spanish cooks, she neither followed recipes nor measured her ingredients and, according to my mother, her recipes varied depending on whatever she happened to have on hand at the moment. This doesn't surprise me in the least as Spanish cooks are notorious for measurement terms along the lines of "a bit of this," "a pinch of that," and "a good spurt of olive oil." As far as I know, measuring cups and spoons do not exist in Spain. My mother is a wonderful American cook who measures everything down to the quarter teaspoon, something I simply can't fathom since I haven't met too many recipes that I don't tamper with in some small way. A recipe to me is little more than a guideline. It's someone pointing me in the right direction. While these recipes do offer measuring guides, they are albeit non-standard ones. When I cook, I use my coffee cup, which is the equivalent of one cup, the spoon I use to stir my coffee, and a soup spoon. I've written this cookbook with that measuring style in mind, so while you will see "cups," you won't see "teaspoons" or "tablespoons;" rather "small spoonfuls" and "large spoonfuls." I know it's not very sophisticated, but it does work and there are no fussy measurements or leveling teaspoons with knives. Nothing that I cook requires such precision. (Please note that I am referring to *slightly rounded* spoonfuls unless otherwise noted.)

Additional Notes for Using this Cookbook

A few other points to keep in mind when using these recipes: Unless otherwise noted, the eggs are large, the fruits and vegetables of medium size, and the herbs and breadcrumbs dried. That doesn't mean that you can't use fresh herbs, if you prefer. I just assume that most people don't have an herb garden readily available to them. Keep in mind that dried herbs are more pungent than fresh and you may need to adjust amounts where these are listed. The one herb I do use that is consistently fresh is flat-leaf parsley. In Spain, parsley is so common that they give it away for free! I buy my fruits and vegetables at a greengrocer's located around the corner from where I live. Every time I go in there—and that would be several times a week—the owner routinely stuffs a bunch of fresh parsley into my bag. In most recipes you will not see specific measurements for salt, pepper, or herbs. These ingredients are simply listed as part of the recipe. That is because I believe that cooks season their food according to individual taste, and just as I would not tell you to sprinkle a chicken breast that you're going to pan sear with exactly ¼ teaspoon of salt, I won't tell you how much thyme to sprinkle on that same cutlet. If when making Rotisserie Chicken, for example, you are particularly fond of thyme and pepper, then it is my supposition that you will load them on. I certainly do! If, on the other hand, you are not, you will go easy on the herbs and spices. It's up to the cook! Only in those cases where the dish requires a particularly heavy hand as regards seasoning, have I listed amounts.

Spanish Ingredients

One of the secrets to Spanish cooking lies in the use of fresh, seasonal products. I always look forward to sweet potatoes, chestnuts, pomegranates, and mushrooms in all their splendor come fall. In the spring, I am reminded of how long it's been since I've eaten fresh apricots and peaches. Late summer brings one of my favorite fruits— figs, with their rich, crimson flesh and delicate outer skin. The sea, just like the garden and orchard, also runs in cycles. As I write this, *bonito del norte*, the fillet mignon of tuna, is in season and available at my local fish market. Regional Spanish cooking moves with the seasons. There are also traditional Spanish dishes that you will only eat at certain times of the year, either because of availability of products or simply due to custom. For example, *turrón*, a nougat candy made with almonds, honey, and sugar, is associated with the Christmas holidays. It appears on grocery store shelves in October and by the end of January it has all but disappeared until the following Christmas.

If the ingredients are not top quality, what could be an extraordinary dish might seem mediocre—or worse, insipid and not worth eating—no matter how good the cook. Spain produces some excellent food products, from spices to wines, sausages to beans, and everything in between. Why they are not more readily available outside of Spain is a mystery to me. Products this good deserve to be known. It is my hope that once you sample Spanish products and become used to cooking with them, you will be as devoted a fan as I am of Spanish cuisine.

Below is a list of Spanish ingredients used in these recipes. Unless otherwise noted, all items are available online in the United States through **www.tienda.com**.

Aguardiente: *Aguardiente* or *orujo*, as it is also known, is a powerful liqueur that is particularly popular in Galicia. The word *aguardiente* is the Spanish contraction of *agua* (water) and *ardiente* (burning), which pretty much says it all. Sorry to begin my list with an exception, but as far as I know, this liqueur is not available through the folks at tienda.com. If you are unable to find a source for it, *grappa*, its Italian equivalent, is a suitable substitute.

Anchovies: In Spain, the best anchovies are said to come from Santoño in Cantabria. Spanish anchovies are packed in sea salt, filleted, and packed again in olive oil. They are sold in small tins or glass jars. The flavor is superbly balanced and I would strongly recommend their use in these recipes over other anchovies.

Bonito del Norte: A breed of white tuna fished from July through October by rod and line in the Bay of Biscay and, therefore, dolphin-friendly. In the case of canned *bonito*, it is cooked and packed in olive oil on board the fishing vessels to preserve the meat's firm texture and fresh flavor. Considered by Spaniards to be the finest, this is canned tuna in a league of its own.

Butifarra: *Butifarra* is the quintessential Catalan sausage. It is heavily seasoned with cinnamon, nutmeg, and cloves, spices not usually associated with meats in Spain, except when it comes to Catalan cooking.

Chorizo: A typically Spanish sausage that is heavily seasoned with garlic and sweet smoked Spanish paprika (*pimentón dulce*). The paprika gives chorizo its deep red coloring and distinctive flavoring and distinguishes it from chorizo sausages from other countries. Chorizo can be dry-cured or moist. Dry-cured chorizo requires no cooking or refrigeration. Simply slice it and serve as a tapa with cheese and wine. Its moist counterpart, however, must be refrigerated and is a common ingredient in many Spanish dishes.

Coarse salt: Most Spanish cooks keep a small ceramic salt jar or box on hand when cooking, as opposed to a salt shaker. That's because the salt they use is no doubt coarse. Coarse salt adds a unique flavor and texture to foods that you won't find if you use only fine salt. In the case of a dish where the salt is going to dissolve, it really doesn't matter if the salt is coarse or fine, but in the case of foods that have already been cooked, or for pan-seared fish, meat, or poultry, reach for the coarse salt. I keep both the fine and coarse varieties on hand, but use sea salt in both cases.

Serrano ham: A culinary masterpiece to be experienced, serrano ham comes in two guises: *jamón ibérico* (Iberian ham) and *jamón serrano* (cured mountain ham). *Jamón ibérico* is produced in the southwestern part of Spain. Iberian pigs, which are descended from wild boars, are allowed to roam stretches of forest and feed mostly on acorns. *Jamón serrano* is produced in the mountains of northeastern Spain from a cross of different breeds with the drying and curing processes occurring at high altitudes; hence the name *serrano* (from the mountains). Both *jamón ibérico* and *jamón serrano* are high-quality hams that are sweet rather than salty in taste. The best hams practically melt in your mouth they're so good. You can substitute Spanish ham's close cousin, Italian prosciutto, though serrano ham has a much deeper flavor and firmer texture than prosciutto. To get the optimal flavor from *jamón serrano*, serve it in very thin slices at room temperature.

Morcilla: This black blood sausage is a typical addition to Spanish stews. When sliced and grilled, it also makes a wonderful appetizer or accompaniment to fried eggs. There is also a rice version of *morcilla*, which is particularly popular in Castile.

Ñora pepper: Small, red, and stubby, these dried sweet peppers look something like wrinkled leather. They are a common ingredient in many rice dishes and stews, and lend an earthy flavor to dishes.

Orange flower water: Known as *agua de azahar* in Spanish, it is an extract made from the natural distillation of orange blossoms. It smells so lovely that I don't know whether to cook with it or bathe in it, though I must say, the taste is quite bitter. It is available through various gourmet specialty retailers. Some possible substitutes are: vanilla extract, orange extract, orange-flavored liqueur, or grated orange peel.

Pimentón: *Pimentón*, or smoked Spanish paprika, can be sweet and mild (*dulce*), bittersweet (*agridulce*), or piquant (*picante*). The mild climate and plentiful rains where the peppers are cultivated, together with the smoke-drying process, give Spanish paprika its unique aroma and flavor.

Pimiento: Pimiento is actually the Spanish word for pepper, though in the United States it has come to mean a red bell pepper that has been roasted, skinned, and seeded. They're so easy to make that it's hardly worth buying them, though it's not a bad idea to have a can in the cupboard, just in case. To make one pimiento, preheat the oven to 425° F. Wash and dry a red bell pepper. Wrap the pepper in parchment paper and place it in a shallow ovenproof dish (the pepper will give off its own juice during baking and some may leak). Bake for 50 to 60 minutes until the pepper has caved in and is soft to the touch. Peel off the skin and remove the seeds. Store the pepper in its own juice in a covered container in the refrigerator. It will keep for several days.

Pimiento del piquillo: *Piquillo* peppers are a variety of red pepper known for their intense red color, small size, and smooth yet meaty texture. Highly prized in Spanish cooking, they manage to be both sweet and deliver a bite at the same time. In Lodosa, a small town in Navarra, these peppers have been granted a denomination of origin.

Saffron: Saffron was first introduced into Spain by the Moors, who referred to it as *az-zafaran*, meaning yellow. The word was later incorporated into Spanish as *azafrán*. Saffron is considered the world's most expensive spice by weight simply because it must be harvested and processed by hand. The crocus flower (*Crocus sativus*) is picked and the stigma are carefully removed and roasted. Saffron comes in two forms: strands and powder. Buy the strand form simply because the powdered version is easier to adulterate. If you want powdered saffron, all you have to do is grind the strands using a mortar and pestle. Accept no substitutes for the real thing. Saffron not only contributes its unusual color to a dish, it also adds a unique flavor and only a small amount is needed.

Salt cod: Salt cod is simply fresh cod that's been cleaned and packed in sea salt to preserve it and is commonly found in supermarkets all over Spain. The gelatinous layer between the skin and the flesh make cod an ideal fish for creating sauces, and this fish is used in a number of traditional Spanish recipes. In order to remove the salt, immerse the fillets in a bowl of cold water (skin side up) and place in the refrigerator for 2 to 3 days. On the second or third day, change the water 4 or 5 times (anywhere from 30 minutes to several hours between changes) until the fish reaches the desired amount of saltiness. Note that the fillets will expand as a result of soaking.

Sherry: *Jerez* ("sherry" in Spanish) takes its name from the Andalusian town of Jerez de la Frontera from which it originates. There are different types of sherry, ranging from the very dry (known as *fino* or *manzanilla*) to the sweeter (*amontillado*) and the very sweet (*oloroso*). Sherry adds a uniquely Spanish flavor to foods. I'm particularly fond of homemade chicken consommé with a bit of *fino* added at the end. This is true comfort food on a cold winter's day!

Sherry vinegar: Spain is a wine-producing country so it's only natural that they would make a deep, intensely flavored vinegar from this emblematic wine.

Short-grain rice: When preparing paella or other Spanish rice dishes, it is important to use only short-grain rice if you want the dishes to retain their original texture and consistency. Special mention should be made of one particular variety of Spanish rice known as *bomba*. This rice is unique because it expands in width—somewhat like an accordion—rather than in length like other rice strains, and absorbs three times its volume in broth, as opposed to the regular two, resulting in particularly flavorful rice dishes and paellas.

Sidra: *Sidra* is a hard, dry cider typical of Asturias, but also produced in the Basque Country. It is used in cooking and drunk in much the same way as one would wine. It has a rich, golden color that is similar to beer, but with *cava*-like bubbles. In fact, the cork and closing on a *sidra* bottle are the same as what you would find on a bottle of *cava*. Watching someone pour a glass of *sidra* is a sight to behold. The bottle of cider is held in one hand and raised high above the head while a stemless glass is held in the other hand at hip level. The cider arches over the pourer's head and lands in the glass without a drop being spilled. *El Gaitero* ("the bagpiper"), a well-known manufacturer of *sidra*, is sold online in the United States. Dry white wine or *cava* can be substituted for *sidra* in recipes.

Tuna: *See Bonito del Norte*

White asparagus spears: White asparagus spears, many with a denomination of origin, are a star product of Navarra and highly prized in Spanish cooking. In order to obtain white asparagus, the spears are manually covered with soil as they emerge, thus shielding them from sunlight. In this way, they maintain their whiteness, as well as tenderness.

Chapter 1

THE ATLANTIC COAST: GALICIA

The interior of Galicia is lush and green as a result of heavy rainfall. The abundance of water colors the landscape and shapes the character of the people who inhabit these lands: hardworking, nose-to-the-grindstone, and humble in their outlook on life. The sea is a constant reference and a source of livelihood. It stretches inland in long, narrow, finger-like waterways called *rías*. On the Atlantic side, there is a stretch of coast with treacherous undercurrents known as "the coast of death" and the seabed there is littered with centuries' worth of shipwrecks. Nowhere is the sea's beauty and savagery more evident than in Finisterre, once believed to be the end of the earth.

The capital city of Galicia, and without a doubt its crown jewel, is Santiago de Compostela ("James of the starry fields"). Legend has it that Saint James spent his early ministry in Spain and was killed by King Herod upon his return to Jerusalem. His body was supposedly returned to Iria Flavia in Galicia in a rudderless boat without sails, and eventually his remains were buried in Santiago de Compostela. For this reason, Santiago has been a place of pilgrimage since the Middle Ages and, along with Rome and Jerusalem, is one of only three great pilgrimage destinations within the Christian world.

Galicia is a land shrouded in legend. When the fog hangs low, it's as if the very air were infused with an almost mystical quality, no doubt the legacy of its ancient Celtic origins, present even today: blond, blue-eyed Galicians, bagpipes, flaming *queimada* accompanied by chants, even the sing-song quality of people's speech. If the Irish are melodic in English, the Galicians are no less so in Spanish and Galego, the native language of Galicia.

Within Spain, Galicia is well-known for the quality of its seafood. I first learned to distinguish different types of fish in the markets of A Coruña. Being a U.S. Midwesterner, I was not accustomed to the wide variety of seafood there or to seeing the entire fish for sale and I can remember walking up and down the market aisles, amazed by the sheer variety and freshness of the products—many caught that same day—not to mention the wooden clogs that the fishmongers wore!

If the shellfish from Galicia is highly prized throughout Spain, the beef is no less regarded. The meat is exceptionally tender and flavorful, and must pass strict controls before it can officially be labeled as Galician beef. The same is true of potatoes or *cachelos* as they're known in Galicia. Or creamy cheeses, such as *Tetilla*. Or *Ribeiro* and *Albariño* wines. And don't forget the little green peppers from Padrón. The Atlantic diet has many devotees, not only for its health benefits, but for the gastronomic ones as well and if you sample Galician cooking, you'll know why.

APPETIZERS
Tapas

Steamed Mussels *(Mejillones al vapor)*
Octopus in Paprika and Olive Oil *(Pulpo á feira)*
Padrón Peppers *(Pimientos de Padrón)*

SOUPS
Sopas

Cream of Swiss Chard Soup *(Crema de grelos)*
Beef, Beans, and Swiss Chard Soup *(Caldo gallego)*

FISH AND SHELLFISH
Pescados y Marisco

Baked Scallops *(Vieiras de Santiago)*
Hake, Galician-Style *(Merluza a la gallega)*
Fillet of Sole in Albariño Wine Sauce *(Lenguado al Albariño)*

MEATS
Carnes

Ham with Greens *(Lacón con grelos)*
Beef Stew *(Ternera gallega estofada)*

BREADS AND SAVORY PIES
Panes y Empanadas

Tuna Pie *(Empanada de atún)*
Galician Rye Bread *(Pan gallego de centeno)*

DESSERTS AND AFTERNOON COFFEE
Postres y Meriendas

Almond Cake *(Tarta de Santiago)*
Crepes *(Filloas)*
Anise-Flavored Fried Pastries *(Orejas)*

DRINKS
Bebidas

Flaming Liqueur *(Queimada)*

Steamed Mussels

Mejillones al vapor

[4 servings]

Mussel farms are a common sight along the *Rías Baixas* in Galicia and I've enjoyed more than one plate of steamed mussels within full view of these *bateas* as they're called in Spanish. A mussel farm is a series of floating rafts with thick ropes suspended from each raft. The young mussels or seeds are attached to the rope and allowed to mature before being harvested. When mussels are this fresh, they require little more than lemon juice. You don't even need water to steam them as they will release their own, flavored with the very essence of the sea.

1 lemon, sliced	2 pounds medium mussels, cleaned*
4 bay leaves	1 lemon, quartered
2 large spoonfuls dry white wine	

Arrange the lemon slices and bay leaves in a saucepan or earthenware dish. Add the wine. Place the mussels on top of the lemon slices, being careful not to stack them too high or they won't cook evenly. Cover the saucepan or dish and place it over low heat until the mussels have opened. Discard any that do not open. Arrange the mussels on a serving platter with the lemon quarters and serve immediately.

Cook's Notes: To clean the mussels, cut away the "beards" using a sharp knife and scrub the shells with a clean steel-wool pad.

Goose Barnacles: A White Water Delicacy

One of the more curious examples of shellfish found in Galicia is the *percebe* or goose barnacle. It consists of a long, soft body—much like the neck of a goose—with a hard shell on top and a "foot" at the bottom that attaches to rocks and resembles a claw. These goose barnacles are savored for their lovely texture and flavor, comparable to crab or lobster. They can only be found in certain parts of the world and on rocks that are exposed to heavy surf, and therein lies the danger for those who harvest them. The job of *percebeiro* entails considerable risk as the *percebes* must be manually cut away from the rocks. Working in teams and outfitted in wet suits, the *percebeiros* use ropes to lower themselves into the sea when the tide goes out and scramble up the rocks when the tide comes in. It is a race against white water and those who lose get thrown against the rocks. Needless to say, *percebes* are an expensive delicacy, but rightly so in my opinion when you see the risk involved for those who collect them.

Like most first-rate seafood, *percebes* are cooked with as few ingredients as possible to preserve the natural flavors that come from the sea. There's no need for complicated recipes when the product is this fresh. If you are fortunate enough to find *percebes*, simply wash them in cold water. Put some water in an earthenware dish—but not enough to actually cover the *percebes*—add a pinch of salt, a bay leaf, and a few drops of white wine. When the water begins to boil, add the *percebes*. They're finished cooking when the water starts boiling again, unless they're particularly large, in which case you might need to let them cook a minute or two more. Drain and cover with a cloth. The steam will help loosen the shells so that they're easier to peel. Serve with an *Albariño* wine and enjoy!

Octopus in Paprika and Olive Oil

Pulpo á feira

[4 servings]

Pulpo á feira in the Galician language takes its name from the custom of serving this dish during traditional fairs. The octopus is cooked in boiling water to tenderize its meat and served on round wooden boards where it is seasoned with *pimentón*, coarse salt, and olive oil. It makes a wonderful tapa with toothpicks inserted in each octopus slice.

1 octopus (approximately 1½ pounds)	*Pimentón dulce* (sweet Spanish paprika)
2 bay leaves	*Pimentón picante* (piquant Spanish paprika)
Extra virgin olive oil for drizzling	Coarse salt

To clean the octopus, cut out the eyes and mouth (located at the center of the body where the tentacles meet the head), remove the entrails, and rinse well.

Put a large pot of salted water with 2 bay leaves on to boil. When the water reaches the boiling point, submerge the octopus in the water and remove it immediately. Repeat twice. Return the octopus to the pot and gently cook for 20 to 25 minutes. Turn the heat off and let the octopus sit for 5 minutes.

Remove the octopus from the water and cool. Remove any loose skin and cut into bite-size pieces using kitchen scissors. Arrange on a wooden board. Drizzle with olive oil. Sprinkle with *pimentón dulce*, *pimentón picante*, and coarse salt. Do not stir. Serve at room temperature.

Cook's Notes: When preparing octopus, it is important not to overcook it. Octopus meat is tough and requires a few tricks (some rather unorthodox) to tenderize it. To begin with, the smaller the octopus, the more tender, so avoid larger ones. Another suggestion: Hurl it into the sink a dozen or so times (this would be the "unusual" tip). If you wish to avoid this last tip, freeze the octopus for at least 48 hours after it's been cleaned. Freezing and thawing help to break down some of this octoped's tough fibers. And finally, when you go to cook the octopus, put it into boiling—never cold—water.

Padrón Peppers

Pimientos de Padrón

[4 servings]

Pimientos de Padrón, as the name implies, come from the area of Padrón in Galicia, specifically the town of Herbón. They are a distant cousin of the jalapeño pepper and were introduced to Galicia by Franciscan monks from Herbón around the sixteenth or seventeenth century. They are small, cone-shaped, and bright emerald green. When they are sweet, they are very, very sweet, but when they are hot, well . . . that's part of their charm too. Sort of a culinary Russian roulette. You simply never know when you're going to bite into a hot pepper. The ratio is about one in ten and there are a multitude of theories as to which peppers will be hot and what makes the peppers hot, but the truth of the matter is that no one really knows until they bite into the pepper. In fact, I find that the pepper is usually halfway down my throat before I realize that, uh oh, I've bitten into a hot one!

---

1 pound Padrón peppers	Coarse salt
½ cup extra virgin olive oil	

Wash the peppers and dry them thoroughly to prevent splattering. Heat the olive oil in a skillet or earthenware dish over medium heat. Add the peppers and stir them until they begin to wrinkle, turn brown, and the clear outer skin separates from the pepper. Drain and sprinkle with coarse salt. Serve immediately. To eat, simply pick the individual pepper up by the stem.

Cook's Notes: Typically these peppers are served as a tapa, but they also make a nice accompaniment to meat, chicken, and fish—even Spanish Omelet (page 222).

Cream of Swiss Chard Soup

Crema de grelos

[4 servings]

Grelos are the tender leaves of the turnip plant and a common ingredient in Galician cooking. Outside of Galicia, though, they can be rather difficult to find, even in the rest of Spain, which is why I've used Swiss chard instead. Typically this soup is made with water or vegetable broth and onion. I find that the flavor is much richer if you use chicken broth, and as for the onion, I prefer its less pungent cousin, the leek. Admittedly, the cheese wedges aren't terribly traditional; however, they are a common ingredient in everyday Spanish *cremas* and, quite frankly, the soup tastes better with them, which is what matters in the end!

4 large spoonfuls extra virgin olive oil plus additional for frying croutons	4 "The Laughing Cow" original creamy Swiss cheese wedges
2 leeks, white part only, coarsely chopped	Salt
2 potatoes, peeled and cut in bite-size pieces	6 baguette slices, ½-inch thick
1 pound Swiss chard, thick stems removed	2 thin slices serrano ham, trimmed and cut in strips
2 cups chicken broth (page 67)	

Sauté the leeks in 2 large spoonfuls of olive oil until tender. Stir in the potatoes, being sure to coat them well with the oil. Add the Swiss chard, along with the chicken broth, and bring to a boil. (Don't worry that the liquid doesn't cover the Swiss chard in the beginning. As it wilts, it will gradually blend in with the broth.) Lower the heat, cover, and cook for 20 minutes. Add the remaining 2 spoonfuls of olive oil, along with the cheese wedges, and blend with an immersion blender until smooth and creamy. Adjust the salt, if necessary.

To make the croutons, simply cut the baguette slices into cubes and fry until golden brown in olive oil. Ladle the *crema* into individual soup bowls, top with the croutons and strips of serrano ham, and serve.

Cook's Notes: Sautéing the vegetables before boiling them in the chicken broth creates a more flavorful soup.

Beef, Beans, and Swiss Chard Soup

Caldo gallego

[6 servings]

In less advantageous times, Galicians had to seek their fortunes far from home and traditional dishes such as this *caldo gallego* accompanied them on their journeys. Years ago when I lived in New York City, I rented an apartment in what was a predominately Latin neighborhood. To my surprise there was a Galician restaurant on the corner. The owner was a *Gallego* who served up typical Galician fare, along with Latin American specialties. Whenever people came to visit me, I invariably took them there for a bowl of *caldo* and a glass of *Albariño* wine.

 START PREPARATION 1 DAY IN ADVANCE.

1 cup dried white beans, rinsed	1 leek, white part only, thoroughly washed,
½ pound beef chuck	quartered
½ pound pork ribs	Salt
¼ pound salt pork or slab bacon	Freshly ground black pepper
1 chorizo sausage	2 potatoes, peeled and cut in bite-size pieces
1 ham bone	½ pound Swiss chard, thick stems removed
1 onion, quartered	and coarsely chopped

Soak the dried white beans in cold water overnight.

Place the beans, beef, pork ribs, salt pork, chorizo, ham bone, onion, leek, salt, and pepper in a large saucepan, along with 8 cups water. Bring to a boil and skim off the foam that forms on the surface. Cover and simmer for 2 hours until the beans are tender. Check the beans periodically to make sure that there's enough water and cut the boil with ¼ cup cold water 3 times during cooking to tenderize the beans.

Add the potatoes and Swiss chard, and continue cooking for another 30 minutes. Adjust the salt, if necessary. Serve in large soup bowls. Be sure to include the different meats, beans, potatoes, and Swiss chard in each serving.

Cook's Notes: For a soup that is low in saturated fats but high in flavor, prepare according to the recipe, then strain the broth, cool, and refrigerate. Degrease the broth and "reunite" it with the other ingredients minus the salt pork and ham bone.

Baked Scallops

Vieiras de Santiago

[4 servings]

The scallop shell is the official symbol of the *Camino de Santiago* (St. James' Way) and can be found on signs along the route pointing the pilgrim in the direction of Santiago de Compostela. Like most symbols, it comes complete with its own legend. The story goes that a devout knight on horseback was riding along the beach when he spotted the boat carrying the remains of St. James. Without hesitating, he began to gallop over the surface of the water, but, of course, this was not possible and both horse and rider sank beneath the waves. St. James miraculously pulled the knight out of the water—covered in scallop shells—and, one would hope, his trusty steed too.

In Galicia, these scallops are presented baked in the shell itself. Given that scallop shells can be rather difficult to come by, I would suggest using small individual earthenware ramekins instead. And if you do visit Galicia, be sure to try the scallops—and save the shells. They're so commonplace in Galicia, that I've even seen them used as ashtrays and soap dishes!

1 pound sea scallops	¼ cup dry white wine
Juice of ½ lemon	Salt
4 large spoonfuls extra virgin olive oil	Freshly ground black pepper
1 small onion, chopped	1 large spoonful minced flat-leaf parsley
1 clove garlic, minced	4 large spoonfuls breadcrumbs
2 thin slices serrano ham, trimmed and minced	

Preheat the oven to 400° F. Sprinkle the sea scallops with lemon juice and reserve.

Place the olive oil in a small sauté pan or skillet. Add the onion and garlic, and cook until tender. Add the ham and cook for another minute. Stir in the wine and cook for a few minutes. Season with salt, pepper, and parsley. Remove from the heat and stir in the breadcrumbs.

Arrange the scallops in individual, greased ramekins or scallop shells. Top with the breadcrumb mixture. Bake for 15 minutes and serve.

Cook's Notes: Scallops are active swimmers, propelling themselves through the water by opening and closing their shells. Since they cannot survive out of water, they are usually shucked from their shells on board the fishing boat, making it difficult to buy fresh scallops with their shells. There are two kinds of scallops: the smaller bay scallop, found in bays, and the larger sea scallop. Bay scallops can easily be substituted for sea scallops in this recipe.

Hake, Galician-Style

Merluza a la gallega

[4 servings]

The term *a la gallega* means that the dish has been prepared with Spanish paprika and olive oil. While Spanish cooking shows a great predilection for *pimentón*, nowhere is it used in more abundance than in Galicia.

5 large spoonfuls extra virgin olive oil
2 onions, thinly sliced
4 potatoes, peeled and cut in ¼-inch slices
1 bay leaf
Salt
2 cloves garlic, minced

1 small spoonful *pimentón dulce* (sweet Spanish paprika)
1 large spoonful all-purpose flour
¼ cup dry white wine
4 hake steaks (approximately 6 ounces each and 1-inch thick)
2 large spoonfuls minced flat-leaf parsley

In a large skillet, gently sauté the onion in 4 large spoonfuls of olive oil until golden brown. Place the potato slices and bay leaf on top of the onions. Season with salt. Add just enough water to cover the potatoes. Cover and cook over low heat for 20 minutes.

In a separate small skillet, gently sauté the minced garlic in the remaining spoonful of olive oil. Remove the skillet from the heat and stir in the paprika, flour, and wine. Stir this mixture into the potatoes, being sure to coat them well.

Salt the hake steaks and sprinkle with parsley. Place on top of the potatoes. Cover and cook for 5 to 7 minutes on each side. To serve, place the hake and potatoes on individual plates and spoon some of the sauce over the top.

Cook's Notes: Spanish paprika burns rather easily. It's always a good idea to remove the pan from the heat before adding it to a dish.

Fillet of Sole in Albariño Wine Sauce

Lenguado al Albariño

[4 servings]

In small amounts, wine is used to highlight and enhance food's natural flavor, and in larger amounts, to create distinctive sauces. Regional dishes demand regional wines, such as the lovely and, until recently, relatively unknown Albariño wine from Galicia.

The albariño grape is cultivated along the shores of the *Rías Baixas*, long, fjord-like estuaries that jut into the landscape. It is the only grape used to produce *Rías Baixas* denomination of origin Albariño wine, a dry, fruity wine that is the perfect accompaniment to the seafood that comes from these same waters. It's no wonder that Albariño wines have been nicknamed "wines of the sea."

4 soles (approximately ½ pound each) or
   1 to 1½ pounds sole fillets
16 large shrimp, in their shells

FISH BROTH:
Reserved fish heads and bones
Reserved shrimp heads
1 carrot, scraped and cut in several pieces
1 leek, white part only, cut in several pieces
1 clove garlic, peeled
1 sprig flat-leaf parsley
1 bay leaf
Salt

SAUCE:
2 large spoonfuls extra virgin olive oil
1 small onion, chopped
2 cloves garlic, minced
2 large spoonfuls all-purpose flour
¾ cup reserved fish broth
¾ cup Albariño wine
Salt
Freshly ground black pepper
2 cups thinly sliced white button
   mushrooms
¾ cup heavy cream
2 egg yolks

SOLE FILLETS:
Juice of ¼ lemon
Salt
All-purpose flour for dusting
4 large spoonfuls extra virgin olive oil
1 large spoonful minced flat-leaf parsley

(continued on next page)

Fillet of Sole in Albariño Wine Sauce *(continued from previous page)*

When buying the sole, ask your fishmonger to fillet the fish and to reserve the bones and heads (for making the fish broth). Clean and peel the shrimp, reserving the heads for the fish broth.

Make the broth: Place the fish heads and bones, along with the shrimp heads, the carrot, leek, garlic, parsley, bay leaf, salt, and 1 cup water in a saucepan. Bring to a boil, lower the heat, cover, and gently cook for 30 minutes. Strain the broth and reserve ¾ cup.

Make the sauce: Sauté the peeled shrimp, onion, and garlic in olive oil until the onion is tender. Remove the shrimp and reserve. Stir in the flour and gradually add the fish broth, wine, salt, and pepper. Add the mushrooms and simmer uncovered.

While the sauce is simmering, prepare the fish fillets: Sprinkle them with lemon juice and lightly salt. Dust the fillets with flour and fry them in olive oil until they are golden brown on both sides. Put on a platter along with the shrimp.

Mix the cream and egg yolks for the sauce. Gradually stir in a small amount of the wine sauce, return this mixture to the pan, and cook for 1 to 2 minutes. Pour the sauce over the fish, sprinkle with parsley and serve. Obviously, an Albariño wine is the perfect accompaniment to this dish.

Cook's Notes: In Spain, fish is sold whole and then prepared to order by the fishmonger. I realize that this is not always the case in the United States. If you are unable to buy an entire sole or shrimp in their shells, follow the recipe for fish broth in Catalan Fish Stew, page 136.

Ham with Greens

Lacón con grelos

[4 servings]

Lacón con grelos, along with *caldo gallego*, are perhaps the most well-known Galician dishes. Traditionally, ham with greens is served during carnival in a meal known as a *laconada*, a sort of "meat fest" before the onset of Lent.

1½ pounds *lacón* (smoked or salted pork hocks)
Freshly ground black pepper
4 chorizo sausages
1 pound Swiss chard, thick stems removed

2 potatoes, peeled and cut in bite-size pieces
1 small spoonful *pimentón dulce* (sweet Spanish paprika)
Salt

If the pork hocks are salty, soak them in cold water for 8 hours. Once soaked, place the *lacón* in an earthenware dish and cover with cold water. Season with pepper. Bring to a boil, reduce the heat, cover, and simmer for an hour.

While the *lacón* is cooking, degrease the chorizo sausages as you would for Lentils with Chorizo Sausage (page 72), and reserve.

Add the Swiss chard to the *lacón*. When the broth begins to boil again, add the potatoes. Dissolve the *pimentón* in a small amount of broth and return to the dish along with the chorizo. Continue cooking until the potatoes are tender, about 20 minutes. Salt to taste.

To serve, arrange the *lacón*, chorizo, potatoes, and Swiss chard on a platter and spoon some of the broth over the meats.

Cook's Notes: Typically this dish is served with just enough broth to moisten the other ingredients; however, true to the waste-not-want-not philosophy of Spanish cooking, the remaining broth gets put to good use too! It is either strained and served as a consommé or turned into a soup with the addition of noodles.

● *La Cazuela:* Spanish Earthenware

It is impossible to imagine Spanish cooking without the *cazuela* or earthenware dish. This basic cooking utensil was first introduced by the Romans and continues strong to this day. A *cazuela* is as simple as clay and water that has been shaped, fired, and glazed. Sizes range from the small, one-serving ramekin to a large, heavy, round piece of cookware that practically requires two burners for heating, though the classic everyday *cazuela* present in Spanish kitchens holds enough food for four to six servings. It is also possible to buy oval and rectangular terracotta baking dishes, as well as serving dishes, plates, cups, mugs, pitchers, bowls, and decorative pieces.

In Spain, *cazuelas* are typically sold in hardware stores, in any shop that carries cookware, and in street markets. Before you can use your *cazuela*, however, it must first be treated to seal the pores and prevent cracking. Begin by soaking it in water overnight. Dry well and rub the unglazed bottom with a garlic clove, followed by olive oil. Use a paper towel to wipe away the excess oil. Fill the *cazuela* almost to the top with water and add a good squirt of vinegar. Slowly bring the water to a boil. Let it boil until almost all of the water has evaporated. Wash your *cazuela* and it's ready to use! Avoid brusque changes in temperature, which could cause cracking, and heat the earthenware gradually. Eventually, terracotta will crack, but if cared for, it should last for a few years.

Spanish cooks swear by their *cazuelas* and you don't have to prepare many dishes in them to see why. Earthenware heats evenly and retains warmth long after the dish has finished cooking. It works equally well with a sizzling tapa as with a cool *gazpacho* or custard. It's highly flexible in the sense that you can cook with it on your stovetop, transfer it to the oven, and place it on the table. Spanish cooks will even tell you that food tastes better cooked in earthenware. Perhaps the earthenware retains the memory of foods savored and enjoyed. Whatever the reason, the aesthetics of eating with earthenware only enhance the culinary experience. Imagine *sopa de ajo* in an earthenware bowl, sizzling garlic shrimp in individual earthenware ramekins, or thick Spanish-style hot chocolate in a clay mug. Great food can only taste better when it is served in cookware with this much history and tradition behind it.

Beef Stew

Ternera gallega estofada

[4 servings]

The traditional style of slow cooking over low heat produces tender, more fla-vorful meat and, as food is not subjected to high temperatures, preserves nu-trients. The combination of locally-raised meat—in this case Galician beef and vegetables—makes for a very complete dish. All that's needed to round out this meal is a salad, good crusty bread for sopping up the sauce, a bold red wine, and a scrumptious dessert.

4 large spoonfuls extra virgin olive oil
1 pound beef for stew, such as chuck, cut in
  bite-size pieces
Salt
Freshly ground black pepper
1 bay leaf
2 carrots, scraped and chopped
1 onion, chopped
2 cloves garlic, minced

1 cup sliced white button mushrooms
4 large spoonfuls tomato sauce (page 119)
1 cup peas, fresh or frozen
2 potatoes, peeled and cut in bite-size
  pieces
1 cup dry white wine
½ cup beef broth (see next page)
1 large spoonful cornstarch

Heat the olive oil in an earthenware dish or large saucepan. Salt and pepper the beef and gently sauté in olive oil, along with the bay leaf.

Start chopping the vegetables and add them to the saucepan in the order listed: first, the chopped carrots, then the onion and garlic, and finally the mushrooms. Stir the meat and vegetables from time to time. Total cooking time will be about 10 minutes.

At this point, add the tomato sauce and cook for a few minutes and then add the peas, potatoes, wine, and beef broth. Cover and simmer for 35 to 40 minutes. Dis-solve 1 large spoonful of cornstarch in ¼ cup water. Add to the stew and cook for a few more minutes until the broth thickens. Adjust the salt, if necessary.

(continued on next page)

Beef Stew *(continued from previous page)*

Beef Broth

[8 cups]

This is my standard recipe for beef broth.

2 beef bones	1 turnip, halved
2 pounds bony cut of meat, such as short ribs or oxtail	1 parsnip, halved
	2 sprigs flat-leaf parsley
2 carrots, scraped and cut in several pieces	2 bay leaves
2 leeks, white part only, cut in several pieces	1 small spoonful thyme
1 celery rib, cut in several pieces with a few leaves remaining	1 small spoonful black peppercorns
	1 small spoonful salt
1 large onion, quartered	

Place all the ingredients in a large pot, along with 10 cups water. Bring to a boil and skim the foam off the top. Lower the heat, cover, and simmer for 4 hours. Strain the broth. Cool and place in the refrigerator. Skim off any fat that has hardened on the surface before using.

Cook's Notes: This stew is a great make-ahead dinner because it actually tastes even better the following day.

Tuna Pie

Empanada de atún

[6 servings]

Empanadas are highly versatile in the sense that they can be made with pork, cod, tuna, sardines, shellfish, or vegetables. In the case of sardine pies, the dough also varies and is made with cornmeal. Regardless of what you use for your filling though, there are still three basic steps involved in making these savory pies. The first is to make the *sofrito*. You will need it for both the dough and the filling. Next comes the dough. And while the dough is rising, the filling.

 START PREPARATION SEVERAL HOURS IN ADVANCE.

SOFRITO:
¾ cup mild extra virgin olive oil
2 onions, thinly sliced
1 green bell pepper, cut in julienne strips
2 cloves garlic, minced

FILLING:
1 (7-ounce) can light tuna, preferably *bonito del norte* tuna
4 large spoonfuls tomato sauce (page 119)

DOUGH:
4 cups all-purpose flour
Pinch salt
1 small spoonful dry yeast
1 small spoonful *pimentón dulce* (sweet Spanish paprika)
1 cup warm water
½ cup oil (from the *sofrito*)
1 egg, beaten

Make the *sofrito*: Gently sauté the onions, pepper, and garlic in olive oil until tender. Reserve ½ cup of the oil for the dough.

Make the filling: Add the tuna and tomato sauce to the sofrito. Set the filling aside to cool before spreading it on the dough or you could end up with a soggy empanada.

Make the dough: Mix the dry ingredients together in a bowl. With a wooden spoon, gradually stir in the warm water and reserved oil. Turn the dough onto a floured surface and knead until elastic, but not sticky, adding more flour, if necessary. Place the dough in a greased bowl, turning once, cover, and let rest in a warm place for an hour.

(continued on next page)

Tuna Pie *(continued from previous page)*

Preheat the oven to 425° F. Divide the dough in half. Roll each half into two rectangles about ½-inch thick. Place the bottom rectangle of the *empanada* on a greased cookie sheet. Top with the filling, leaving a 1-inch border all the way around. Use a brush to paint the border of the dough with the beaten egg. (The egg acts like glue to keep the dough together.) Cover with the other piece of dough. Seal the edges and prick the dough to allow the air to escape. You can also decorate the top of the *empanada* with any scraps of dough that you have left over. Simply cut the leftover dough in strips and place on top to form squares (like a tic-tac-toe board). Paint the top of the *empanada* with the beaten egg. Bake for 20 to 25 minutes until the dough is a golden brown color. Cool before serving or serve at room temperature. Cut in squares.

Cook's Notes: "Sofrito" is the mother of all sauces when it comes to Spanish cooking and the base for innumerable dishes. "Sauté a bit of chopped onion and garlic in olive oil" requires only one word in Spanish: "sofrito."

Galician Rye Bread

Pan gallego de centeno

[Makes 1 large round loaf]

When I started looking into how some Spanish breads are made, at least those that follow traditional methods, I realized that many use a bread starter, much like sourdough bread. Flour is fermented over a period of several days to create a *masa madre* (mother sponge). In many cases, bakers also work compressed yeast into the sponge, though I've used dry yeast, which is much more common in the United States. I find the combination of a starter and dry yeast works amazingly well, even for people who do not usually have good results with one or the other (like yours truly). Below you will find a step-by-step description of how to create your own starter and mother sponge. This sponge can then be used to make anything from rye bread to sweetbread and is the starter that I've used throughout this book.

   This particular bread uses rye flour. The end result is a hearty, round loaf with its characteristic "top knot" that, like most Galician breads, is rather rustic in nature and the perfect complement to Galician dishes and seafood. Try it with a slice of *Tetilla* cheese.

 START PREPARATION 4 TO 5 DAYS IN ADVANCE.

DAY 1 – CREATE THE STARTER:
½ cup wheat bran
2 large spoonfuls raisins
1½ cups warm water
1 cup all-purpose flour

DAYS 2, 3, AND 4 – FEED THE STARTER:
1½ cups water
1½ cups all-purpose flour

DAY 4 OR 5 – CREATE THE MOTHER SPONGE:
1 cup warm water
1 cup all-purpose flour

MAKE THE BREAD:
2 cups mother sponge
¼ cup warm water
1 package dry yeast
1 large spoonful sugar*
1 small spoonful salt*
2 large spoonfuls extra virgin olive oil*
2 cups rye flour
1 cup unbleached all-purpose flour
1 cup cornmeal or breadcrumbs

(continued on next page)

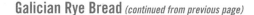
Galician Rye Bread *(continued from previous page)*

Day 1 – Create the starter: Soak the wheat bran and raisins in the water at room temperature for an hour. Use either a glass, plastic, or earthenware container, but avoid metal as it can interfere with the fermentation process. Drain and reserve 1 cup of the liquid. Mix the reserved liquid together with the flour. Keep the starter in a warm place such as a cupboard or an oven that is turned off.

Days 2, 3, and 4 – Feed the starter: Discard half the starter (¾ cup) and add ½ cup water and ½ cup flour. Do the same on the third and fourth days. You know that the starter is ready when it has lots of bubbles and a yeast-like smell to it. It can take any-where from 2 days to a week to develop a starter, but 4 days is the average; however if it takes more time, simply continue the same procedure until the starter is ready and, if it takes less, proceed to creating the mother sponge. You will also notice that the starter produces a certain amount of liquid that forms its own layer on top. If the starter is dry, simply stir the liquid back in, and if it's already moist, pour it off.

Day 4 or 5 – Create the mother sponge: Now that you've created your own bread yeast in the form of a starter, you will need to make a "sponge" from that starter. To do so, simply add water and flour to the starter and let it sit in a warm place for 2 to 3 hours. The sponge is ready when a white froth forms on the surface. (See Cook's Note below.)

Day 4 or 5 – Make the bread: Place two cups of sponge in a large mixing bowl. In a separate bowl, dissolve the yeast in warm water. Use a wooden spoon to mix the sugar, salt, and olive oil with the yeast and then with the sponge. Gradually add the rye and unbleached flours to the sponge until the dough comes together to form a firm ball. Turn onto a floured surface and knead for 5 minutes, adding more flour as needed. Place the dough in a greased bowl, cover, and let rise until it doubles in size, about 2 hours. (The dough is ready when you press it with a finger and the indent doesn't bounce back.)

Punch the dough down and knead for another 5 minutes. Shape into a round loaf and twist the center to create a little bun on top. Sprinkle the cornmeal or bread-crumbs on a cookie sheet and place the bread on top. Place the loaf in a warm place and let rise until it doubles in size, about an hour.

Preheat the oven to 400° F. Bake the bread on the middle-upper rack for 35 to 40 minutes. The crust should be brown and the loaf should make a hollow sound when tapped on the bottom. Cool before slicing.

Cook's Notes: This recipe makes 2½ cups mother sponge, 2 cups for this recipe with ½ cup left over, which you can continue "feeding" for future loaves. Simply refrigerate the leftover sponge and once a week, stir in ½ cup water and ½ cup flour.

*When it comes to bread baking, many cooks are more comfortable with exact measurements as too much or too little of a particular ingredient can alter the texture of the final product. The sugar measures out to exactly 1 level tablespoon plus ½ level teaspoon, the salt to 1 level teaspoon, and the oil to 2 tablespoons.

Almond Cake

Tarta de Santiago

[8 servings]

This cake doesn't have a bit of flour in it; rather, it uses ground almonds. Though almonds come from Andalusia and I have seen recipes for this cake that include sweet sherry (also from Andalusia), it is the quintessential Galician dessert.

5 eggs
½ cup powdered sugar
Grated peel of 1 lemon
Dash ground cinnamon

2 cups finely ground almonds (approximately ½ pound blanched almonds)
Powdered sugar for dusting

Preheat the oven to 350° F. Grease and flour a 9-inch round cake pan.

Beat the eggs until they are light and fluffy. Add the sugar, lemon peel, and cinnamon and continue beating. Stir in the ground almonds a little at a time to avoid lumps. Pour the batter into the cake pan and bake for approximately 45 minutes, until a toothpick inserted in the middle comes out clean.

Allow the cake to cool and dust with powdered sugar just before serving. Typically this cake is served with a dessert wine known as *vinho des meus amores* ("wine of my loves"), but a sweet sherry (*oloroso*) also works well.

Cook's Notes: Whenever you decorate a cake using powdered sugar, be sure to sprinkle the sugar on just as you're going to serve the cake; otherwise, the cake will absorb the sugar and you'll be left wondering where it went! For a uniform powdered coating, use a sifter or strainer.

Crepes

Filloas

[Makes 9 crepes]

Though their beginnings are uncertain, crepes are probably of Celtic origin. Traditionally this dessert was served during carnival and again when it came time to sacrifice animals for meat and sausages. In fact, some old recipes even use animal blood to make crepes, and even today, there are recipes that call for chicken broth. These crepes, however, are sweet and light with a dusting of powdered sugar and cinnamon.

2 eggs	½ cup all-purpose flour
½ cup milk	Powdered sugar for dusting
3 large spoonfuls butter, melted	Ground cinnamon for dusting
1 small spoonful sugar	

Beat the eggs, milk, butter, sugar, and flour together until smooth. Heat a small skillet over medium-high heat and grease (I use a few drops of extra virgin olive oil). Pour 3 large spoonfuls of batter into the hot skillet and swirl the skillet around so that the bottom of the pan is completely covered. When the crepe is set, turn it over, and cook on the other side. To serve, either fold the crepe in half or roll it. Dust with powdered sugar and cinnamon, and serve.

Cook's Notes: These crepes can be made ahead of time and stacked on a platter with a paper towel in between each crepe.

Anise-Flavored Fried Pastries

Orejas

[Makes about 24 pastries]

Orejas—ears in Spanish—are so named because of their shape and are especially popular during carnival. More than a dessert in themselves, they typically accompany coffee *after* dessert!

1 small spoonful dry yeast*	2 large spoonfuls anisette liqueur
¼ cup warm milk	Pinch salt
3 large spoonfuls sugar	2½ cups all-purpose flour
2 eggs	Mild extra virgin olive oil for frying
¼ cup butter, melted	Powdered sugar for dusting

Dissolve the yeast in warm milk. Add the sugar, eggs, butter, anisette liqueur, and salt. Mix well. Gradually stir in the flour until the mixture forms a firm ball. Cover and let rest in a warm place for 30 minutes.

Roll the dough out on a floured surface until it is about ¼-inch thick. Cut the dough into 4-inch by 5-inch pieces and roughly shape them to look like ears. Fry in abundant hot olive oil (about 1 finger deep) until golden on both sides. Drain on paper towels and dust with powdered sugar.

Cook's Notes: Add a few strips of orange and/or lemon peel to the skillet to keep the oil from acquiring a burnt taste.

*The dry yeast measures out to exactly 1 level teaspoon.

LA BUENA MESA • CHAPTER 1 The Atlantic Coast: Galicia

Flaming Liqueur

Queimada

[4 servings]

Queimada is a mystical drink which conjures up images of *meigas* (Galician witches) and chanting. It is a potent brew made with what can only be described as firewater or *aguardiente*. The flaming liquid is prepared in an earthenware punch bowl made especially for *queimada*, with individual cups that hang from the sides and an earthenware ladle, but any earthenware dish will do the trick.

---

2 cups *aguardiente* (also known as *orujo*)
   or Italian *grappa*
½ cup sugar

Peel of 1 orange
4 coffee beans

Mix the *aguardiente*, sugar, orange peel, and coffee beans together in an earthenware dish. Use a ladle to scoop up some of the liquid. (If the ladle is metal, wrap a pot-holder around the handle to protect your hand.) Light the *aguardiente* in the ladle and slowly lower the blue flame into the earthenware dish to ignite the rest of the liquid. Gently stir the *queimada* and continue burning for a few more minutes. The longer you burn the *queimada*, the lower the alcohol content will be. Once the flames have been extinguished, ladle the queimada into small earthenware cups and serve.

Cook's Notes: A typical Galician setting for preparing queimada *might be a beach at night, and because of the flames, you might want to consider a controlled outdoor setting or perhaps your kitchen. When I prepared it in my kitchen—without any breeze—the flames leapt as high as a foot and it took nearly 10 minutes before all the alcohol had burned out.*

Chapter 2

THE BAY OF BISCAY: ASTURIAS, CANTABRIA, AND THE BASQUE COUNTRY

The north of Spain is characterized by gently rolling green hills, the rugged Cantabrian Mountains, and cliffs that drop abruptly to the sea. Asturias, Cantabria, and the Basque Country all border the Bay of Biscay and this close communion with the sea is reflected in a diet rich in seafood. Fish, shellfish, fruits and vegetables, cereals, and legumes abound in both the Atlantic and Mediterranean diets; however, these two styles of eating differ on two major points. Northern regions consume more shellfish than the rest of Spain—and Spain is a country where people eat a lot of seafood—and meat and dairy products have a heavier presence in the Atlantic diet. This is not surprising because while Asturias, Cantabria, and the Basque Country are coastal regions, their interiors are largely pasture lands, ideal for grazing. The north is dairy country, as evidenced by the many fine cheeses and milk-based desserts so typical of these areas.

Asturias, in particular, produces a number of notable cheeses that are available in the United States and well worth trying. *Cabrales*, a blue cheese made primarily from cow's milk and aged in mountain caves, is probably the most well-known. There are also a number of smooth creamy cheeses, perfect for accompanying Asturian cider or *sidra*. And one cannot leave Asturias without trying what has to be its signature dish, *fabada*, a bean stew flavored with chorizo and *morcilla* sausages and salt pork. Spaniards love their legumes and it is in this dish that the lowly bean achieves culinary excellence.

My maternal grandparents came from Cantabria, and this region served as my own initiation to Spain when I visited there for the first time at the impressionable age of sixteen. Seafood fished from the cold Bay of Biscay waters dominates the local diet: hake, *bonito del norte* tuna, sardines, porgy, turbot, and anchovies from Santoño, considered to be the best in Spain. *Quesada pasiega*, made from cheese produced in the Valley of Pas, is a typical Cantabrian cheese custard. It's surprisingly easy to make and satisfies a sweet tooth.

The Basque Country has a long culinary tradition and an internationally recognized cuisine. The Basques are a rather mysterious people whose origins have been lost in the mists of time. They also have their own language, *Euskara* or Basque, of unknown origin as well. Basques take their food seriously and in Euskadi there are men-only cooking societies that go back generations. In the 1970s, Basque chefs Juan Mari Arzak and Pedro Subijana, both still active today, initiated a movement known as the New Basque Cuisine (*la nueva cocina vasca*). Heavily influenced by their French neighbors, they used traditional Basque dishes as a starting point to create a new style of cooking. This philosophy of cooking uses high-quality, traditional, seasonal products as is the norm in regional Spanish cooking, but incorporates different ingredients and methods of preparation. Many Spanish chefs have embraced this new cuisine and this trend has interestingly led to increased international awareness of Spanish food.

Though people in the north have easy access to fresh fish, one of the most common foods is cod that has been preserved in coarse sea salt. Salt cod is popular all over Spain, but it is the Basques who developed this system of preserving fish during the Middle Ages, a method that is used to this day. A supreme example of Basque cookery is *bacalao a la vizcaína*, dry salt cod covered in a sauce of dried sweet red peppers and onions. In fact, lightly scented sauces are a trademark of the north. There are sauces made with wine, such as the young green *txakolí* from the Basque Country or the hard dry cider known as *sidra* in Asturias. Green sauce, so typical of the north of Spain, owes its distinctive color to the large quantity of parsley used. Then there is that ingenious minimalist sauce known as *pil pil*, created by using a combination of olive oil, cod gelatin, and a wrist motion that has to be just right for these two ingredients to emulsify. These sauces are light, never overpowering, and serve to highlight impeccably fresh fish. Once you sample the seafood in Spain, you'll wonder how you ever ate anything less.

APPETIZERS

Tapas

Chorizo Sausages in Cider *(Chorizo a la sidra)*
Clams in White Wine Sauce *(Almejas a la marinera)*
Baby Eels in Garlic Sauce *(Angulas a la bilbaína)*

SALADS

Ensaladas

Marinated Cod and Lobster Salad *(Ensalada koshkera)*

SOUPS AND MEALS-IN-A-POT

Sopas y Potajes

Fish and Seafood Soup *(Sopa de pescado)*
Basque Tuna Soup *(Marmitako)*
Asturian Bean Stew *(Fabada)*
White Beans with Clams *(Fabes con almejas)*

EGG DISHES

Huevos

Soft-Set Eggs with Red Peppers, Tomatoes, and Serrano Ham *(Piparrada)*

FISH AND SHELLFISH
Pescados y Marisco

Baked Sardine Fillets *(Sardinas a la santanderina)*
Salmon in Cider Sauce *(Salmón a la ribereña)*
Hake in Green Sauce *(Merluza a la vasca)*
Salt Cod, Basque-Style *(Bacalao a la vizcaína)*
Salt Cod in Creamy Garlic Sauce *(Bacalao al pil pil)*
Stuffed Crab *(Txangurro)*
Baby Squid in Ink Sauce *(Chipirones en su tinta)*

MEATS
Carnes

Filet Mignon in Blue Cheese Sauce *(Solomillo al Cabrales)*
Pork Chops in Cider Sauce *(Chuletas de cerdo a la sidra)*

DESSERTS AND AFTERNOON COFFEE
Postres y Meriendas

Cheese Custard *(Quesada pasiega)*
Fried Custard Squares *(Leche frita)*
Rice Pudding *(Arroz con leche)*

Chorizo Sausages in Cider

Chorizo a la sidra

[4 servings]

While the wet, cool summers and mild winters in Asturias are not conducive to wine production, they are perfect for growing apples and fermenting hard apple cider. This cider, or *sidra* as it is known in Spanish, can accompany food or be used as a cooking sauce, as is the case with these chorizo sausages.

---

4 chorizo sausages
1 large spoonful extra virgin olive oil

1 cup *sidra*

Slice the chorizo sausages into ½-inch slices. Heat the olive oil in a skillet over medium-high heat and brown the chorizo slices on both sides. Remove the chorizo and place in an earthenware ramekin. Cover with the cider and cook over medium-high heat for 5 minutes. Insert toothpicks in each slice and serve.

Cook's Notes: It's also possible to substitute a dry white wine or "cava" for the cider.

Clams in White Wine Sauce

Almejas a la marinera

[4 servings]

In Spanish cooking, a *marinera* sauce is not synonymous with tomatoes; rather, it refers to a white wine sauce with flecks of parsley and a hint of onion and garlic. While these clams can be found in other parts of Spain, they are a specialty of northern regions.

---

2 large spoonfuls extra virgin olive oil
1 onion, chopped
2 cloves garlic, minced
Salt
1 large spoonful all-purpose flour

1 cup dry white wine
2 pounds small clams, cleaned (see Cook's Notes below)
2 large spoonfuls minced flat-leaf parsley

Put the olive oil in a large skillet and sauté the onion and garlic until the onion is transparent. Sprinkle with salt and stir in the flour. Gradually add the wine, stirring constantly to avoid lumps. Add the clams and cook uncovered over medium-high heat until they open. Discard any clams that do not open. Sprinkle with parsley and serve immediately.

Cook's Notes: Whenever you use clams in a dish, there is always the possibility that they'll have traces of sand. To remove any sand particles, place the clams in a bowl of salted water and soak for several hours or overnight. A faster option is to place the clams in the freezer for 3 to 4 minutes. This will cause the shells to open slightly. Remove them from the freezer and place them in a bowl of cold water for a few minutes.

LA BUENA MESA • CHAPTER 2 The Bay of Biscay: Asturias, Cantabria, and the Basque Country

Baby Eels in Garlic Sauce

Angulas a la bilbaína

[1 serving]

Angulas, or baby eels, are a delicacy in Spain. Though no thicker than a strand of cooked spaghetti and a few inches long, their price can be exorbitant. Typically they are prepared in individual *cazuelitas* or earthenware ramekins and eaten with a small wooden fork.

---

2 large spoonfuls extra virgin olive oil
1 clove garlic, thinly sliced
½ dried red chili pepper, seeds removed and
   cut in rings

Salt
¼ pound baby eels

Place the olive oil, garlic, chili pepper, and some salt in an individual, earthenware ramekin. Heat over medium-high heat until the garlic turns golden brown. Add the baby eels and stir them once with a wooden fork. Cover with a saucer and serve immediately.

Cook's Notes: If you find a local source for baby eels, it's more than likely that they will be frozen. Thaw them as you would shrimp by placing them in the refrigerator overnight and drying them between paper towels.

Baby Eels: Marathon Swimmers

It is not unusual to find aquariums with eels in Spanish restaurants in the north, much as one would lobster tanks in seafood
restaurants in the United States. I must admit that I find the eel's slippery texture and appearance off-putting, and for this reason, have never
sampled this Spanish dish. Sorry. One can't always be a gourmand. I have
tried snails, tripe, and even brains, but I draw the line on eels; however, not
so their offspring!

Gastronomic considerations aside, what amazes me so about these
tiny little elvers, as they're also known, is just that: their miniscule size—
about a quarter of an inch when they begin their journey home—and the
Herculean effort required to spend no less than three years crossing the
Atlantic Ocean.

How eels reproduce and where has been one of natural history's great
mysteries. Even Aristotle couldn't figure out where the eels he loved to eat
came from and in *Historia Animalium* (350 B.C.) wrote that, "the eels come
from the entrails of the earth." Another theory claimed that eels reproduced
by rubbing up against rocks and that the bits of skin that peeled off came
to life. There were even some rather poetic hypotheses such as dew or
floating horse hairs that transformed into elvers. However, the real story of
how the eel spawns turns out to be even more fantastic than these theories
and is in itself the stuff of great epic odysseys. A dogged Danish scientist
by the name of Johannes Schmidt was given the task of finding the eels'
spawning grounds by the Danish government. Resourceful and thorough,
he enlisted the help of transatlantic shipping companies to help him collect
specimens. After all, the Danish government had only given him one small
ship with which to comb the entire Atlantic Ocean! In 1922, after sixteen
years and excruciatingly detailed records, he narrowed the area for both
American eels (*Anguilla rostrata*) and their European counterpart (*Anguilla
anguilla*) to the weed-choked Sargasso Sea, roughly in the area known as
the Bermuda Triangle. Ah, the mystique!

In the case of the European eel, the journey begins thousands of miles
away when the females meet the males at the river's mouth and mate
before embarking on a journey that will take them across the Atlantic to
their *presumed* breeding ground. I say *presumed* because no one has ever
seen the female eels spawn. We'll need another Johannes Schmidt for that!
It is believed that the females deposit their eggs at inaccessible depths

beneath the tangled seaweed and then die. As soon as they are born, the tiny transparent larvae must fend for themselves as they begin the journey back to their ancestral waters. In the case of the American eel, the final destination is much closer and the elvers are too small for eating purposes. Their European cousins, however, will have grown to about three inches in length as they are carried on the ocean's surface to the north of Spain where fishermen await them. The elvers are fished on moonless nights in estuaries. Slippery and able to breathe out of water, they are not easy to catch. The *anguleros*, as the fishermen are called, trap the *angulas* in large metal sieves, plunge them into water that has been deoxygenated with a tobacco infusion, and parboil them in salted water; hence, there really is no such thing as "fresh" *angulas*. Their slippery nature makes it practically impossible. *Angulas* do, however, freeze well, though purists would no doubt scoff at eating frozen fare.

The elvers have a very delicate texture and flavor—not at all fishy—that is overpowered by too many ingredients. Simple is best here. The classic method for preparing *angulas* is *a la bilbaína*. The baby eels are quickly sautéed in olive oil with slivers of browned garlic and dried red chili pepper in an earthenware ramekin. They are covered and, still sizzling, whisked to the table where they are eaten with a wooden fork so as not to taint their delicate flavor, not to mention to get a grip on them!

Marinated Cod and Lobster Salad

Ensalada koshkera

[4 servings]

This seafood salad is a signature dish of Basque cooking. Though it's intended as a first course, I find that it works well as a main course for a light summer meal.

1 pound fresh cod
1 lemon slice
1 onion slice
Thyme
Salt
1 pound cooked lobster meat, thinly sliced
2 pimientos, cut in strips (page xv)
20 pitted green olives
4 hardboiled eggs, quartered

MARINADE:
4 large spoonfuls extra virgin olive oil
2 large spoonfuls red wine vinegar
1 clove garlic, minced
Salt
Freshly ground black pepper

Place the cod in a pan with just enough water to cover. Add the lemon and onion slices, some thyme, and salt. Cover and cook gently for 15 minutes.

While the cod is cooking, prepare the marinade. In a small bowl, mix together the olive oil, vinegar, garlic, salt, and pepper. Reserve.

Drain, cool, and shred the cod. Mix the cod, lobster, pimientos, and green olives together. Combine with the marinade and refrigerate. To serve, decorate with egg wedges.

Cook's Notes: You can also use salt cod, if you wish, but you will need to start preparation 2 to 3 days in advance in order to desalt the cod. In the case of salt cod, I would also suggest omitting the salt in the marinade. For an everyday version of this salad, substitute canned tuna for the lobster.

Fish and Seafood Soup

Sopa de pescado

[6 servings]

The secret to this soup's robust flavor lies in its broth. I prefer monkfish for making fish broth, and when buying fish, always request that the fishmonger separate the head and bones for this purpose. On top of using an already flavorful fish for stock, there is the addition of shrimp and mussels, making this a fish broth with substance. This soup is so satisfying that I usually don't make a second course. I simply round it off with some good bread, cheese, and fruit.

 START PREPARATION SEVERAL HOURS IN ADVANCE.

1 small monkfish (approximately 3 pounds),
   or 1 pound monkfish fillets
10 medium shrimp, in their shells

FISH BROTH:
Reserved monkfish head and bones
Reserved shrimp heads
10 medium mussels
1 carrot, scraped and cut in several pieces
1 leek, white part only, halved
1 large onion, quartered
2 cloves garlic, peeled
1 ripe tomato, halved
1 sprig flat-leaf parsley
1 bay leaf
6 black peppercorns

½ cup dry white wine
Salt

SOUP:
1 onion, chopped
1 clove garlic, minced
4 large spoonfuls extra virgin olive oil
1 large spoonful all-purpose flour
3 large spoonfuls tomato sauce (page 119)
¼ pound small clams
1 hardboiled egg, chopped
¼ cup cooked short-grain rice
1 large spoonful minced flat-leaf parsley
8 baguette slices, ½-inch thick
Extra virgin olive oil for frying

Prepare the fish: When buying the monkfish, ask your fishmonger to fillet it and set the bones and the head aside to make fish broth. Clean and peel the shrimp. (If you are unable to buy the monkfish and shrimp whole, substitute 2 pounds of whitefish.) Chop the shrimp meat and reserve the heads. Use kitchen scissors to cut the monkfish into bite-size pieces. Reserve.

Make the broth: Place the monkfish head and bones, along with the shrimp heads, the mussels, carrot, leek, onion, garlic, tomato, parsley, bay leaf, peppercorns, wine, salt, and 8 cups water in a pot. Bring to a boil and skim the foam off the top. Gently cook for 1½ to 2 hours, until the liquid has been reduced by half. Strain the broth and reserve.

Make the soup: Gently sauté the onion and garlic in olive oil until the onion is tender. Stir in the flour and tomato sauce, followed by the reserved fish broth. Add the monkfish, shrimp, clams, chopped egg, and rice (see Cook's Notes). Adjust the salt, if necessary. Cook until the clams have opened.

In the meantime, fry the bread slices in olive oil until golden brown on both sides and drain on paper towels. To serve, ladle the soup into individual bowls, sprinkle with parsley, and top with the fried bread.

Cook's Notes: When used in soup, pasta and rice have a way of acting like small sponges that absorb a lot of liquid. If you are going to make this soup ahead of time or foresee having leftovers, then you might want to add the cooked rice right before serving the soup.

Basque Tuna Soup

Marmitako

[6 servings]

This tuna soup is typically made using a variety of tuna known as *bonito del norte*, combined with potatoes and peppers. It probably takes its name from the Basque word *marmita*, which is a soup pot that is taller than it is wide. Traditionally fishermen prepared *marmitako* on board the fishing vessels with the fish not deemed apt for canning. With time—and better cooking conditions than a fishing boat on the high seas can offer—this soup has become more sophisticated. A little brandy, dried sweet red peppers, a smidgeon of *pimentón* . . . you get the idea!

2 dried *ñora* peppers, stems and seeds removed	2 large potatoes, peeled and diced
4 large spoonfuls extra virgin olive oil	Salt
2 onions, chopped	Freshly ground black pepper
2 cloves garlic, minced	½ cup dry white wine
3 green Italian frying sweet peppers,	4 cups fish broth (page 34)
or 1½ green bell peppers, seeded and	8 baguette slices, ½-inch thick
cut in julienne strips	Extra virgin olive oil for frying
1 small spoonful *pimentón dulce* (sweet	1 pound tuna fillets, cut in bite-size pieces
Spanish paprika)	2 large spoonfuls minced flat-leaf parsley
2 ripe tomatoes, grated and drained	
1 large spoonful brandy, preferably Spanish	

Soak the *ñora* peppers in warm water for an hour. Drain, chop, and reserve.

In a large saucepan or soup pot, sauté the onions, garlic, and Italian peppers in olive oil until tender. Add the chopped *ñora* peppers, *pimentón*, tomatoes, and brandy, stirring until the alcohol evaporates. Stir in the potatoes, being sure to coat them thoroughly with the oil. Season with salt and pepper. Cover the potatoes with the wine and fish broth. Bring to a boil, lower the heat, and simmer until the potatoes are tender, about 30 minutes.

In the meantime, fry the bread slices in olive oil until golden brown on both sides and drain on paper towels.

Add the tuna to the soup and cook for 5 minutes. To serve, ladle the soup into individual bowls, sprinkle with parsley, and top with the fried bread.

Cook's Notes: Wine and its more potent cousin, brandy, are common ingredients in Spanish cooking. Used in small amounts, they highlight a dish's natural flavors in everything from meat and fish to legumes, rice, pastries, and, in this case, soup. When a recipe calls for an alcohol-based liquid, it is important to allow for a cooking time of at least 5 minutes to ensure that all of the alcohol evaporates.

Asturian Bean Stew

Fabada

[4 servings]

Fabada is probably the most emblematic dish from Asturias. It takes its name from the word *faba*, which means "bean" in Bable, a romance language native to this region. *Fabes*, however, are no ordinary beans. They are large, flat white beans that also go by the name of *alubias de granja* in Spanish. There is no substitute for them when making *fabada*. Creamy and buttery in texture, they have a unique ability to absorb the other flavors in this bean stew, particularly the chorizo and *morcilla* sausages. This Asturian Bean Stew is a meal in itself and, like most hearty legume dishes, is best served during the cold winter months.

 START PREPARATION 1 DAY IN ADVANCE.

1½ cups very large dried white beans (*fabes*), rinsed	1 *morcilla* sausage
1 onion, peeled	¼ pound salt pork or slab bacon
2 whole cloves garlic, peeled	2 large spoonfuls extra virgin olive oil
1 carrot, scraped and cut in thirds	2 cloves garlic, minced
1 sprig flat-leaf parsley	½ small spoonful *pimentón dulce* (sweet Spanish paprika)
2 chorizo sausages	Salt

Soak the white beans in cold water overnight in an earthenware dish.

Add the onion, whole cloves garlic, carrot pieces, and parsley to the beans. (These ingredients will be removed once the beans are cooked. For this reason, you may want to wrap them in cheesecloth for easy removal.)

Degrease the chorizo sausages as you would for Lentils with Chorizo Sausage (page 72). Add the chorizo, *morcilla*, and salt pork to the beans. The water covering the beans should be about 1 finger deep. Bring to a gentle, rolling boil. Skim the white foam that forms on the surface of the water. Add ¼ cup cold water to the beans to cut the boil. Cover and cook over low heat until the beans are tender, 2½ to 3 hours. Check the beans periodically to make sure that there's enough water and cut the boil with cold water at least twice during cooking to tenderize the beans.

(continued on next page)

Asturian Bean Stew *(continued from previous page)*

Gently sauté the minced garlic in olive oil in a small skillet until the garlic begins to brown. Remove from the heat and stir in the *pimentón*.

Remove the onion, whole garlic cloves, carrot pieces, parsley, and salt pork from the beans. Add the sautéed garlic mixture to the beans, season with salt, cover, and let sit for 30 minutes. To serve, cut up the sausages and arrange them on top of the beans.

Cook's Notes: Here are a few tips for cooking tender beans. First of all, soak them overnight in cold water that completely covers the beans. If you see any beans floating on the surface, remove them as this means that they're dry and tough. When you go to cook the beans, begin with cold water. Finally, interrupt the cooking process about three times by adding enough cold water that you break the boil. (In Spanish, this is known as "scaring" the beans.) Having to reach the boiling point again tenderizes them.

White Beans with Clams

Fabes con almejas

[4 servings]

This bean dish, also made with *fabes*, is often overlooked due to the popularity of *fabada* (see page 37). While the combination of beans with seafood might sound odd, it does work and is a perfect example of just how intuitive healthy traditional cooking can be. Beans are a vegetable source of protein, which the addition of vegetables and seafood rounds out to make White Beans with Clams a meal in itself!

 START PREPARATION 1 DAY IN ADVANCE.

1½ cups very large dried white beans (*fabes*), rinsed
2 carrots, scraped and cut in several pieces
1 celery rib, cut in several pieces with a few leaves remaining
2 cloves garlic, peeled
1 bay leaf
Salt
Pinch saffron

¼ cup dry white wine
4 large spoonfuls extra virgin olive oil
½ red bell pepper, chopped
½ green bell pepper, chopped
1 onion, chopped
4 thin slices serrano ham, trimmed and cut in small pieces
1 pound small clams

Place the beans in a pan with cold water to cover and soak them overnight.

Add the carrots, celery, garlic, and bay leaf to the beans. (These ingredients will be removed once the beans are cooked. For this reason, you may want to wrap them in cheesecloth for easy removal.) The water covering the beans should be about 1 finger deep. Bring to a gentle, rolling boil. Skim the white foam that forms on the surface of the water. Cover and cook over low heat until the beans are tender, 2½ to 3 hours. Check the beans periodically to make sure that there's enough water and cut the boil with ¼ cup cold water at least 3 times during cooking to tenderize the beans.

(continued on next page)

LA BUENA MESA • CHAPTER 2 The Bay of Biscay: Asturias, Cantabria, and the Basque Country

White Beans with Clams (continued from previous page)

Once the beans are cooked, remove the carrot and celery pieces, bay leaf, and garlic cloves. Season with salt. Heat the saffron for 1 minute in a warm oven and grind, using a mortar and pestle. Add the wine to the saffron. Pour the wine and saffron over the beans, mixing well. Continue cooking for another 5 minutes.

In a large skillet, gently sauté the peppers, onion, and ham in olive oil until the peppers and onion are tender. Add the clams, cover, and steam on low until the clams have opened, about 3 to 5 minutes. Discard any clams that do not open. Add the clam and pepper mixture to the beans and serve.

Cook's Notes: Traditionally, legumes in Spain are prepared with salt pork or slab bacon; however, I have prepared this dish without either and, quite frankly, didn't miss them!

Soft-Set Eggs with Red Peppers, Tomatoes, and Serrano Ham

Piparrada

[4 servings]

In Spain, eggs are usually served as the main course of a light supper. With its pimiento and subtle ham flavor, these soft-set eggs make an ideal evening meal, along with a glass of wine and fresh fruit for dessert.

8 baguette slices, ½-inch thick
3 large spoonfuls extra virgin olive oil plus additional for frying baguettes
1 onion, chopped
2 cloves garlic, minced
2 thin slices serrano ham, trimmed and cut in small pieces

2 pimientos, cut in thin strips (page xv)
4 small tomatoes, seeded, grated, and drained
Salt
Freshly ground black pepper
8 eggs (your choice whether to beat or not)

Fry the bread slices in olive oil and drain on paper towels. Reserve.

Gently sauté the onion and garlic in the 3 large spoonfuls of olive oil until tender. Add the ham and pimientos and cook for another minute. Stir in the tomatoes, salt, and pepper. Continue cooking for another 5 minutes. Add the eggs and stir until set, but not dry. Serve with the fried bread slices.

Cook's Notes: I hardly ever chop tomatoes. I find it a rather annoying task which takes too long. Normally, I simply halve the tomatoes crosswise and press my hand on them as I grate them over a bowl. If I don't want the liquid, then I take a flat grater and place it on top of a strainer placed on top of a bowl! In this case, I'd prefer them without seeds, so what I do is cut the seeds out with a sharp knife before grating. It's so much faster and easier than peeling and chopping, and the end result is the same.

Baked Sardine Fillets

Sardinas a la santanderina

[4 servings]

I've eaten sardines at outdoor festivals where they are prepared over a charcoal fire and I must say they are exquisite that way. I also enjoy them grilled in a bit of olive oil; however, one of the great advantages to baking them is that you avoid the strong odor they give off during cooking without losing any of their characteristic flavor.

16 fresh sardine fillets	4 large spoonfuls minced flat-leaf parsley
Juice of 1 lemon	4 cloves garlic, minced
4 large spoonfuls extra virgin olive oil	Salt
3 large spoonfuls breadcrumbs	1 lemon, quartered

Preheat the oven to 325° F. Place sardine fillets in a shallow ovenproof dish, skin side down. Mix the lemon juice, olive oil, breadcrumbs, parsley, garlic, and some salt together to make a paste. Spread 1 small spoonful of paste on each sardine fillet. Bake for 15 minutes and then run the sardines under the broiler to brown them. Serve with lemon wedges.

Cook's Notes: If, like me, you have to fillet the sardines yourself, well, just remember all the heart-friendly omega 3 oils that they have. Begin by cutting the head off, slice along the belly, and gently push the sardine open so that the backbone is in the center. Peel the backbone off towards the tail and, as you reach the tail, you'll find that it will come off as well. Rinse the fillets and soak them in cold water for at least 10 minutes. This removes any trace of blood from the fish and makes the flesh firmer. Drain the fillets and place them between paper towels to absorb the excess water.

Salmon in Cider Sauce

Salmón a la ribereña

[4 servings]

In Asturias, the fishing season for salmon begins in March and ends around mid-July. The salmon fished from the rivers of this principality reach high prices on the market, in part because of the high quality of the meat, and in part due to the scarcity of the fish. There is a story that during the eighteenth century, the villagers who worked in the Benedictine monastery of San Pedro de Villanueva in Cangas de Onís asked that they not be served salmon more than twice a week. Obviously there were a lot more salmon then, and in those days, no one had heard of salmon's heart-friendly omega 3 oils!

In the case of these fish steaks, a Spanish cook would never serve them alone without any type of garnish, which in Spain means a small serving of something, usually a vegetable or perhaps rice, served on the same plate. A lone salmon steak simply looks too sad and incomplete. You could accompany this dish with a few new potatoes or grilled asparagus spears, as I've done here.

4 salmon steaks (approximately 6 ounces each and 1-inch thick)
1 large spoonful extra virgin olive oil plus additional for grilling

2 cups *sidra**
24 asparagus spears
Coarse salt

Brown the salmon steaks in olive oil for about a minute on each side. Add the *sidra*, lower the heat, cover, and simmer for 5 minutes. Remove the salmon steaks from the cider and serve with grilled asparagus spears.

To prepare the asparagus, heat a non-stick skillet or griddle over medium-high heat. Drizzle olive oil over the cooking surface. Place the spears on the cooking surface. Cook for approximately 10 minutes, turning frequently. Season with coarse salt.

*Cook's Notes: You can substitute dry cava *(Spanish sparkling wine) for the* sidra *in this recipe, if you wish.*

LA BUENA MESA • CHAPTER 2 The Bay of Biscay: Asturias, Cantabria, and the Basque Country

Hake in Green Sauce

Merluza a la vasca

[4 servings]

Subtle white wine sauces such as this green sauce are typical of the north of Spain. The large amount of parsley gives the sauce its characteristic green color. Fresh minced parsley is present in a myriad of Spanish dishes. In fact, parsley is so common in Spanish cooking that stores and markets usually give it away!

4 hake steaks (approximately 6 ounces each and 1-inch thick)
Salt
Freshly ground black pepper
4 large spoonfuls extra virgin olive oil
1 onion, chopped
4 cloves garlic, minced
1 large spoonful all-purpose flour

¾ cup dry white wine
¾ cup fish broth (page 136)
¾ cup peas, fresh or frozen
5 large spoonfuls minced flat-leaf parsley
½ pound small clams
1 hardboiled egg, chopped
4 white asparagus spears

Season the fish steaks with salt and pepper, and reserve.

Heat the olive oil in an earthenware dish and gently sauté the onion and garlic until tender. Stir in the flour and gradually add the wine and fish broth, stirring constantly until the sauce is smooth. Add the peas and 4 large spoonfuls of parsley. Season with salt.

Place the fish steaks in the sauce and add the clams. Cook for 10 minutes, occasionally shaking the dish gently from side to side to ensure that the fish steaks don't stick. Turn the fish over and continue cooking for another 5 minutes.

To serve, place the fish steaks on individual plates. Spoon some sauce over the fish and decorate with the remaining spoonful of minced parsley, chopped egg, and a white asparagus spear.

Cook's Notes: As herbs go, parsley is more than a pretty face. I always have it on hand in my kitchen. Rinse the parsley well with water and store in an airtight container in the refrigerator. It will keep for up to a week. Apart from looking nice when sprinkled on foods or garnishing plates, parsley helps to highlight a food's natural flavor. This humble little herb is also rich in vitamins and minerals.

Salt Cod, Basque-Style

Bacalao a la vizcaína

[4 servings]

This emblematic Basque dish combines salt cod—so highly prized in the north—with a dried red pepper and onion sauce, known as "Basque-style." The pepper used to create this unusual sauce goes by the name of *pimiento choricero* and, as far as I know, is not available in the United States. In its place, I have simply listed dried sweet red peppers, which is what *pimientos choriceros* are. Please note that the pepper should not be at all spicy, but sweet.

 START PREPARING SALT COD 2 TO 3 DAYS IN ADVANCE.

---

1 pound thick-cut salt cod fillets
4 dried sweet peppers, stems and seeds
    removed
3 baguette slices, ½-inch thick
4 large spoonfuls extra virgin olive oil plus
    additional for frying baguettes
2 onions, chopped

4 cloves garlic, crushed
4 ripe tomatoes, grated
Pinch sugar
1 bay leaf
Salt
Freshly ground black pepper

Begin soaking the salt cod 2 to 3 days in advance (see salt cod, page xv).

Soak the dried peppers in warm water for an hour. Drain and reserve.

Place the salt cod in a pot with cold water to cover. Heat to boiling, and as soon as the water begins to boil, skim the white foam off the top and immediately remove the fish. Reserve the fish and cooking liquid separately.

Fry the baguette slices in olive oil until golden brown on both sides and drain on paper towels. Reserve.

Gently sauté the onions and garlic in the 4 spoonfuls of olive oil until tender. Add the dried peppers, tomatoes, sugar, and bay leaf. Cover and simmer for 30 minutes. Check periodically, and if the sauce is too thick, adjust by adding a few spoonfuls of the water in which you've cooked the cod.

(continued on next page)

Salt Cod, Basque-Style *(continued from previous page)*

Add the fried baguette slices to the onion and pepper mixture, along with 1 cup of the reserved cod cooking liquid. Remove the bay leaf and blend until smooth using an immersion blender. Season with salt and pepper.

Spread the sauce in an earthenware dish. Place the fish on top, skin side up, so that the sauce covers the fish. Slowly bring to a boil and cook for 3 to 4 minutes, gently moving the dish from side to side. Turn the fish over and continue cooking for another 3 to 4 minutes. To serve, spread the sauce on individual serving plates and place the fish on top.

Cook's Notes: Of course you can use pots and skillets to prepare this dish, but I find that Spanish earthenware is ideal for everything from cooking the cod in water to sautéing the vegetables to bringing the sauce and the fish together. It is optimal for simmering, distributes heat evenly throughout the cooking process, and offers the perfect aesthetic backdrop to this classic dish.

Salt Cod in Creamy Garlic Sauce

Bacalao al pil pil

[4 servings]

Cod in Creamy Garlic Sauce is a perfect example of minimalism in cooking. The gelatinous juices in the cod skin emulsify with the olive oil to create a creamy white sauce flavored with garlic and specks of dried red pepper. The trick to creating this sauce lies in not overheating the oil, in slowly mixing the cod juices and oil together, and in the back and forth movement of the *cazuela* (earthenware dish), along with some really good wrist motion. First-rate ingredients are one of the secrets to Spanish cooking, nowhere more evident than in dishes such as this that use a minimum of ingredients. Use only good quality salt cod, preferably the loin cut.

 START PREPARING SALT COD 2 TO 3 DAYS IN ADVANCE.

1 pound thick-cut salt cod fillets with skin
½ cup extra virgin olive oil
4 cloves garlic, thinly sliced

½ dried red chili pepper, seeds removed and
cut in rings

Begin soaking the salt cod 2 to 3 days in advance (see salt cod, page xv).

Heat the olive oil slowly in a *cazuela* or non-stick skillet and then gently sauté the garlic and chili pepper just until the garlic begins to brown. Remove with a slotted spoon to a platter and reserve.

Place the salt cod skin side up in the same oil and slowly cook—practically simmer—4 minutes on each side. The fish should fit snugly in the *cazuela* or non-stick skillet so that the oil and juices are concentrated in the smallest space possible. Remove the fish to a platter. Drain the olive oil into a separate bowl and reserve. Make sure that there are no stuck bits remaining in the pan or oil. Allow the oil to cool for a few minutes.

(continued on next page)

Salt Cod in Creamy Garlic Sauce *(continued from previous page)*

Place 1 large spoonful of the reserved oil in the pan and then the cod fillets, skin side down. Constantly move the pan in circular movements until the oil emulsifies. Add the rest of the oil one large spoonful at a time and don't add any more oil until the previous addition has emulsified. Continue until all the oil has been added and the sauce has thickened. To serve, spoon the sauce over the fish and decorate with the fried garlic slivers and chili pepper rings.

Cook's Notes: This is not an easy sauce to make and you may need to make it several times before getting the hang of it. If the sauce does not thicken as expected, all is not lost. You have two options. You can serve the cod with the garlic slivers and flecks of pepper and a few drops of the olive oil it's been cooked in drizzled over the top. Or, if you really want that sauce, dissolve 1 envelope (¼ ounce) of unflavored gelatin in 2 large spoonfuls of cold water and stir into the sauce.

Stuffed Crab

Txangurro

[4 servings]

Txangurro is literally "spider crab" in the Basque language. (Basque has an inordinate fondness for consonants.) The cooked crabmeat is mixed with onion, tomatoes, and leeks and then spooned into the crab shell, which then becomes its own baking dish. Because fresh spider crabs are not readily available in the United States, I've used fresh crabmeat instead and individual earthenware ramekins in place of the shell. Another eye-pleasing alternative, if you have them, would be scallop shells.

---

2 day-old baguette slices, ½-inch thick
2 large spoonfuls extra virgin olive oil plus
   additional for frying baguettes
1 onion, finely chopped
1 leek, white part only, finely chopped

1 carrot, scraped and finely chopped
2 large spoonfuls brandy, preferably Spanish
1½ pounds fresh crabmeat
1 cup tomato sauce (page 119)
Salt

Fry the baguette slices in olive oil until golden brown on both sides and drain on paper towels. Use a mortar and pestle or other appropriate kitchen appliance to grind the fried bread. Reserve.

Sauté the onion, leek, and carrot in the 2 spoonfuls of olive oil until tender. Add the brandy, crabmeat, and tomato sauce. Salt to taste. Continue cooking for another 2 to 3 minutes.

Fill individual ramekins with the crabmeat filling, sprinkle with the fried breadcrumbs, and place under the broiler until golden brown. Serve immediately.

Cook's Notes: If you are able to find a source for live spider crabs, choose small ones and cook them in boiling salted water for 15 to 20 minutes. Allow them to cool before removing the meat, and best of luck to you, because they're rather spiny creatures!

Baby Squid in Ink Sauce

Chipirones en su tinta

[4 servings]

Do not be put off by the black color of the sauce used in this squid dish or by the squid itself. Squid has a taste and texture somewhere between fish and meat, and when they are this small, they are especially tender. These small squid are cooked in an onion, garlic, and tomato sauce to which the black ink from the squid sacs has been added, giving this dish its characteristic color. Apart from its color, the ink also adds a subtle flavor to the sauce. Once you've conquered Baby Squid in Ink Sauce, you'll be ready for Black Rice (page 126), another dish that uses squid ink, typical of the Mediterranean region of Spain.

16 small squid (approximately 3 inches in length)
2 baguette slices, ½-inch thick
4 large spoonfuls extra virgin olive oil plus additional for frying baguettes
2 onions, chopped

3 cloves garlic, minced
1 bay leaf
4 ripe tomatoes, grated
Pinch sugar
Salt
¼ cup dry white wine

Clean and prepare squid: Separate the body from the tentacles by holding the body in one hand and pulling the tentacles out with the other. You will need to remove the ink sac, which is silvery in color and located beneath the tentacles. Place the sacs in a small bowl and reserve. Cut the tentacles off and discard the eyes, mouth, and other waste material. Roughly chop the tentacles and reserve. Peel the skin off the body and pull off the fins. Roughly chop the fins and reserve. Remove the clear piece of cartilage and discard. Place the squid under cold running water and turn inside out. To do so, push down on the pointy end of the squid with your index finger until the squid is turned inside out. Wash away any material that adheres to the body, turn the squid to the outside again using your index finger, and dry on paper towels. Stuff the squid with the chopped tentacles and fins and close with toothpicks.

Fry the baguette slices in olive oil until golden brown on both sides and drain on paper towels. Reserve.

Gently sauté the onions, garlic, and bay leaf in the 4 spoonfuls of olive oil until the onions are tender. Add the tomatoes, a pinch of sugar, and some salt. Simmer for 20 minutes.

Press down on the ink sacs with the back of a wooden spoon to release the ink. "Wash" the ink out of the bowl and into the onion mixture by gradually pouring the wine over the ink. Add the fried bread slices and remove the bay leaf. Blend the sauce with an immersion blender or in a regular blender and return it to the pan. Place the squid in the sauce, cover, and simmer for 30 minutes.

Traditionally, this dish is accompanied by rice. A recipe for plain rice is included below. To serve, cover the bottom of individual plates with sauce. Spoon the rice into individual molds and place the molded rice in the center of each plate. Arrange the squid around the rice so that the open ends are pointing towards the edge of the plate.

Basic Rice

2 large spoonfuls extra virgin olive oil	1 cup short-grain rice
1 small onion, finely chopped	1 cup chicken broth (page 67)

Sauté the onion in olive oil until tender. Stir in the rice, being sure to coat well with the olive oil. Heat 1 cup water and chicken broth to boiling and pour over the rice. Cook uncovered over medium-high heat for approximately 15 minutes (the broth should boil rapidly) until almost all of the broth has been absorbed. Avoid stirring the rice; instead, move the pan from side to side if you need to redistribute the cooking liquid. During the last 5 minutes or so of cooking, as the liquid is absorbed, you may need to lower the heat a bit to keep the rice from cooking too fast. Remove from the heat and let sit for 5 minutes before serving.

Cook's Notes: If you are unable to buy uncleaned squid with the ink sacs intact, you can get squid ink online at tienda.com and it's even the same brand of ink that is available at the local supermarket in Spain where I normally shop! Use 2 packets (0.14 ounces each) of squid ink for this recipe.

LA BUENA MESA • CHAPTER 2 The Bay of Biscay: Asturias, Cantabria, and the Basque Country

Filet Mignon in Blue Cheese Sauce

Solomillo al Cabrales

[4 servings]

This dish combines simplicity with elegance: a good cut of meat grilled to perfection and topped with a sauce made from *Cabrales*, an Asturian blue cheese.

4 filets mignons	**BLUE CHEESE SAUCE:**
Extra virgin olive oil for grilling	8 ounces *Cabrales* cheese
Coarse salt	1 small spoonful butter
Freshly ground black pepper	1 cup heavy cream
	1 large spoonful brandy, preferably Spanish

Make the blue cheese sauce: Melt the blue cheese with the butter. When it's almost melted, but a few chunks of cheese remain, stir in the cream and brandy. Simmer for 5 minutes.

To grill the meat, heat a non-stick skillet or griddle over medium-high heat. When the cooking surface is hot, add just enough olive oil to keep the meat from sticking. Place the filets mignons on the hot surface. Cook on both sides and season with coarse salt. Remove filets to a platter and let rest about 5 minutes.

Add the meat juices that remain on the platter to the cheese sauce. To serve, spoon the blue cheese sauce over the meat and sprinkle with pepper.

Cook's Notes: If you prefer your blue cheese sauce with a few visible pieces of blue cheese and the intense blue cheese flavor that comes with biting into one of those chunks of cheese, instead of melting all of the blue cheese with the butter, reserve a few bite-size morsels to add at the end.

Pork Chops in Cider Sauce

Chuletas de cerdo a la sidra

[4 servings]

Hard dry cider, known as *sidra*, is a common ingredient in sauces such as this onion and tomato sauce with pork chops. It's also a nice alternative to wine and the perfect accompaniment to this dish.

4 loin pork chops, 1-inch thick
Salt
Freshly ground black pepper
4 large spoonfuls extra virgin olive oil

2 onions, thinly sliced
4 ripe tomatoes, grated and drained
Pinch sugar
1 cup *sidra*

Preheat the oven to 350º F. Salt and pepper the pork chops. Heat the olive oil in an earthenware dish. Brown the chops on both sides and remove to a platter.

Sauté the onions in the same oil until tender. Stir in the tomato, along with a pinch of sugar, and cook for 5 minutes. Season with salt and pepper. Add the *sidra* and pork chops, covering the meat with the onions and tomatoes. Cover and transfer to the oven. Bake for 30 minutes until the meat is tender.

To serve, spoon the onions and tomatoes over the pork chops, along with a few spoonfuls of the cooking liquid.

Cook's Notes: When grilling or browning meat, it is important to use a cooking surface that has been preheated and is at its optimal (hot) temperature. The heat seals the pores in the meat and keeps the juices from escaping.

Cheese Custard

Quesada pasiega

[4 servings]

The term *pasiega* implies that this dessert comes from the valley of Pas in Cantabria. Cantabria and Asturias are milk-producing regions in Spain, which explains the predominance of dairy desserts.

---

4 eggs
8 ounces cream cheese, softened
½ cup sugar

¼ cup milk
Grated peel of 1 lemon

Preheat the oven to 350° F and grease an 11-inch by 7-inch rectangular baking pan. Beat together all the ingredients, pour into the pan, and bake until set, about 40 minutes.

Cook's Notes: Try serving with fresh berries or a dollop of berry jam.

Fried Custard Squares

Leche frita

[4 servings]

These fried custard squares are crunchy on the outside and pure sweet creaminess on the inside. They don't turn up that often on restaurant menus and tend to be more of a homemade dessert. While several regions claim *leche frita* as their own, the Basque city of San Sebastian is generally considered home to this dessert.

2 cups milk
1 cinnamon stick
4 strips lemon peel (approximately ½-inch wide and the length of the lemon)
4 eggs, at room temperature
4 large spoonfuls sugar

4 large spoonfuls cornstarch
Mild extra virgin olive oil for frying
Breadcrumbs
Powdered sugar for dusting
Ground cinnamon for dusting

Place the milk, cinnamon stick, and lemon peel in a saucepan and gradually bring to a boil. Lower the heat and simmer for 10 minutes. In a separate bowl, beat together 2 eggs, the sugar, and cornstarch. Discard the lemon peel and cinnamon stick, and *gradually* stir the warm milk into the egg mixture. Return to the saucepan and stir constantly over low heat until the custard thickens.

Pour into a greased, 10-inch square pan, being sure to create a smooth even surface approximately 1 inch thick. Cool, cover with plastic wrap, and refrigerate for at least 2 hours.

Heat the olive oil over medium to medium-high heat. It should be about 1 finger deep. Cut the custard into 8 portions. Beat the 2 remaining eggs. Dip the custard squares in the beaten egg, coat them with breadcrumbs, and fry in the hot olive oil until golden brown on both sides. Drain on paper towels and dust with powdered sugar and cinnamon. Serve immediately.

Cook's Notes: It's much easier to cut the custard if you dip the knife in cold water first.

Rice Pudding

Arroz con leche

[4 servings]

While *arroz con leche* is served in other parts of Spain, Asturias lays claim to this creamy pudding. Though it is doubtful that the dish actually originated there, it is true that the best rice pudding comes from this region. It is possible to prepare rice pudding without using eggs to thicken it, but I have yet to achieve this feat without burning the pudding at some stage simply because to do so involves cooking large quantities of milk down over two to three hours. I've tried non-stick saucepans, double boilers, and earthenware, but the pudding invariably sticks. For this reason, I prefer to use eggs. No burnt taste and the end result is a nice creamy pudding for dessert. And as the saying goes, "The proof of the pudding is in the eating!"

½ cup short-grain rice	½ cup sugar
3 cups milk	1 large spoonful brandy, preferably Spanish
1 stick cinnamon	2 eggs, at room temperature, beaten
4 strips lemon peel (approximately ½-inch wide and the length of the lemon)	1 small spoonful butter
	Ground cinnamon for dusting

Bring 2 cups water to a boil in a small sauepan. Add the rice and cook for 3 minutes. Drain the rice and rinse. Reserve.

Place the milk, cinnamon stick, and lemon peel in a saucepan and gradually bring to a boil. Lower the heat and simmer for 10 minutes. Stir in the rice and cook for another 10 minutes, stirring occasionally. Add the sugar and brandy, and cook for another 5 minutes, stirring occasionally.

Discard the lemon peel and slowly add half the hot milk to the beaten eggs, stirring constantly to keep the eggs from curdling. Return the mixture to the saucepan, add the butter, and gradually bring to a boil, stirring constantly. Boil for one minute, stirring constantly. (The pudding will be thick and creamy, though not as thick as a custard. It will continue to thicken as it cools.)

To serve, spoon into dessert dishes and sprinkle with cinnamon. Serve warm. Any leftover pudding should be covered and refrigerated and can be served cold.

Cook's Notes: Be sure to use only short-grain rice. Long-grain rice produces a different texture and consistency that is not at all suitable for this pudding.

● The Spanish Style of Eating

Traditionally, Spaniards eat five meals a day: the three that any American would recognize as breakfast, dinner, and supper, and two snacks, one mid-morning and the other mid-afternoon. You will notice that I've written "dinner" instead of "lunch" and "supper" as opposed to "dinner." That's because in Spain, people eat their main meal around 2 or 3 p.m. and a lighter supper late in the evening around 9 or 10 p.m. In fact, don't expect to get a restaurant reservation before half past one in the afternoon or half past eight in the evening, not if you want to eat traditional Spanish fare. With such late eating hours, it's only natural that people need mid-morning and mid-afternoon snacks.

Breakfast in Spain is a light affair. A proper Mediterranean breakfast might include toast with a bit of extra virgin olive oil drizzled over the top, fruit, yogurt, and *café con leche*. Plain cookies, known as *galletas María*, or small cake-like muffins called *magdalenas* are also typical breakfast foods in Spain. You're not likely to see eggs served at this time of day. In Spain, eggs are usually eaten in the evening for supper. When you order coffee in Spain, it's necessary to specify if you want your coffee *solo, cortado,* or *con leche. Café solo* translates into an espresso and a *cortado* is an espresso that has been "cut" with a bit of hot milk, both of which are served in demitasse cups. The typical breakfast coffee, *café con leche*, is a large cup of coffee with half espresso and half hot, frothy milk. Ah, the scent of fresh coffee wafting from Spanish bars in the morning! Of course, not everyone eats a proper breakfast—sound familiar?—and there are those who settle for something along the lines of a croissant and coffee. Which brings us to breakfast number two, known as *el almuerzo.* I say this because it's not unusual to walk into an office and find that the person you wish to speak to is "having breakfast"—and it's 11:00 in the morning! In the case of children, this second breakfast usually consists of a sandwich made with baguette-style bread and juice or chocolate milk. School children typically carry their morning snack to school in small drawstring bags on which their names have been embroidered. In Spain, sandwiches are considered snack food and no self-respecting Spaniard would make a meal out of one!

Dinner is the main meal of the day. It is usually served around 2 or 3 p.m. and consists of a first course, second course, dessert, bread, wine or water, and coffee. Business comes to a screeching halt and most stores, with the exception of larger chain stores, close during this time and don't reopen until 4 or 5 o'clock. The restaurants offer a set menu, known as the *menú del día*, which is a great way to sample regional dishes at an economical price.

At 5:00 p.m. when most Americans are thinking about what to fix for dinner, Spaniards are wondering what to have for *merienda* or mid-afternoon snack. After all, supper is still a few hours away and the second part of the day is just beginning after the lunch break. You will notice the bakeries and cafés filling up at this hour as people nip in for a quick pastry or baguette-style sandwich. While supper is a three-course meal, the courses are much lighter than those served at midday. Given the late hour, it would be inadvisable to eat a heavy meal. The first course usually consists of soup, vegetables, or a salad. Eggs and fish, both lighter forms of protein, are often the main course, with fruit or yogurt for dessert.

Chapter 3

INLAND SPAIN: NAVARRA, ARAGON, LA RIOJA, CASTILE, AND EXTREMADURA

When I think of Spain as a whole, my mind invariably wanders to the austere landscapes of the central plateau, to the large expanses of wheat fields, and to the somber character of its people. The climate there is one of extremes. In summer, the sun is unforgiving, and in winter, the dry cold pierces right through you. "*Hace un frío que pela*", they say ("It's a cold that strips you bare"). Central Spain is the birthplace of the Spanish language, and I would even dare say, of the Spanish character in general. I have included both Castiles, Extremadura, Navarra, Aragon, and La Rioja in this decidedly broad category. Culturally Navarra looks towards the Basque Country and Aragon finds itself sandwiched between Castile and Catalonia. However, all of these regions are landlocked and, for purposes of this book, I have opted to include them under one heading.

When one looks at the dishes that are emblematic of Aragon, Navarra, and La Rioja, the use of peppers in cooking is what stands out. In Aragon, there is *chilindrón*, a sauce made with red peppers that is used to create distinctive dishes such as chicken or lamb *al chilindrón*. Navarra is famous for its *pimientos del piquillo*, small ruby-red peppers with a smooth, meaty texture and slight bite. The *piquillo* peppers from the town of Lodosa have been granted a denomination of origin and are highly prized in Spanish cooking. La Rioja, apart from its world-famous wines, produces a variety of vegetable products, many of which are present in a vegetable medley known as *menestra riojana*.

Castilla, which takes its name from the Spanish word for castle, is home to what can only be described as two gastronomic jewels of Spanish cooking: roast baby lamb and roast suckling pig. If you find yourself in *Castilla-León*, be sure to order them because their special characteristics make it impossible to recreate these roasts outside of Spain. (See Roast Suckling Lamb and Pig: Culinary Masterpieces, page 95.)

La Mancha, immortalized by Miguel de Cervantes in *Don Quijote de la Mancha*, produces what is probably the quintessential Spanish cheese, *Queso Manchego*. The central plains of Spain in general are pastoral and the practice of transhumance, where livestock are taken to higher pastures in summer and moved back to warmer foothills in winter, is still alive today. Nowhere is the contrast between the modern bustle of city life and this timeworn practice more noticeable than in Madrid. Each year on a particular Sunday in November, a couple thousand sheep stop traffic in the center of Spain's capital as they travel ancient *cañadas* or cattle passageways towards their winter grazing lands. While this practice may seem little more than a quaint, picturesque custom, it actually plays an active role in maintaining the area's natural ecosystems.

Extremadura is the land of conquistadores and its capital city, Mérida, is home to some of the world's most important Roman ruins, including a theater which still stages plays in summer. Gastronomically, pork and game are very present in traditional dishes here. While chorizo sausage can be found all over Spain and is a Spanish sausage—unlike *butifarra*, for example, which is clearly a Catalan sausage—the chorizo sausage from Spain's interior regions is considered to be the best. Traditionally, pigs were slaughtered with the first cold winds of winter in a ritual known as *la matanza* (the slaughter). Spanish even has a proverb to this effect: *A cada cerdo le llega su San Martín* ("Martinmas arrives for every pig") which roughly translated means that all pigs—of the two- and four-legged variety—have their day of reckoning.

Madrid offers a synthesis of Spanish cooking and, surprisingly, some of the best seafood in Spain. Such is the Spanish passion for seafood that the day's catch is shipped in fresh from the coast. Several dishes are particularly emblematic of Spain's capital city, the most well-known being *cocido madrileño*, a beef and chickpea stew. In Madrid, there is no shortage of restaurants when it comes to avant-garde Spanish cuisine; however, the discerning gourmand needn't worry about having to choose between cosmopolitan upscale and old world charm, because in Madrid it's possible to have your Scorched Squab over Melon and eat your Tripe, Madrid-Style too.

APPETIZERS
Tapas

Tripe, Madrid-Style *(Callos a la madrileña)*
Snails in Spicy Red Pepper Sauce *(Caracoles con salsa picante)*
Ham-Stuffed Mushroom Caps *(Champiñones rellenos)*

SALADS
Ensaladas

Lettuce Hearts with Anchovies *(Cogollos con anchoas)*

SOUPS AND MEALS-IN-A-POT
Sopas y Potajes

Chicken Consommé with Sherry *(Caldo de pollo con jerez)*
Garlic Soup *(Sopa de ajo)*
Cream of White Asparagus Soup *(Crema de espárragos)*
Beef and Chickpea Stew *(Cocido madrileño)*
Lentils with Chorizo Sausage *(Lentejas estofadas con chorizo)*
White Beans with Chorizo Sausage *(Judías con chorizo)*
Potato and Chorizo Sausage Stew *(Patatas riojanas)*

VEGETABLES
Verduras y Hortalizas

Red Peppers Stuffed with Cod *(Pimientos del piquillo rellenos de bacalao)*
Vegetable Medley, Rioja-Style *(Menestra riojana)*
Vegetable Medley, Manchego-Style *(Pisto manchego)*
Oven-Roasted Potatoes *(Patatas panaderas)*

EGG DISHES

Huevos

Fried Eggs and Potatoes with Chorizo Sausage *(Huevos fritos con patatas y chorizo)*
Scrambled Eggs with Bacon and Chorizo Sausage *(Duelos y quebrantos)*

FISH

Pescados

Trout with Serrano Ham *(Truchas a la Navarra)*
Salt Cod in Tomato and Pepper Sauce *(Bacalao al ajo arriero)*
Butterflied Porgy *(Besugo a la espalda)*

POULTRY AND GAME

Aves y Caza

Chicken in Saffron-Scented Sherry Sauce with Almonds *(Pollo en pepitoria)*
Chicken with Tomato and Red Pepper Sauce *(Pollo al chilindrón)*
Ham-Stuffed Quail *(Codornices rellenas de jamón)*
Roast Partridge *(Perdiz a la toledana)*

MEATS

Carnes

Lamb and Red Pepper Stew *(Cordero al chilindrón)*
Roast Leg of Lamb *(Paletilla de cordero asada)*
Stewed Pig's Feet *(Manos de cerdo estofadas)*

BREADS

Panes

Round Castilian Loaf *(Pan candeal)*

DESSERTS AND AFTERNOON COFFEE

Postres y Meriendas

Peaches in Wine Syrup *(Melocotón con vino)*
Buttery Cupcakes *(Mantecadas de Astorga)*
Fresh Cheese with Walnuts and Honey *(Queso de Burgos con nueces y miel)*

Tripe, Madrid-Style

Callos a la madrileña

[4 servings]

Like so many classic foods, this tripe dish is of lowly birth. Much less expensive than meat, tripe was typically eaten by mule drivers and hustlers trying to scratch out a living. Tripe refers to the stomach tissue of ruminant animals; in this case, of cows. Because bovine tripe is lacking in gelatin, it is often cooked in combination with a calf's hoof or pig's trotter. It is one of those dishes that you leave to simmer for hours. The longer it cooks, the more flavorful and tender the tripe. *Callos a la madrileña* has risen from its humble origins to become one of the gastronomic symbols of Madrid and today is served in some of the city's finest restaurants.

 START PREPARATION 6 TO 7 HOURS IN ADVANCE OR THE DAY BEFORE.

1 pound beef tripe, cleaned and cut in
   bite-size pieces (see Cook's Notes below)
1 pig's foot, split in half lengthwise
1 whole onion, peeled; plus 1 onion, chopped
2 whole cloves garlic, peeled; plus 2 cloves
   garlic, minced
1 ripe tomato, grated
1 bay leaf
2 cloves
3 sprigs parsley
10 black peppercorns
Dash ground nutmeg

Salt
1 chorizo sausage
2 large spoonfuls extra virgin olive oil
¼-pound piece serrano ham, trimmed and
   diced
1 *morcilla* sausage, sliced
1 small spoonful *pimentón dulce* (sweet
   Spanish paprika)
1 large spoonful all-purpose flour
½ cup dry white wine
1 dried red chili pepper, seeds removed
   and crumbled

Place the tripe in a saucepan with water to cover. Bring to a boil, drain, and rinse with cold water. Place the tripe in an earthenware dish, along with the pig's foot, whole onion, whole garlic, tomato, bay leaf, cloves, parsley, peppercorns, nutmeg, some salt, and water to cover. (The water should be about 1 finger deep.) Cover and cook slowly for 4 hours. (If you want to break this recipe into two parts, you could prepare the tripe up to this point and finish cooking it the following day.)

Degrease the chorizo sausages as you would for Lentils with Chorizo Sausage (page 72), slice, and reserve. Sauté the chopped onion and minced garlic in olive oil until tender. Add the chorizo, ham, and *morcilla*. Continue cooking for another 5 minutes. Stir in the *pimentón* and flour, followed by the wine. Add this mixture, along with the chili pepper, to the tripe. Cover and cook slowly for 2 more hours.

Discard the whole onion, whole garlic cloves, bay leaf, and parsley sprigs (and the peppercorns and cloves, if you can find them!). Remove the bone from the pig's foot and discard. Serve in individual earthenware ramekins.

Cook's Notes: To make sure that the tripe has been thoroughly cleaned, rinse well with cold water. Place in a bowl with water to cover and add a cup of vinegar and a small spoonful of salt to the water. Repeat if necessary.

Snails in Spicy Red Pepper Sauce

Caracoles con salsa picante

[4 servings]

Snails are used in a number of regional Spanish dishes and are readily available in Spain; in fact my local supermarket stocks them in the frozen foods section. These snails are seasoned with dried red chili pepper and piquant Spanish paprika to give them a slightly spicy bite. I have used frozen snails in this recipe for reasons of availability, as well as to avoid having to purge the little creatures. This is a great make-ahead tapa as it tastes even better the following day.

2 large spoonfuls extra virgin olive oil
1 onion, finely chopped
2 cloves garlic, minced
1 bay leaf
¼ pound dry-cured mild or piquant chorizo sausage, diced
¼-pound piece serrano ham, trimmed and diced
1 dried red chili pepper, seeds removed and crumbled

1 small spoonful *pimentón picante* (piquant Spanish paprika)
1 small spoonful all-purpose flour
Salt (optional)
1½ pounds frozen snails, thawed
1 cup dry white wine
½ cup tomato sauce (page 119)
2 large spoonfuls minced flat-leaf parsley

In an earthenware dish, sauté the onion, garlic, and bay leaf in olive oil until tender. Stir in the chorizo, ham, chili pepper, *pimentón*, flour, and some salt. Add the snails, wine, and tomato sauce. Bring to a boil, lower the heat, and simmer uncovered for 30 minutes, stirring occasionally. Sprinkle with parsley and serve.

Cook's Notes: If you do find a source for fresh snails, they will need to be purged before cooking. Storing them in a wicker basket with a lid makes it easy to clean them without having to worry that they'll get away from you. Purging consists of fasting (the snails, not the cook!) for 2 to 3 days, followed by a diet of white flour for another several days until "everything" comes out white.

Ham-Stuffed Mushroom Caps

Champiñones rellenos

[Makes 12 mushrooms]

According to a friend of mine from Burgos, these tasty little mushrooms go by the name of *botones* or buttons in the bars there.

12 white button mushrooms
4 large spoonfuls extra virgin olive oil
1 scallion, chopped
2 cloves garlic, minced
2 thin slices serrano ham, trimmed and minced

1 large spoonful dry sherry (*fino*)
Salt (optional)
2 large spoonfuls minced flat-leaf parsley
4 large spoonfuls dry white wine

Wash and dry the mushrooms. Separate the stems from the caps. Chop the stems and reserve the caps.

Sauté the scallion and garlic in olive oil until tender. Add the minced mushroom stems and ham, and continue cooking until tender. Stir in the dry sherry and cook for a few minutes until the alcohol has evaporated. Salt to taste.

Spoon the stuffing into the mushroom caps and return the caps to the same pan where you sautéed the filling. Sprinkle the caps with parsley, add the wine, cover, and simmer for 5 minutes. Spoon any remaining sauce over the mushroom caps and serve.

Cook's Notes: To prevent any discoloration, sprinkle the mushroom caps with a few drops of lemon juice.

Lettuce Hearts with Anchovies

Cogollos con anchoas

[4 servings]

Lettuce hearts from the town of Tudela in Navarra are well-known in Spain. They are small—approximately six inches in length—with dark outer leaves and light, almost yellow inner leaves. They are characterized by a slightly bitter taste. Typically they are served with anchovy fillets, pimiento, and a cooling sherry vinaigrette.

4 lettuce hearts
4 hardboiled eggs, quartered
1 pimiento, cut in thin strips (page xv)
8 large spoonfuls extra virgin olive oil
2 large spoonfuls sherry vinegar

1 large spoonful minced flat-leaf parsley
Salt (optional)
16 olive oil-packed anchovy fillets,
   preferably Spanish

Wash the lettuce hearts to remove any earth between the leaves. Cut them in quarters lengthwise and arrange on individual salad plates. Place the egg slices between the lettuce quarters. Arrange the pimiento strips on top of the lettuce.

Mix the olive oil, vinegar, parsley, and salt together in a small bowl. (Keep in mind that the anchovies are very salty so a light hand should be used if adding salt to the vinaigrette.)

Pour the vinaigrette over the lettuce. Arrange the anchovies on top of the lettuce quarters and serve.

Cook's Notes: Another option is to use canned tuna instead of anchovies. You can also make an anchovy vinaigrette by blending three or four anchovy fillets with the olive oil and vinegar.

Chicken Consommé with Sherry

Caldo de pollo con jerez

[Makes about 8 cups]

In the central part of Spain where the winters are quite cold, it's not uncommon to find homemade chicken broth served in coffee cups with a bit of dry sherry added at the end. A few years ago when I was walking the Saint James' Way (*Camino de Santiago*) with a group of friends, we took a break mid-morning to get something to eat. The bar where we stopped advertised homemade chicken broth. A cup of this consommé after several hours of walking in the cold, dry Castilian winter can only be described as nourishment for body *and* soul. This is my standard recipe for homemade chicken broth that I turn to time and time again. It's heavily flavored with bay leaf, rosemary, thyme, and peppercorns.

 START PREPARATION SEVERAL HOURS IN ADVANCE.

2 pounds chicken pieces
2 carrots, scraped and cut in several pieces
2 leeks, white part only, cut in several pieces
1 celery rib, cut in several pieces with a few leaves remaining
1 large onion, quartered
2 sprigs flat-leaf parsley

2 bay leaves
2 small spoonfuls rosemary
2 small spoonfuls thyme
1 small spoonful black peppercorns
1 small spoonful salt
Dry sherry (*fino*)

Make chicken broth: Place all the ingredients, with the exception of the dry sherry, in a large pot, along with 10 cups water. Bring to a boil and skim the foam off the top. Lower the heat, cover, and simmer for 4 hours. Strain the broth. Cool and place in the refrigerator. Skim off any fat that has hardened on the surface.

To serve, pour into mugs or soup bowls and add 1 to 2 large spoonfuls of dry sherry per serving (or use the broth in any recipe calling for chicken broth).

Cook's Notes: This is one of the few times I would advise not skinning the chicken before cooking. The reason is that a thick layer of fat will form on the surface of the broth once it's refrigerated and a thick layer is infinitely easier to remove than droplets of fat scattered here and there.

Garlic Soup

Sopa de ajo

[4 servings]

Garlic soup was originally a poor man's soup, born of the necessity to use bread that had turned stale. Over the years, Spanish cooks have invented several rather ingenious ways of using up stale bread: *Torrijas* (page 237), *Pa amb tomàquet* (page 110), and this garlic soup, to name a few. Originally garlic soup was—and, in many cases, still is—made with nothing more than olive oil, garlic, bread, Spanish paprika, and water. In the wintertime, it's not uncommon to see bars advertise that they serve *sopa de ajo* and consommé. It's a great way to come out of the cold!

6 large spoonfuls extra virgin olive oil	8 day-old baguette slices, ½-inch thick
8 cloves garlic, thinly sliced	4 cups chicken broth (page 67)
4 thin slices serrano ham, trimmed and minced	2 large spoonfuls dry sherry (*fino*)
1 large spoonful *pimentón dulce* (sweet Spanish paprika)	4 eggs
	Salt

Preheat the oven to 450° F. Heat 2 large spoonfuls of olive oil in an earthenware dish. Gently sauté the garlic and ham until the garlic begins to brown. Remove the garlic and ham from the oil and grind, using a mortar and pestle or appropriate kitchen appliance. Mix in the *pimentón* and reserve.

Add the rest of the olive oil to the earthenware dish and fry the bread until golden brown on both sides. Return the garlic and ham mixture to the earthenware dish with the bread. Pour in the chicken broth and sherry. Cook over medium heat for 10 minutes, stirring frequently.

Crack the eggs on top of the soup. Season with salt. Place in the oven until the eggs are set, about 10 minutes. Ladle into individual soup bowls and serve.

Cook's Notes: Garlic cloves can be difficult to peel. If the clove is a bit dry, simply place it under the flat edge of a cutting knife and give the blade a quick, light punch with your fist. The skin should pull away easily from the clove. If the clove is fresh, then soak it in warm water for about 10 minutes before peeling. There's also a nifty little gadget for peeling garlic cloves that looks something like a plastic crepe. You simply place the clove inside, roll it back and forth, and you have a peeled clove!

Cream of White Asparagus Soup

Crema de espárragos

[4 servings]

White asparagus, many with a denomination of origin, are a star product of Navarra and highly prized in Spanish cooking. In order to obtain white asparagus, the spears are manually covered in soil as they emerge, thus shielding them from sunlight. In this way, they maintain their whiteness, as well as tenderness. In Spain, these tender white spears, which practically melt in your mouth, are eaten as is, with a dollop of mayonnaise, or atop a green salad (see Green Salad, Spanish-Style, page 219).

4 large spoonfuls extra virgin olive oil
1 leek, white part only, coarsely chopped
1 small onion, coarsely chopped
1 potato, peeled and sliced
2 pounds fresh white asparagus spears
2 cups chicken broth (page 67)

1 cup heavy cream
White pepper
Salt
2 thin slices serrano ham, trimmed and
  cut in thin strips

Gently sauté the leek, onion, and potato in olive oil for 8 to 10 minutes. Add the asparagus and chicken broth to the vegetables. Bring to a boil, lower the heat, and cook for 20 minutes.

Blend the soup with an immersion blender until smooth (or use a standing blender and blend in batches). Place a strainer over a saucepan and press the mixture through the strainer using the back of a wooden spoon. Add the heavy cream and heat through, but be sure not to boil or the cream could curdle. Season with white pepper and salt. Ladle the soup into individual bowls and garnish with strips of ham.

Cook's Notes: White asparagus spears are a staple on Spanish supermarket shelves and they're available online in the United States. If fresh white asparagus is not in season, simply substitute 2 (8.8-ounce) cans.

LA BUENA MESA • CHAPTER 3 Inland Spain: Navarra, Aragon, La Rioja, Castile, and Extremadura

Beef and Chickpea Stew

Cocido madrileño

[6 servings]

Cocido, in one form or another, can be found all over Spain. For example, in Cantabria it is known as *cocido montañés*, in Catalonia as *escudella*, and in the Canary Islands as *puchero canario*. The origins of *cocido* (literally "cooked") probably date back to an old Jewish recipe known as *adafina* that was prepared on Friday and left to cook overnight in order to observe the Sabbath. The dish was later Christianized and pork was added. This meal-in-a-pot is traditionally served as three separate courses. The first course consists of soup, which is the broth from the stew, with or without noodles. The second course is made up of chickpeas, potatoes, and vegetables, and for the third course, meat is served.

 START PREPARATION OF THE CHICKPEAS 1 DAY IN ADVANCE.

CHICKPEAS, MEATS AND BROTH:
2 cups dried chickpeas, rinsed
1 chicken breast with bone, skinned
1 pound beef chuck
¼ pound salt pork or slab bacon
4 chorizo sausages
2 *morcilla* sausages
¼-pound slice serrano ham
1 ham bone
1 beef bone
Salt
Freshly ground black pepper
2 carrots, scraped
4 potatoes, peeled
1 onion, peeled and halved
1 leek, white part only
2 cloves garlic, peeled
6 large spoonfuls very fine noodles (optional)

MEATBALLS:
1 large spoonful breadcrumbs
1 large spoonful milk
3 large spoonfuls beaten egg
1 clove garlic, minced
1 large spoonful minced flat-leaf parsley
Salt
Freshly ground black pepper
¼ pound ground beef
2 large spoonfuls extra virgin olive oil

CABBAGE:
1 head cabbage, center vein removed and
  coarsely chopped
2 large spoonfuls extra virgin olive oil
1 clove garlic, minced
Salt
Freshly ground black pepper

The day before you plan to serve *cocido*, soak the chickpeas overnight in salted water to cover.

Make the broth: Place the chicken, beef, salt pork, chorizo, *morcilla*, ham, ham bone, beef bone, salt, and pepper in a large pot with 8 cups water. Bring to a gentle, rolling boil. Skim the white foam that forms on the surface of the water. Lower the heat, cover, and simmer for 1½ hours. Discard the bones and salt pork. Remove the meats and allow the broth to cool slightly. Place the meats and broth in the refrigerator until cool.

Skim off the fat that has hardened on the surface of the broth. Drain the chickpeas and put them in a mesh bag or cheesecloth. Place them in the soup pot with the degreased broth. Add the carrots, potatoes, onion, leek, garlic, and 4 cups water. Bring to a gentle, rolling boil. Skim the white foam that forms on the surface. Lower the heat, cover, and simmer for 2 hours. If your soup pot is large enough, you can also add the meats at this point; if not, add them later, as indicated below.

Drain off 4 cups of broth from the soup and place in another pot. Add the cabbage to this broth. Bring to a boil, cover, and cook for 30 minutes. Drain the cabbage and reserve, returning any leftover broth to the chickpeas.

Make the meatballs or *pelotas* (as they're known in Spanish): Mix the breadcrumbs, milk, egg, garlic, parsley, and some salt and pepper together in a bowl. Fold in the ground beef. Shape into 6 small meatballs and fry in olive oil. Drain and add to the chickpeas, along with the meats. Continue cooking for another 30 minutes to an hour, until the meatballs are cooked and the chickpeas are tender.

Make the cabbage: Heat the olive oil in a skillet. Gently sauté the garlic. Add the cabbage, and some salt and pepper. Continue cooking until the cabbage is tender.

Remove the meats, chickpeas, and vegetables from the soup pot. Strain the broth in order to remove any loose food particles. Reserve ½ cup to moisten the meats. Place the rest of the broth back in the pot and bring to a boil. If you are going to use noodles in the soup, add them to the broth and cook according to package directions. Serve this soup as a first course.

Arrange the chickpeas and vegetables on one platter and the meats and meatballs on another. Cut the meats and vegetables (with the exception of the meatballs) into thick slices. Moisten the meat with the reserved broth. Serve the cabbage with either the meats or vegetables. Place a cruet of extra virgin olive oil on the table for those who wish to drizzle a bit of olive oil over their vegetables. A good crusty bread and a bold, full-bodied red wine are the perfect accompaniments to this hearty *cocido*.

Cook's Notes: Adding cold water to cut the boil is a good way to tenderize beans, but not chickpeas. If you need to add more water during cooking, use only hot water.

Lentils with Chorizo Sausage

Lentejas estofadas con chorizo

[4 servings]

Legumes in Spain are typically cooked with slabs of salt pork and sausages, such as chorizo or *morcilla*. While I certainly enjoy the flavor of these Spanish *embutidos*, I'm not overly fond of the saturated animal fats they contain. Since I believe it's possible to enjoy traditional fare and keep an eye out for your arteries at the same time, I have eliminated salt pork from these lentils and degreased the chorizo sausages before adding them to the pot. In this way you get the flavor and very little of the fat. Lentils and beans are typically served as a first course in Spain; however, given their overall heartiness, they work perfectly well as a main course.

1½ cups dried lentils, preferably the *Pardiñas* or *Puy* variety, rinsed
1 whole onion, peeled; plus 1 onion, chopped
2 whole cloves garlic, peeled; plus 2 cloves garlic, minced
1 carrot, scraped and cut in thirds; plus 1 carrot, scraped and chopped
1 sprig parsley
1 bay leaf

4 chorizo sausages
4 large spoonfuls extra virgin olive oil
1 small spoonful *pimentón dulce* (sweet Spanish paprika)
6 large spoonfuls tomato sauce (page 119)
3 large spoonfuls red wine vinegar
Salt
2 potatoes, peeled and cut in bite-size pieces

Place the lentils in a pot along with the whole onion, whole garlic cloves, carrot pieces, parsley, and bay leaf. Cover with water (about 2 fingers deep). Bring to a gentle rolling boil. Lower the heat, cover, and gently cook for 30 minutes.

Degrease the chorizo sausages: Prick the sausage with a fork and place in a saucepan with water to cover. Bring to a boil and cook for 5 minutes. Drain and cut into ½-inch slices.

In a separate pan or skillet, sauté the chopped onion, minced garlic, and chopped carrot in the olive oil until the onion is transparent. Remove from the heat and stir in the *pimentón*, tomato sauce, vinegar, and some salt.

Remove the parsley, bay leaf, carrot pieces, whole onion, and whole garlic cloves from the lentils. Add the chorizo and potatoes along with the sautéed vegetable mixture to the lentils. If need be, add more water—there should be enough water in the pot to cover the potatoes and chorizo. Cover and continue cooking until the potatoes are tender, about 20 minutes. Serve with a good crusty bread.

Cook's Notes: Vinegar used in small amounts helps food to release its full flavor. This trick works with sweet foods, such as strawberries, and with savory foods, such as these lentils or "Poor Man's Potatoes."

White Beans with Chorizo Sausage

Judías con chorizo

[4 servings]

Legumes are a staple of the Spanish diet. In summer, they're served as salads with cooling vinaigrettes, and in winter, as hearty meals-in-a-pot. Just as I did in the previous recipe for Lentils with Chorizo Sausage, I have not used salt pork and have degreased the chorizo sausages before adding them to the beans.

 START PREPARATION THE DAY BEFORE BY SOAKING THE BEANS.

1½ cups dried white beans, rinsed
1 whole onion, peeled; plus 1 onion, chopped
2 whole cloves garlic, peeled; plus 2 cloves
   garlic, minced
2 carrots, scraped and cut in thirds
1 leek, white part only
1 sprig parsley
1 bay leaf

4 chorizo sausages
4 large spoonfuls extra virgin olive oil
1 pimiento, chopped (page xv)
1 small spoonful *pimentón dulce* (sweet
   Spanish paprika)
1 large spoonful red wine vinegar
Salt

Place the white beans in a large pot with cold water to cover and soak them overnight.

Add the whole onion, whole garlic cloves, carrots, leek, parsley, and bay leaf to the beans. The water covering the beans should be about 2 fingers deep. Bring to a gentle, rolling boil. Skim the white foam that forms on the surface of the water. Lower the heat, cover, and cook for 2 hours. Check the beans periodically to make sure that there's enough water and cut the boil with ¼ cup cold water 3 times during cooking to tenderize the beans.

Degrease the chorizo sausage: Prick the sausage with a fork and boil in water to cover for 5 minutes. Drain and cut into bite-size pieces.

In a small skillet, sauté the chopped onion and minced garlic in olive oil until tender. Stir in the pimiento and cook for another minute. Remove from the heat and stir in the *pimentón*, vinegar, and salt.

Remove the whole onion, whole garlic cloves, carrot pieces, leek, parsley, and bay leaf from the beans. Add the chorizo, along with the onion mixture to the beans, cover, and continue cooking for another 30 minutes. If the broth is too watery and needs to be thickened, either cook uncovered so that some of the water evaporates or remove some of the beans and broth, puree them, and return the mixture to the pot. Serve with a good crusty bread.

Cook's Notes: Rinse beans well before soaking and cook them in the same water that they've soaked in. It contains nutrients from the beans.

Potato and Chorizo Sausage Stew

Patatas riojanas

[4 servings]

This potato stew is one of those dishes that has small variations depending on the cook. Some make it with bell peppers, others without; some use sweet dried peppers or even *piquillo* peppers. As for the chorizo sausage, I've used a dry-cured chorizo known as *sarta* in reference to the string that holds the sausage loop together. Typically, each sausage loop weighs about half a pound, so you will need two for this recipe. And yes, it's available online. Potatoes are great flavor sponges and these soak up all the essence of the sausage, chopped vegetables, *pimentón*, and broth. Simply add a salad or fresh fruit and you have a complete meal.

4 medium potatoes, peeled
Salt
1 pound dry-cured mild chorizo sausage,
    cut in ½-inch slices
6 large spoonfuls extra virgin olive oil
1 onion, chopped
2 cloves garlic, minced

1 green bell pepper, chopped
1 red bell pepper, chopped
1 bay leaf
1 small spoonful *pimentón dulce* (sweet
    Spanish paprika)
4 large spoonfuls dry white wine
4 cups chicken broth (page 67)

Break the potatoes into eighths. To do so, insert a small knife in the center of the potato and cut a slit that is deep enough that you can wedge your thumb in and pull the potato apart. Continue this process until each potato has been broken into 8 pieces. Season the potatoes with salt and reserve.

Degrease the chorizo: Place the slices in a saucepan and cover with cold water. Bring to a boil and cook for 5 minutes. Drain the chorizo slices and reserve.

Gently heat the olive oil in a large earthenware dish or saucepan. Add the onion, garlic, peppers, and bay leaf. Cover and simmer for 10 minutes. Remove from the heat and stir in the *pimentón*. Add the potatoes and stir, being sure to coat them thoroughly with the oil. Return to the heat and add the wine. Cook for a few minutes until the wine has evaporated. Add the chorizo and chicken broth. Bring to a boil, lower the heat, and cook uncovered for 40 minutes. Allow the stew to sit 5 minutes before serving.

Cook's Notes: There is a reason that the potatoes in this recipe are broken into pieces as opposed to cut. It's because the starch does a better job of thickening the broth when the potato is broken. Another trick is to gently move the earthenware dish or saucepan back and forth from time to time during cooking.

Red Peppers Stuffed with Cod

Pimientos del piquillo rellenos de bacalao

[4 servings]

Pimientos del piquillo, small ruby red peppers from Navarra (page xv), can be prepared with a variety of stuffings ranging from *morcilla* to crabmeat to squid, but typically they are stuffed with cod. I've used salt cod in this recipe, but you can also use fresh cod, in which case, there's no need to desalt the fish.

 START PREPARING SALT COD 2 TO 3 DAYS IN ADVANCE.

8 ounces salt cod
4 large spoonfuls extra virgin olive oil
1 spring onion, chopped
1 green bell pepper, chopped
16 *piquillo* peppers

BÉCHAMEL SAUCE:
2 large spoonfuls mild extra virgin olive oil*
3 large spoonfuls all-purpose flour*
1 cup milk
Salt

Freshly ground black pepper
Several generous dashes ground nutmeg

RED PEPPER SAUCE:
2 large spoonfuls extra virgin olive oil
1 onion, chopped
2 homemade pimientos, cut in strips and
   juices reserved (see page xv)
½ cup reserved pepper juice
Salt

Begin soaking the salt cod 2 to 3 days in advance (see salt cod, page xv). Once the cod has been desalted, dry well with paper towels, shred, and reserve.

Make the béchamel sauce: Mix the olive oil and flour together in a saucepan over low heat to make a smooth paste. Gradually add the milk, stirring constantly to avoid lumps. Season with some salt, pepper, and nutmeg. Increase the heat to medium. Stir constantly until the sauce begins to thicken and reaches the boiling point, approximately 10 minutes. Remove from the heat and reserve.

Prepare the stuffed peppers: Sauté the spring onion and green pepper in olive oil until tender. Add the shredded cod and continue stirring for another few minutes. Remove the cod mixture with a slotted spoon (to drain off excess liquid). Mix together with the béchamel sauce and stuff each *piquillo* pepper with 1 large spoonful of the mixture. Arrange the stuffed peppers in an ovenproof dish and reserve. Preheat the oven to 325° F.

Prepare the Red Pepper Sauce: Sauté the onion in olive oil until tender. Stir in the pimiento strips and continue cooking for another few minutes. Add ½ cup of the reserved juice from the peppers and cook uncovered for 15 minutes.

While pepper sauce is cooking, place the stuffed peppers in the oven to warm for 10 minutes.

Blend the pepper mixture with an immersion blender (or puree in a regular blender) and season with salt. Spoon 4 large spoonfuls of sauce onto 4 individual serving plates and arrange 4 peppers each on top of the sauce. Serve.

Cook's Notes: "Béchamel" is normally made with butter, but you can also make it with olive oil. The taste is slightly different, but I find that béchamel made with olive oil is less heavy on the stomach—and arteries too.

*If you like exact measurements for your sauce, the oil measures out exactly to 2 tablespoons and the flour to 3 level tablespoons.

Vegetable Medley, Rioja-Style

Menestra riojana

[4 servings]

The vegetables you use for this dish may vary depending on what's in season. For example, snap peas make a lovely and tasty addition in spring. What doesn't vary is that certain vegetables—namely the cauliflower, artichoke hearts, and Swiss chard stems—are breaded and fried or that the vegetables are bathed in a serrano ham and garlic-flavored sauce. The pimiento and egg garnish is also quite typical.

1 carrot, scraped
1 potato, peeled and cut in ½-inch slices
½ small head cauliflower, cut in medium-size flowerets
8 asparagus, trimmed and halved
4 ounces broad green beans, trimmed and cut in 2-inch pieces
½ cup peas, fresh or frozen
½ cup lima beans, fresh or frozen
4 artichoke hearts, halved
4 leaves Swiss chard, thick stems trimmed
1 small spoonful all-purpose flour plus additional for dusting

4 large spoonfuls extra virgin olive oil plus additional for frying
1 leek, white part only, chopped
2 cloves garlic, minced
4 thin slices serrano ham, minced
2 eggs, beaten
Salt
2 large spoonfuls minced flat-leaf parsley
1 pimiento, cut in thin strips (page xv)
2 hardboiled eggs, quartered

Put just enough salted water in a pot to cover the vegetables that you're going to cook and bring to a boil. Add the carrot, potatoes, cauliflower, asparagus, green beans, peas, lima beans, artichoke hearts, and Swiss chard. Gently boil for 10 minutes. Using a slotted spoon, remove the vegetables and set them aside. Reserve ½ cup cooking liquid.

Separate the Swiss chard, cauliflower, and artichoke hearts from the other vegetables for frying. Take the Swiss chard and separate the leaves from the white portion. Coarsely chop the leaves and reserve with the vegetables that you won't be frying.

Take the white portion and cut into 2-inch pieces. Dust with flour, dip in beaten egg, and fry in abundant olive oil. Follow the same procedure for the cauliflower and artichokes.

Gently sauté the leek and garlic in 4 large spoonfuls of olive oil until the leek turns golden brown. Add the ham and stir for a minute. Sprinkle 1 small spoonful of flour over the leek mixture. Gradually stir in the reserved cooking liquid. Season with salt. Add the vegetables, stirring to coat well with the sauce. Sprinkle with parsley. To serve, decorate with pimiento strips and egg wedges.

Cook's Notes: In order to minimize the loss of vitamins and flavor, use the minimum amount of water necessary when cooking the vegetables. Also, add the vegetables to boiling water rather than cold water and cook them until they're "al dente." Another trick is to steam the vegetables or cook them in the microwave, though remember that you do need a bit of cooking liquid for the sauce.

Vegetable Medley, Manchego-Style

Pisto manchego

[4 servings]

Versatile dish that it is, *pisto manchego* can be served as a starter, as the accompaniment to a main course, or used as a filling in omelets or turnovers. It's also a great make-ahead dish and freezes quite well. This vegetable medley, as its name implies, hails from La Mancha, the land of Don Quijote.

6 large spoonfuls extra virgin olive oil	Salt
1 green bell pepper, diced	Freshly ground black pepper
1 red bell pepper, diced	2 ripe tomatoes, grated
1 onion, chopped	Pinch sugar
1 zucchini, unpeeled and diced	

Heat the olive oil in a skillet or earthenware dish. Sauté the peppers, onion, and zucchini until tender, about 20 minutes. Season with salt and pepper. Add the grated tomato along with a pinch of sugar. Cover and simmer for 15 minutes, stirring occasionally.

Cook's Notes: Turn this vegetable medley into a light supper by adding some chopped serrano ham, cracking 4 to 6 eggs over the vegetables, and stirring until the eggs are soft-set.

Oven-Roasted Potatoes

Patatas panaderas

[4 servings]

These potatoes are the perfect accompaniment to the roasted meats typical of central Spain. They also work well with chicken and fish.

4 potatoes, peeled and cut in ¼-inch-thick slices	2 cloves garlic, minced
1 small onion, thinly sliced	Salt
	3 large spoonfuls extra virgin olive oil

Preheat the oven to 350° F. Mix all the ingredients together in an earthenware dish, being sure to coat the potatoes thoroughly with the olive oil. Bake for an hour, turning occasionally. The potatoes should be tender and a few of them will even be brown and crispy.

Cook's Notes: If you're pressed for time, you can cook these potatoes (and "Poor Man's Potatoes" or potatoes for a Spanish omelet) in the microwave. I won't say that the microwave method is as good as the traditional stovetop or oven method, but it's not bad either. Place the potatoes (and other ingredients, depending on the recipe) together in a microwave-proof bowl. Stir to coat the potatoes with the olive oil. (In the case of potatoes for a Spanish omelet, use 3 large spoonfuls of extra virgin olive oil.) Cover and microwave on high for 10 minutes.

Fried Eggs and Potatoes with Chorizo Sausage

Huevos fritos con patatas y chorizo

[4 servings]

It's amazing what Spaniards can do with eggs and just how satisfying they can be when served as a main course. This is comfort food, Spanish-style.

4 chorizo sausages	Coarse salt
4 potatoes	8 eggs
Extra virgin olive oil for frying	

Degrease the chorizo sausages: Prick the sausage with a fork and place in a saucepan with water to cover. Bring to a boil and cook for 5 minutes. Drain.

Peel the potatoes and cut in ⅛-inch round slices or French fries. Heat the olive oil over medium-high heat. The olive oil should be about 1 finger deep. Fry the potatoes until their edges are golden and crispy. Remove from the oil and drain on paper towels. Sprinkle with coarse salt.

Use the same oil in which you've just fried the potatoes and heat in a non-stick skillet over medium-high heat. The oil should be about ½ finger deep. When the oil is hot (not smoking), add an egg or two (no more as they cook quickly and will be hard to control). Using a slotted pancake turner, "splash" the oil onto the eggs until the yolks are set. The whites will be light and crunchy around the edges. Remove the eggs using the slotted pancake turner and drain on paper towels. Sprinkle with coarse salt.

To serve, arrange the fried potatoes, eggs, and chorizo on the same plate.

Cook's Notes: Once you've eaten eggs that have been fried in hot olive oil, you won't want to go back to butter-fried eggs. Butter produces a rubbery fried egg that can't begin to compare to one that's been fried in extra virgin olive oil.

Scrambled Eggs with Bacon and Chorizo Sausage

Duelos y quebrantos

[1 serving]

Duelos y quebrantos—something akin to mourning and suffering—is a dish with a literary pedigree. Miguel de Cervantes makes reference to these scrambled eggs in the opening lines of *Don Quijote de la Mancha*:

> In a place in La Mancha, whose name I do not wish to recall, lived a gentleman who owned a lance, an old shield, a weak horse and a racing hound. Three parts of his income were consumed in food—a stewpot of beef, leftover ground meat on other nights, *duelos y quebrantos* on Saturdays, lentils for Fridays and perhaps a pigeon on Sundays.

Normally these scrambled eggs are translated into English as "hash," an all too unfortunate and inaccurate description. Don Quijote was simply scrambling up some eggs with what he had on hand—bacon and chorizo sausage.

½ chorizo sausage, thinly sliced (approximately 1½ ounces)
2 large spoonfuls diced slab bacon

2 eggs
Extra virgin olive oil

Cut the chorizo slices into quarters. (What you want are bits of chorizo sausage and bacon in your scrambled eggs.) Sauté the chorizo and bacon until brown. Drain on paper towels. Beat the eggs and add the cooked bacon and chorizo.

In a separate skillet, add enough olive oil to keep the eggs from sticking and heat over medium-high heat. Add the egg mixture and stir until soft-set. Serve immediately.

Cook's Notes: I'm quite sure that in Cervantes' time, they didn't bother cooking the meat in a separate skillet or draining the fat; however I find that this is a way to enjoy all the flavor that the bacon and sausage give to the eggs without the added fat. Given that both of these meats are salty, I've intentionally not added more.

Trout with Serrano Ham

Truchas a la Navarra

[4 servings]

Regional dishes are born of regional products as is the case with these trout, fished from the rivers and streams of Navarra. And the best-known recipe for preparing this fish is a la Navarra, which means with serrano ham.

4 freshwater trout (approximately ¾ pound each), cleaned with heads on Salt Freshly ground black pepper 8 thin slices serrano ham, trimmed	All-purpose flour for dusting Extra virgin olive oil for frying 2 large spoonfuls minced flat-leaf parsley 1 lemon, quartered

Season the trout inside and out with salt and pepper. Place a slice of serrano ham in each trout cavity. Dust the trout with flour and wrap each fish in a slice of ham. Secure the ham with a string or toothpicks.

Heat the olive oil in a skillet over medium-high heat (oil should be about 1 finger deep). Fry the trout on both sides until well browned and cooked through. Remove the string or toothpicks, sprinkle the trout with parsley, and serve with a lemon wedge.

Cook's Notes: If you're buying fresh fish whole, ask yourself the following questions: Are the scales close to the body and shiny? Do the eyes stick out and are they bright? Is the body rigid? Are the gills a vivid red? If you answered "yes" to these questions, then chances are you've got a fresh catch.

Salt Cod in Tomato and Pepper Sauce

Bacalao al ajo arriero

[4 servings]

Even though the interior of Spain is landlocked, it has some excellent fish dishes, among them this cod cooked in a tomato and pepper sauce. The name in Spanish makes reference to the mule drivers (*arrieros*) who transported goods in the days before eighteen wheelers. While the mule drivers may have stopped at inns along the way, the midday meal invariably found them on the road. Salt cod was a food that would keep without refrigeration and so this traditional dish was born.

 START PREPARING THE SALT COD 2 TO 3 DAYS IN ADVANCE.

1 pound thick-cut salt cod fillets
4 large spoonfuls extra virgin olive oil
6 cloves garlic, thinly sliced
1 (8 ounce) jar *piquillo* peppers, cut in thin strips

4 ripe tomatoes, grated
Pinch sugar

Soak the salt cod for 2 to 3 days in advance (see salt cod, page xv).

Heat the olive oil in an earthenware dish and gently sauté the garlic until it begins to brown. Add the *piquillo* peppers, tomatoes, and a pinch of sugar. Simmer for 8 to 10 minutes.

Add the salt cod, skin side up. Cover and cook for 10 minutes. Turn the fish over and cook for another 8 to 10 minutes. To serve, arrange the cod fillets on individual plates and spoon the peppers and garlic over the fish, along with some of the broth. This dish is often served with cubed potatoes that have been fried in olive oil.

Cook's Notes: I'm particularly fond of piquillo *peppers because of their meaty texture, and find that they contrast nicely with the strong-flavored salt cod; however, you can also use regular pimientos in this recipe.*

Butterflied Porgy

Besugo a la espalda

[4 servings]

While Madrid is a landlocked city, it has some of the best seafood in Spain thanks to modern shipping methods. *Besugo*, fished from the Bay of Biscay and the Mediterranean Sea, is popular in the interior of Spain, particularly at Christmas time, and so I've included it in this chapter. While porgy isn't an exact translation of *besugo*, both fish do belong to the same family. A *besugo (Pagellus bogaraveo)* is salmon-colored and characterized by a black spot above its pectoral fin. It is similar in appearance to sea bream. This method of preparing fish requires that you use only the freshest of fish. There are no adornments or sauces and so the fish must be top quality. Ask to have the fish sliced down the middle and opened so that it lies flat. Any fish that is prepared this way is said to be *a la espalda* or "on its back."

1 dried red chili pepper, seeds removed and crumbled

4 cloves garlic, minced

4 large spoonfuls minced flat-leaf parsley

4 large spoonfuls extra virgin olive oil

2 porgies (approximately 2 pounds each), cleaned, heads removed, and butterflied

2 lemons, quartered

4 large spoonfuls dry white wine

Coarse salt

Preheat the oven to 375° F. Mix together the chili pepper, garlic, parsley, and olive oil. Reserve.

Heat a non-stick skillet or griddle over medium-high heat and lightly grease with a few drops of extra virgin olive oil. Place the fish skin side down on the hot cooking surface and cook for 3 to 4 minutes on that side only.

Remove the fish and arrange them skin side down in an ovenproof dish. Squeeze 2 lemon wedges over each fish and pour 2 large spoonfuls of wine over each fish. Spread half the olive oil mixture over each fish. Bake for 10 minutes. Lightly season with coarse salt and serve with the remaining lemon wedges.

Cook's Notes: Other fish that lend themselves to this type of preparation and that are similar to porgy are sea bream, sea bass, and red snapper.

Chicken in Saffron-Scented Sherry Sauce with Almonds

Pollo en pepitoria

[4 servings]

Chicken prepared with a *pepitoria* sauce is a classic of Spanish cooking. The presence of saffron and almonds suggests Arab roots, though the word itself comes from the French *petite-oie* according to the very official *Real Academia Española* dictionary. There are references to *pepitoria* sauce in cookbooks that date from the Middle Ages and this dish appears in literary works by Cervantes and Quevedo, among others. Traditionally, a *pepitoria* sauce contains saffron, nuts (usually almonds, but some recipes call for pine nuts), and cooked egg yolk to thicken the sauce. The combination of almonds, saffron, garlic, and dry sherry creates a seasoning so uniquely Spanish that it's no wonder this dish has been around for centuries and that its preparation has varied so little over time.

1 chicken (3 to 3½ pounds), cut in serving pieces and skinned	1 bay leaf
Salt	20 blanched almonds, finely ground
Freshly ground black pepper	Pinch saffron
4 large spoonfuls extra virgin olive oil	2 large spoonfuls minced flat-leaf parsley
1 onion, chopped	¾ cup chicken broth (page 67)
3 cloves garlic, minced	¼ cup dry sherry (*fino*)
	2 hardboiled eggs

Season the chicken pieces with salt and pepper. Heat the olive oil in a large earthenware dish and brown the chicken pieces. Remove to a platter and reserve.

Add the onion, garlic, and bay leaf to the same oil and sauté until the onion is tender. Stir in the ground almonds, saffron, 1 large spoonful parsley, chicken broth, sherry, and 1 egg yolk. Return the chicken to the earthenware dish. Cover and simmer for 40 minutes, turning the chicken pieces halfway through cooking.

Chop the remaining hardboiled egg and egg white. To serve, sprinkle the chicken with the remaining spoonful of parsley and chopped egg.

Cook's Notes: For even better results, use a free range chicken.

Chicken with Tomato and Red Pepper Sauce

Pollo al chilindrón

[4 servings]

In Aragon, Navarra, and La Rioja, *chilindrón* denotes a sauce that is prepared using red peppers, tomatoes, and onion, which means colorful as well as flavorful!

1 chicken (3 to 3½ pounds), cut in serving pieces and skinned
Salt
Freshly ground black pepper
4 large spoonfuls extra virgin olive oil
1 onion, chopped

2 cloves garlic, minced
2 thin slices serrano ham, trimmed and minced
2 ripe tomatoes, grated
2 pimientos, cut in thin strips (page xv)

Salt and pepper the chicken pieces, and brown them in olive oil on both sides. Remove the chicken to a platter and reserve.

Sauté the onion and garlic in the same oil. Stir in the ham, tomatoes, and pimientos. Return the chicken to the sauce. Cover and simmer for 20 minutes. Turn the chicken over and continue cooking for another 20 minutes.

Cook's Notes: I keep an oil cruet with extra virgin olive oil on hand when cooking. The cruet makes adding oil to a skillet or dish much easier than pouring it directly from the bottle as the oil comes out in a fine stream and is much easier to control.

Ham-Stuffed Quail

Codornices rellenas de jamón

[4 servings]

Quail is not just a dish for special occasions in Spain. It's a common game bird and readily available in local grocery stores, along with quail eggs. These ham-stuffed quail, typical of Aragon, are surprisingly easy to prepare.

---

8 quail, butterflied
Salt
Freshly ground black pepper
4 thin slices serrano ham, trimmed and cut
  in small pieces
4 large spoonfuls extra virgin olive oil

2 onions, chopped
1 clove garlic, minced
¼ cup dry white wine
2 cups chicken broth (page 67)
2 large spoonfuls minced flat-leaf parsley

Lightly salt and pepper the outside of the quail. Fill the inside cavities with the ham and fold the quail over on their sides. Heat the olive oil in an earthenware dish and brown the quail on both sides. Remove to a platter and reserve.

Sauté the onion, garlic, and bay leaf in the same oil until tender. Place the quail on top of the sautéed onions and add the wine. Pour in the chicken broth, cover, and simmer for 30 minutes, turning the quail halfway through cooking. To serve, spoon a bit of the broth over each quail and sprinkle with parsley.

Cook's Notes: Given that the birds are so small, I don't find it necessary to tress them.

Roast Partridge

Perdiz a la toledana

[4 servings]

Hunting is a long-standing tradition in *Castilla-La Mancha* and this is reflected in the local cuisine with traditional game dishes such as hare, deer, wild boar, and these well-known partridges, prepared in either a white wine or sherry sauce and delicately scented with bay leaf, pepper, garlic, and thyme.

4 young partridges, split open	2 carrots, scraped and cut in ½-inch slices
Salt	8 small onions, peeled
Freshly ground black pepper	2 bay leaves
Thyme	10 black peppercorns
8 large spoonfuls extra virgin olive oil	8 new potatoes
1 onion, chopped	1 cup dry sherry (*fino*) or dry white wine
4 cloves garlic, peeled and lightly crushed	

Preheat the oven to 350° F. Wash the partridges thoroughly and dry with paper towels. Season with salt, pepper, and thyme. Heat the olive oil in a large earthenware dish and brown the partridges on all sides. Remove to a platter and reserve.

Add the chopped onion to the dish and sauté until tender. Add the garlic, carrot slices, French onions, and bay leaves. Sauté for a few minutes. Return the partridges to the dish, add the peppercorns and new potatoes, and pour in the dry sherry or wine. Cook for a few minutes. Cover and transfer the dish to the oven. Bake for 1 to 1¼ hours.

To serve, arrange the partridges on individual plates or on a platter, along with the vegetables, and spoon some of the sauce over the birds.

Cook's Notes: Baking time may vary depending on the size of the partridges. In this recipe, I use young partridges, which usually weigh between 1 and 1½ pounds. It is important to cook the birds until they are well done. To see if the meat is done, pierce the partridge with a fork. The fork should go in easily and you should be able to wiggle the leg with ease. Take care not to overcook though as partridge dries out quickly.

Lamb and Red Pepper Stew

Cordero al chilindrón

[4 servings]

Instead of chicken (page 90), try preparing lamb *chilindrón*-style. Again, this means with plenty of red peppers and slow cooking that allows the flavors to mingle, creating tender juicy meat.

2½-pound leg of lamb, cut in 2-inch to 3-inch pieces with the bone	2 cloves garlic, minced
Salt	4 ripe tomatoes, grated
Freshly ground black pepper	2 pimientos, cut in strips (page xv)
2 large spoonfuls extra virgin olive oil	1 large spoonful minced flat-leaf parsley
1 onion, chopped	1 bay leaf
	¼ cup dry white wine

Salt and pepper the lamb and sauté in olive oil until browned on both sides. Add the onion and garlic and continue cooking until the onion is tender. Stir in the tomatoes, pimientos, parsley, bay leaf, and wine. Cover and simmer for 15 minutes. Turn the lamb pieces over and continue cooking for another 15 minutes.

Cook's Notes: I usually buy a 2½ pound lamb shank and have my butcher cut it into small pieces. Another option is to buy lamb that has been cut up for stew without the bone. In that case, you will need 1 to 1½ pounds of meat for this recipe.

Roast Leg of Lamb

Paletilla de cordero asada

[4 servings]

While sampling roast suckling lamb may require a trip to Spain, you can still enjoy lamb Spanish-style without having to board a plane. (See Roast Suckling Lamb and Pig: Culinary Masterpieces, page 95.) Lamb is a common meat in Spain and is eaten year-round, but roast leg of lamb is especially popular during the Christmas holidays in many parts of Spain.

3½- to 4-pound leg of lamb or shank	Salt
4 cloves garlic, minced	Freshly ground black pepper
Rosemary	2 large spoonfuls lard
Thyme	1 cup dry white wine

Preheat the oven to 450° F. Place the lamb in a roasting pan or earthenware dish. Rub the lamb with garlic. Season with rosemary, thyme, salt, and pepper. Rub with lard. Roast for 15 minutes.

Pour ¼ cup wine over the lamb. Reduce the heat to 350° F and continue basting with the remaining wine every 10 minutes until the meat is done, approximately 15 to 20 minutes per pound, depending on the desired doneness. (For best results, use a meat thermometer.)

Cook's Notes: It's important that the meat start to roast before adding any liquid to it; otherwise you end up stewing the meat as opposed to roasting it. What you want is a leg of lamb that is crusty and brown on the outside, but tender and juicy on the inside.

Roast Suckling Lamb and Pig: Culinary Masterpieces

If Spanish cooking is good—and it's better than good—then there are several dishes that deserve a place in the food hall of fame. Two such examples await the traveler to *Castilla-León*: roast baby lamb and roast suckling pig. Both are culinary masterpieces of Spanish cooking, but, alas, masterpieces that must be experienced in Spain. Animals this young are simply not available in the United States and most people don't have access to a wood-burning baker's oven either, which is where the meat is roasted in oval earthenware dishes. Both of these factors are key to producing the succulent meat and crackling skin characteristic of the roasts from this area of Spain.

The lambs used for *lechazo* (which takes its name from *leche* or milk) are less than a month old and have received only mother's milk for nourishment. Discerning gourmands will even go so far as to say that the left forequarter is superior to the right since the lamb generally lies on its right side, making the meat there a smidgen tougher. There are only four ingredients needed to make roast suckling lamb: first and foremost, a lamb which meets the previously described conditions, then lard, salt, and water.

In the case of roast suckling pig, known as *cochinillo* or *tostón* in Spanish, the animal is between fifteen and twenty days old. The pig is opened down the middle and cleaned out, but the head is left on. The *cochinillo* is roasted sprawled out using the simplest, most exquisite ingredients: a newborn pig, salt, fresh herbs such as bay leaf or thyme, lard, perhaps a few cloves of garlic, and white wine. When roasted, the meat must be tender enough that it can be cut with a plate, a spectacular sight to behold: first the head, then down the middle, and finally, along the sides.

A word about lard.

I know. The thought of it alone makes you cringe, which is why I've buried this four-letter word in the middle of the book; however, I'd be remiss if I didn't point out that lard is used in Spanish cooking, particularly where roasts and pastries are concerned. We know that lard refers to pig fat; however, the quality of lard can vary depending on which part of the pig the fat was taken from and how it was processed. Industrially-produced lards can be rendered from a combination of fats and are typically hydrogenated to improve shelf life, which means trans fats. (Two *very* ugly words.) You can either purchase artisan lard or render your own, preferably from the premium fat deposits surrounding the kidneys. This type of lard is known as leaf lard and is considered to be of superior quality. Because the lard you make at home has not been treated, it will need to be refrigerated. You could, of course, use extra virgin olive oil, but for culinary purposes, lard works best.

So, while I use extra virgin olive oil for everything from homemade muesli to meat, fish, vegetables, and even cake, I am going to use lard for the Roast Leg of Lamb (page 94) because it's not everyday that I eat lamb and I want the most tender, flavorful meat possible. Tomorrow I'll return to my more Mediterranean ways.

Stewed Pig's Feet

Manos de cerdo estofadas

[4 servings]

Spaniards will tell you that nothing goes to waste with a pig. If you're looking for something a little different, look no further. These little trotters have a gelatinous consistency and the white wine sauce only enhances their tenderness. These stewed pig's feet are typical of Extremadura, which should come as no surprise given that this region of Spain is home to the Iberian pig and the *pata negra* ("black hoof") variety of cured Iberian hams.

---

4 pig's feet, split in half lengthwise
2 onions, coarsely chopped
1 whole clove garlic, peeled; plus 2 cloves
    garlic, minced
2 bay leaves
2 cups dry white wine

Salt
2 large spoonfuls extra virgin olive oil
1 small spoonful *pimentón dulce* (sweet
    Spanish paprika)
1 large spoonful all-purpose flour
1 large spoonful minced flat-leaf parsley

Tie the pig's feet with string so that they maintain their shape during the cooking process.

Place the pig's feet in a large saucepan, along with 1 chopped onion, whole clove garlic, 1 bay leaf, 1 cup wine, some salt, and water to cover. (The water should be about 1 finger deep.) Gradually bring to a boil, lower the heat, cover, and cook over low heat for 3 hours.

Once cooked, remove the pig's feet from the broth, untie them, and carefully take out the bones, all the while maintaining the original shape of the trotters. Reserve. Drain the broth and reserve. (If you want to break this recipe into two parts, you can prepare the pig's feet up to this point and finish cooking them the following day.)

In an earthenware dish, sauté the remaining chopped onion, minced garlic, and 1 bay leaf in olive oil until tender. Stir in the *pimentón*, flour, parsley, and some salt. Gradually add remaining 1 cup wine and 4 cups of the reserved broth. Add the pig's feet to the broth, cover, and simmer for 30 minutes.

To serve, arrange the trotters on individual serving plates and spoon some of the sauce on top. This dish is often served with mashed potatoes.

Cook's Notes: Pig's feet contain surprisingly very little fat. What's particularly noticeable with this broth is just how much gelatin there is.

Round Castilian Loaf

Pan candeal

[Makes 1 round loaf]

If cake were bread, this is what it would look like, round and compact. The secret to creating this dense Castilian loaf lies in not allowing the bread to ferment and rise too much, which would create air bubbles, giving the bread an entirely different texture.

 START PREPARING THE SPONGE SEVERAL DAYS IN ADVANCE.

¼ cup warm water	2 cups unbleached all-purpose flour
1 package dry yeast	1 cup mother sponge (page 19)
Pinch sugar	1 cup cornmeal or breadcrumbs
1 small spoonful salt	Egg white

If you do not already have a mother sponge, then you will need to create one first. To do so, see recipe for Galician Rye Bread, page 19.

Dissolve the yeast in warm water, along with a pinch of sugar. Mix together the salt and 1 cup flour, and using a wooden spoon, add it to the yeast along with the sponge. Gradually stir in the remaining cup of flour until the dough comes together to form a firm ball. Turn onto a floured surface and knead for 5 minutes, adding more flour as needed. Place the dough in a greased bowl, cover, and let rise until it's almost, but not quite, double in size, about 1½ hours.

Punch the dough down and knead for another 5 minutes. Shape the dough into a round loaf about 1 inch thick. Sprinkle the cornmeal or breadcrumbs on a cookie sheet and place the loaf on top. Dip a sharp knife in cold water and cut a square just inside the circle that is the loaf. Place the dough in a warm place and let it rest for another 15 minutes.

Preheat the oven to 425° F. Bake bread on the middle-upper rack for 10 minutes. Lightly brush the bread with egg white and continue baking for another 20 minutes. The loaf should make a hollow sound when tapped on the bottom.

Cook's Notes: This loaf is usually round. Typically, the baker uses a knife to draw a large square that fits snugly inside the circle that is the loaf before baking. When doing this, the parameters of the square should practically meet those of the circle. But it's also possible to buy this bread or bake this bread in an elongated form or as small individual rolls, perfect for entertaining.

Peaches in Wine Syrup

Melocotón con vino

[4 servings]

Denomination of origin Calanda peaches from Aragon prepared in wine syrup are a classic dessert. These lovely yellow peaches even come complete with their own popular saying:

La casadica en su casa,	The eligible young woman at home,
los curas en el pulpito,	the priests in the pulpit,
el militar en la guerra,	the soldier at war,
y el melocotón en vino.	and peaches in wine.

3 cups full-bodied red wine	Peel of 1 lemon
½ cup brandy, preferably Spanish	1 cinnamon stick
1 cup sugar	4 large ripe peaches (yellow flesh), peeled

Mix the wine, brandy, sugar, lemon peel, and cinnamon stick together in saucepan or earthenware dish. Heat over medium heat, stirring until the sugar dissolves. Add the peaches, bring to a boil, lower the heat, and simmer for 20 minutes. Cool for a few minutes. Spoon the warm syrup over the peaches and serve.

Cook's Notes: Use any leftover syrup as a marinade for cut-up fresh fruit.

Buttery Cupcakes

Mantecadas de Astorga

[Makes 12 cupcakes]

These buttery cupcakes are the perfect accompaniment to morning or afternoon coffee. Their name in Spanish comes from the word *manteca* or lard as that was the fat that was originally used when making them. Like so many Spanish desserts, this one originated in a convent kitchen. *Mantecadas* are typically baked in rectangular paper molds, though they taste just as good round.

¼ pound butter, softened	1 large spoonful baking powder*
½ cup sugar	Pinch salt
3 eggs	Ground cinnamon (the tip of a small spoonful)
1 cup all-purpose flour	Sugar for sprinkling

Preheat the oven to 350° F. Beat the butter and sugar together. Beat in the eggs. Stir in the flour, baking powder, salt, and cinnamon. Fill cupcake liners ⅔ full. Sprinkle with sugar. Bake for 20 minutes until lightly golden.

Cook's Notes: To achieve authentic rectangular mantecadas, *you can either use foil cupcake liners and miter the corners or make your own molds using parchment paper.*

The baking powder measures out to exactly 4 level teaspoons.

Fresh Cheese with Walnuts and Honey

Queso de Burgos con nueces y miel

[1 serving]

Spaniards can be rather irreverent at times when it comes to nicknames. This dessert is a perfect example as it is also known as *el postre del abuelo* (grandpa's dessert) because this fresh cheese is easy to chew.

2 ounces *Queso de Burgos* or another fresh cheese, such as ricotta, fromage blanc, or fromage frais

Handful of walnut pieces
1 large spoonful honey

Place the *Queso de Burgos* on a dessert plate. Top with the walnuts and drizzle with honey.

Cook's Notes: Fresh Queso de Burgos *has no smell whatsoever, so if the cheese starts to smell a little sour, then it has probably gone bad. Once opened, wrap the cheese in a paper towel, run it under the tap, and place it on a plate in the refrigerator. It will keep up to 3 days this way. Another way to keep the cheese for up to 10 days is to store it in extra virgin olive oil in a glass jar in your refrigerator. If you'll be using it in salads, you can also add some aromatic herbs to the oil for extra flavor.*

Spanish Cheeses: Regional Delights

Spain is home to a wide variety of regional cheeses. Here are a few available in the United States that you might enjoy trying.

Arzúa-Ulloa: A mild, creamy, pale yellow cheese made using cow's milk and produced in Galicia. This cheese has a soft rind and, when it is young, spreads easily.

Cabrales: A blue cheese made primarily from cow's milk and aged in the mountain caves of Asturias.

Garrotxa: A mild-flavored goat's milk cheese produced in the Catalan Pyrenees. This smooth-textured, pale white cheese is covered with a thick, natural gray rind. Enjoy it with Catalan *cava*.

Ibores: A zesty, semi-cured goat's milk cheese from Extremadura. The goats are left to roam the countryside and feed on the aromatic herbs and grasses that grow there, infusing the cheese with herbal flavors. During the aging period, the rind is rubbed with olive oil and paprika, creating a visually striking cheese wheel.

Idiazábal: A smoked sheep's milk cheese from the Basque country.

Mahón: A traditional, semi-soft cow's milk cheese from the island of Menorca.

Manchego: Queso Manchego is the quintessential Spanish cheese. It is available all over Spain and is probably the best-known Spanish cheese outside of Spain. Made from sheep's milk, this cheese ranges from semi-soft and mild to hard and sharp. Pair *Manchego* with *jamón serrano* and throw in a bold Rioja red and you have a taste combination that's hard to beat.

Ovin: This cheese comes from the northern Asturian province of Nava. It is an artisan cheese made primarily with goat's milk, though it can also be made with sheep's or cow's milk, as well as with a blend. No less than four varieties! Because it has a short maturation time—30 to 40 days—it is not a sharp cheese, but creamy with a hint of herbs.

Queso de Burgos: This fresh cheese takes its name from the Castilian city where it is made, though it is commonly eaten throughout Spain. Made from sheep's milk, *Queso de Burgos* is low in cholesterol and easy to digest. It's also a remarkably versatile cheese and can be eaten alone, used in salads or, if accompanied by walnuts and honey or quince, served as a dessert.

Roncal: A cured cheese from the valley of Roncal in Navarra made from sheep's milk. The elaboration of this cheese is a closely guarded secret passed on from generation to generation. *Roncal* has a smooth buttery texture and slightly sharp taste and was the first Spanish cheese to be granted a denomination of origin in 1981.

San Simón: A smoked cheese made from cow's milk and produced in Galicia.

Taramundi: A smooth, buttery cheese with a slightly toasted flavor, *Taramundi* comes in several versions: a semi-cured blend of sheep's, goat's, and/or cow's milk; semi-cured with goat's milk only; and a mild cow's milk cheese with hazelnuts and walnuts. Try pairing it with Asturian *sidra*.

Tetilla: A mild and creamy cow's milk cheese from Galicia. This cheese bears a striking resemblance to a woman's breast; hence the name *Tetilla*. *Queso de Tetilla* makes a wonderful accompaniment to fruits. Try a few slices with apples, pears, or grapes.

Torta del Casar: A creamy artisan cheese in the shape of a cake (*torta* means "cake") from Extremadura made from raw sheep's milk. The flavor is intense, infused with the flavor of the herbs and grasses the ewes graze on right before the milk is collected. Peel back the top of the cheese and spread over good crusty bread for a memorable taste experience.

Tupí: A bold-flavored cheese made from sheep's and cow's milk mixed with *aguardiente*. The cheese is left to ripen in a small earthenware pot known in Catalan as a *tupí;* hence, the cheese's name.

● The Spanish Kitchen

You may be surprised to learn that none of the recipes in this book requires special equipment or a sophisticated kitchen. In fact, I have prepared each and every one of them in the decidedly less than state-of-the-art kitchen of my not-so-roomy apartment in Tarragona. Kitchens in Spain are small by American standards and most are not stocked with every kitchen appliance known to man. Famed chef Ferran Adrià waxes poetic about the food served at the Pinotxo bar in La Boqueria market in Barcelona and it doesn't even have what could be called a proper kitchen! A narrow aisle separates customers seated on bar stools from the cooking area and yet they manage to turn out dishes that make a world-famous chef swoon. Appliances don't make the cook; top-notch ingredients, technique, and the more ethereal heart and soul do.

Here are a few utensils that are common in Spanish kitchens, but that you might not think about when stocking your own kitchen:

Earthenware dish: The versatility and unique properties that this cooking dish offers have made it a standard since Roman times. Talk about tradition! (See *La Cazuela:* Spanish Earthenware, page 14.)

Griddle: The modern Spanish kitchen uses an electric griddle for grilling fish, meat, chicken, and vegetables. Of course, you can just as easily use a non-stick skillet, but with a griddle, you can cook everything at once.

"Minipimer": This is a case where the brand name has become the name of the object itself. This little one-legged immersion blender is a staple in Spanish kitchens—perfect for making mayonnaise and blending sauces—and I've become so used to cooking with it that I wonder how I ever lived without it.

Mortar and pestle: Typically wooden or ceramic, a mortar and pestle are perfect for grinding ingredients in small quantities, such as saffron, garlic, herbs, or nuts. This little utensil also comes in handy for creating pastes for certain Spanish sauces.

Oil cruet: A cruet is perfect when you simply want to drizzle a few drops of olive oil onto a hot griddle, over food that you're cooking, or atop a salad, because, quite frankly, there's a lot of drizzling in Spanish cooking. I drizzle all the time and a cruet is infinitely more precise than pouring directly from the bottle.

Paellera: The pan used to make paella is called a *paellera*. There is a certain amount of controversy surrounding this term in Spain. Purists will say that a *paellera* is a woman who prepares paella and, conversely, a *paellero* is a man who prepares this same dish, but it's confusing, even in Spain! Especially in Spain! I recently tried to buy a *paellera* at a local shop and, when I asked if they carried this pan, the shopkeeper showed me a skillet, which in Catalan (known as *Valenciano* in Valencia and another bone of contention) is called a paella (and the origin, by the way, of the name of this rice dish). Are you confused yet? It is not my intention to enter into linguistic arguments or to offend sensibilities, but using two separate terms to distinguish the food from the pan does avoid confusion, so I will henceforth use the term *paellera* or its English equivalent, paella pan, when alluding to the cooking utensil and paella when referring to that exquisite rice dish.

To get back to the cooking utensil, it is a two-handled, round, metal pan with low, sloping sides. The bottom of the pan is slightly dimpled in order to spread heat evenly and enhance the rice's absorption of liquid. Most *paelleras* are made of carbon or stainless steel. To prevent rust, the paella pan should be treated before using it for the first time. Fill your *paellera* with water and boil to remove any remaining dirt or glue. Coat the pan with olive oil and place it in a 350° F oven for two hours. After that, simply wash and dry well after each use and lightly re-oil.

Pressure cooker: This is a great time-saver that Spanish cooks regularly use to cut down on the time required to prepare stews and legumes. It's also a very effective way to tenderize cheaper cuts of meat.

Salt jar: I'm not quite sure what term to even use for this nifty little box, typically ceramic, with a wooden lid. It sits on the countertop and all the cook has to do is lift up the lid, pinch a bit of salt, and continue preparing the dish. Some people even keep two in their kitchen: one for coarse salt and the other for fine.

Vegetable chopper: I have an embarrassing little secret. I can't chop vegetables the way professional cooks do. I have never mastered that rapid-fire chopping motion with impressive-looking stainless steel knives. In fact, I don't even have impressive-looking stainless steel knives! For this reason, I have added vegetable chopper to this list without worrying about tradition. I find a vegetable chopper to be a *big* time-saver given that Spanish cooking involves a fair amount of sautéing, not to be outdone by its close cousin, chopping. For the same reason that I have a vegetable chopper, I also have a garlic press because I can't mince garlic either!

Chapter 4

There's a lot of talk these days about the health—and I might add taste—benefits of the Mediterranean diet. More than a specific diet plan, the Mediterranean diet is a collection of eating habits and lifestyles from the different cultures bordering the Mediterranean Sea. Spain is without a doubt a Mediterranean country and many of the components of the Mediterranean diet are present in traditional Spanish dishes from all over Spain; yet nowhere is this presence more noticeable than in the areas bathed by the Mediterranean itself: Catalonia, the Balearic Islands, Valencia, and Murcia. (Andalusia, Ceuta, and Melilla also have Mediterranean coastlines; however, I've included these regions in separate chapters.) Three of these regions (Catalonia, the Balearic Islands, and Valencia) have two official languages, Catalan and Spanish, though the people of Valencia prefer the term *Valenciano* and in Baleares, they say *Mallorquín*.

Catalans are immensely proud of their cultural heritage and are quick to point out that theirs is a Mediterranean cuisine. Perhaps it's because I live in Catalonia and am more familiar with this part of Spain than with any other, but I have to say that, in my opinion, Catalan food is the most ingenious of regional Spanish cuisines. It never ceases to delightfully surprise and amaze me. Seasoning meats with fruits and cinnamon. Flavoring sauces with ground almonds or hazelnuts. Moistening bread with tomato pulp and olive oil. It's creative and satisfying, but seldom heavy, and it's the food I regularly turn to for both everyday and special-occasion meals.

Traditional cooking in the Balearic Islands, like the rest of the Mediterranean, reflects the generous coastline and the delicacies that the sea provides, as well as a more agricultural interior with meat, cheese, and vegetable products. Coastal cooking, as one might expect, favors seafood, while the interior produces heavier dishes that tend to rely more on meat and legumes.

Valencia is home to what is probably the most widely known and emblematic of all Spanish dishes: paella, which takes its name from the Catalan word for skillet. There is no one recipe for paella, just as there is no one type of paella. Rather, there are innumerable interpretations because this versatile dish simply uses rice as a base for any workable combination of ingredients from snails, meat, and rabbit to seafood, legumes, and vegetables. While American cooks tend to approach paella with a certain amount of trepidation, Spanish cooks are pretty nonplussed about the whole thing. It really is not a difficult or complicated dish to make. The secret to good paella is the rice and knowing how to cook it. There's also the noodle version of paella: *fideuà*. And lest you mistakenly think that Valencia is a one-dish region, keep in mind that all that coastline translates into first-class seafood, freshly grilled vegetables, and one of my favorite summer refreshments, *horchata*, a sweet, milky, white beverage made from tiger nuts (see *Horchata*: It's Gold, Baby!, page 156).

With a benevolent climate, ideal for growing fruits and vegetables, Murcia is known as the orchard of Spain. Like Valencia, Murcia is rice-growing country. Put fresh vegetables and rice together and you have one of Murcia's most well-known dishes: vegetable paella.

The Mediterranean region of Spain, more than any other, reflects the richness and variety that make up the Mediterranean diet. Olive oil, fresh fruits and vegetables, bread, pasta, rice, fish, nuts, cheese, meat, and wine in moderation make for a way of eating that transcends trends and can lead to a lifetime of pleasurable meals and the good health that accompanies eating well.

APPETIZERS
Tapas

Bread with Tomato and Olive Oil *(Pa amb tomàquet)*

SALADS
Ensaladas

Potato and Orange Salad *(Ensalada valenciana)*
Escarole Salad with Cod, Tuna, and Anchovies *(Xató)*

MEALS-IN-A-POT
Potajes

Lobster Stew *(Caldereta de llagosta)*

VEGETABLES AND LEGUMES
Verduras y Legumbres

Roasted Eggplant, Red Pepper, and Onion *(Escalivada)*
Spinach with Raisins and Pine Nuts *(Espinacs amb panses i pinyons)*
Majorcan Vegetable Casserole *(Tombet mallorquí)*
Chickpeas, Catalan-Style *(Cigrons a la catalana)*
Spicy Lima Beans *(Michirones)*

RICE AND PASTA DISHES
Arroces y Pasta

Chicken and Seafood Paella *(Paella mixta)*
Vegetable Paella *(Paella huertana de Murcia)*
Black Rice *(Arroz negro)*
Seafood-Flavored Rice *(Arròs a banda)*
Black Beans and Rice *(Moros y cristianos)*
Noodle and Seafood Paella *(Fideuà marinera)*
Cannelloni with Spinach and Pine Nut Filling *(Canelons d'espinacs)*

FISH AND SHELLFISH
Pescados y Marisco

Sea Bream Baked in Salt with Alioli *(Orada a la sal amb allioli)*
Catalan Fish Stew *(Suquet de peix)*
Monkfish in Romesco Sauce *(Cassola de peix amb romesco)*

POULTRY
Aves

Chicken with Vegetable Medley *(Pollastre amb samfaina)*

MEATS
Carnes

Braised Beef with Wild Mushrooms *(Fricandó)*
Butifarra Sausage with White Beans *(Botifarra amb mongetes)*

BREADS AND SAVORY PIES
Panes y Empanadas

Country Bread *(Pa de pagès)*
Catalan Pizza with Roasted Peppers, Eggplant, and Onion *(Coca de recapte)*
Murcian Meat Pie *(Pastel murciano)*

DESSERTS AND AFTERNOON COFFEE

Postres y Meriendas

Catalan Custard *(Crema catalana)*
Catalan Almond Pastries *(Panellets)*
Sweet Bread with Sugar and Pine Nut Topping *(Coca de Sant Joan)*
Sweet Spiral-Shaped Yeast Rolls *(Ensaimadas)*

DRINKS

Bebidas

Catalan Coffee *(Cremat)*

Bread with Tomato and Olive Oil

Pa amb tomàquet

[4 servings]

Pa amb tomàquet ("bread with tomato" in Catalan) is simple, practical, and typically Catalan. Its ingredients are nothing more than a large slice of coarse-textured country bread that has been toasted, a vine-ripened tomato, extra virgin olive oil, salt, and, if you're a garlic lover, a clove of garlic that you rub on the toast before adding the other ingredients. Thrifty people that they are, the Catalans invented "bread with tomato and olive oil" as a way to eat bread that had turned stale. The tomato and olive oil softened the bread and made it much easier to eat—and no food was wasted! In Catalonia, there are specialized taverns called *llescaries* (a *llesca* is a slice of bread) that serve *pa amb tomàquet* with a variety of toppings, such as serrano ham, a plain omelet, tuna, anchovies, *escalivada* (another typical Catalan dish that consists of roasted peppers, onions and eggplant) . . . the possibilities are endless.

4 large slices coarse-textured country bread (see page 145)
2 cloves garlic, peeled or unpeeled and cut in half crosswise (optional)

4 ripe tomatoes, cut in half crosswise
Extra virgin olive oil
Salt

Toast the bread slices. Rub each toasted bread slice with a garlic half on one side. Gently squeeze one of the tomato halves on each slice as you rub it on the bread. You will leave a light coating of tomato juice, pulp, and seeds. Drizzle the slices with extra virgin olive oil and then rub another tomato half on each slice to blend the olive oil and tomato together. Sprinkle with salt.

Cook's Notes: Pa amb tomàquet *is the Catalan answer to fast food. It works for breakfast, for a light lunch or supper, and as a snack. If you're planning on making large quantities of this bread, mix the tomatoes, oil, and salt together to make a paste that you can then spread on the bread.*

Potato and Orange Salad

Ensalada valenciana

[4 servings]

You would expect a salad with oranges to come from Valencia. The contrast between the sweetness of the oranges and onion slices and the slightly bitter bite of the vinegar gives this salad its particular appeal. You can serve this salad as a first course or as a tapa, if you wish.

3 potatoes
1 orange, peeled and cut in bite-size pieces; plus 1 orange, peeled and separated into wedges
8 thin slices Spanish onion

4 large spoonfuls extra virgin olive oil
2 large spoonfuls red wine vinegar
Salt
Freshly ground black pepper

Boil the potatoes in their jackets in salted water until tender. Cool, peel, and cut in bite-size pieces. Gently mix the potatoes, orange pieces, and onion slices together. Mix together the olive oil, vinegar, and some salt and pepper. Fold into the salad and refrigerate until well chilled.

Arrange the salad on individual plates or on a platter. Decorate with orange wedges before serving.

Cook's Notes: It is also possible to make this salad using mayonnaise, though I prefer the lighter vinaigrette dressing. For homemade mayonnaise, see page 204.

Escarole Salad with Cod, Tuna, and Anchovies

Xató

[4 servings]

As usually happens with so many traditional recipes, more than one town or area claims ownership and it becomes practically impossible to trace the origins of the dish. Such is the case with *Xató*. One of the more popular theories regarding this salad is that it originated in the wine-producing region of Penedès, close to Barcelona. When it was time to taste the wine, a small spout was inserted into the wineskin in a process known in Catalan as *aixetonar la bòta*. Since wine is a drink that typically accompanies food, a dish was created with whatever happened to be on hand, in this case escarole from the garden and olives and dried fish, typical items in most Spanish cupboards. There are various versions of this salad, depending on where you happen to sample it, but they all combine escarole, salt cod, olives, anchovies, and tuna topped with a dressing that bears a strong resemblance to *salsa romesco*. Traditionally the tuna is salt tuna that has been soaked, just like the cod; however, salt tuna is not commonplace, even in Catalonia, and most people use tuna that has been preserved in extra virgin olive oil. *Xató* is an elegant salad, pleasing to the eye, as well as the palate.

 START PREPARING SALT COD 2 TO 3 DAYS IN ADVANCE.

¼ pound salt cod fillet
1 small head escarole, chopped
1 (4-ounce) can light tuna, preferably *bonito del norte* tuna
16 olive oil-packed anchovy fillets, preferably Spanish
32 *Arbequina* olives*

DRESSING:
4 dried *ñora* peppers, stems and seeds removed

2 day-old baguette slices, ½-inch thick, fried in olive oil
15 blanched almonds, toasted
15 hazelnuts, toasted
2 cloves garlic, peeled
4 ripe tomatoes, grated
1 large spoonful minced flat-leaf parsley
2 large spoonfuls white wine vinegar
Salt
Freshly ground black pepper
6 large spoonfuls extra virgin olive oil

Begin soaking the salt cod 2 to 3 days in advance (see salt cod, page xv).

Drain the salt cod and place in a saucepan with water to cover. Gradually bring to a boil and as soon as the water begins to boil, remove the saucepan from the heat. Cover and let sit for 10 minutes. Drain, cool, and shred the fish. Reserve.

Make the dressing: Soak the *ñora* peppers in warm water for an hour. Drain. Blend the peppers, baguette slices, almonds, hazelnuts, garlic, tomatoes, parsley, vinegar, and some salt and pepper together using either a mortar and pestle or an appropriate kitchen appliance. Gradually pour in the olive oil as you would to make mayonnaise and continue blending until the olive oil has emulsified with the rest of the ingredients, creating a thick dressing.

Place the escarole on individual plates. Arrange the cod, tuna, anchovy fillets, and olives on top of the escarole. Top with the dressing and serve.

Cook's Notes: I've used Arbequina olives, small greenish brown olives that are very popular in Catalonia. They are available online. However, you can substitute black and/or green olives, if you prefer.

Lobster Stew

Caldereta de llagosta

[4 servings]

The broth in this stew bears a striking resemblance to a French bouillabaisse and yet *caldereta de llagosta* is one of the most emblematic dishes of the Balearic Islands. The small fishing village of Fornells in Menorca is said to serve the best.

4 live lobsters (approximately 1 pound each)
2 dried *ñora* peppers, stems and seeds removed
6 large spoonfuls extra virgin olive oil
2 onions, finely chopped
2 cloves garlic, minced
1 large spoonful minced flat-leaf parsley

8 ripe tomatoes, seeded and grated
1 bay leaf
Salt
Freshly ground black pepper
4 cups fish broth (page 136)
2 large spoonfuls brandy, preferably Spanish
8 baguette slices, ½-inch thick, toasted

Prepare the lobster as follows or, better yet, have your fishmonger do this for you: Using a sharp knife or cleaver, sever the spinal cord at the point where the body meets the tail using a quick sharp blow. Cut the tail into rings, separate the claws, and lightly crush them. Slice the head in half lengthwise and discard the stomach sac. Scoop out the tomalley and reserve.

Soak the *ñora* peppers in warm water for an hour. Drain and blot dry with paper towels.

Heat the olive oil in an earthenware dish over medium-high heat. Sauté the lobster pieces for just a few minutes, remove to a platter, and reserve.

Lower the heat and sauté the *ñora* peppers, onions, garlic, and parsley until tender. Add the tomatoes and continue cooking for another 10 to 15 minutes, until the sauce has thickened. Using an immersion blender or regular blender, blend the tomato mixture and the lobster tomalley together until smooth and return to the earthenware dish. Add the lobster pieces, bay leaf, some salt and pepper, and fish broth. Cook over low heat for 10 to 15 minutes.

Stir in the brandy, increase the heat, and cook for another 5 minutes. To serve, place 2 baguette slices in each soup dish, along with the lobster pieces, and pour the stew over all.

Cook's Notes: To seed the tomatoes, cut them in half crosswise. Cut the seeds out and grate them over a bowl.

Roasted Eggplant, Red Pepper, and Onion

Escalivada

[4 servings]

Escalivada is healthy, easy to prepare, and tastes great. What more could you ask for? It works on its own, served on slices of *pa amb tomàquet* (page 110), or as a topping for *coques*, Catalan pizzas.

1 red bell pepper	Juice of ¼ lemon
1 eggplant	Coarse salt
1 Spanish onion, peeled	Freshly ground black pepper
2 large spoonfuls extra virgin olive oil	

Preheat the oven to 450° F. Wash the bell pepper, eggplant, and onion. Wrap them in parchment paper and place in a roasting pan. Roast for 45 minutes, turning the vegetables halfway through roasting to prevent scorching. (The vegetables should "sweat" while they are in the oven and will release a lot of juice. The eggplant will be soft to the touch when cooked and the bell pepper will have "caved in.")

Split the eggplant in half lengthwise and scrape out the seeds. Skin the bell pepper and remove the seeds. Cut the eggplant, bell pepper, and onion roughly into thin strips using a knife and fork. Arrange on a serving platter and drizzle with olive oil and lemon juice. Season with salt and pepper. Serve at room temperature.

Cook's Notes: I sometimes find red peppers difficult to skin. My trick for peeling them is to remove the seeds and slice the pepper in quarters lengthwise before roasting. The skin just seems to peel right off.

● La Boqueria: A Market for the Senses

A visit to Barcelona would not be complete without a stroll down the emblematic Ramblas and, if you find yourself walking down the Ramblas, just veer right when you reach La Boqueria. You won't be disappointed. The market's official name is *Mercat de Sant Josep* (St. Joseph's Market) due to the convent of Sant Josep that existed on this site but that burned down in 1835. Everyone refers to it as La Boqueria, though the origins of its name are unclear as usually happens with a place whose existence dates back to the thirteenth century. The market is constantly a-hum with people in motion. Customers range from camera-toting tourists to renowned chefs. It's no secret that chefs from the best restaurants in Barcelona do their shopping here or that master chef Ferran Adrià has a laboratory a stone's throw from the market.

La Boqueria is for those who enjoy the pleasure of shopping for food and being able to consult with vendors who know their product and throw a bit of conversation and human touch into the exchange. A variety of fresh, high quality products artfully arranged are the order of the day and you can buy just about anything from exotic fruits to suckling pig. Its aisles offer a veritable feast for the eyes and, if you get hungry, for the stomach too. Not only can you do your shopping here, but you can also dine on some very good food at one of the market's several bars or at La Gardunya, a restaurant adjacent to the market that serves up *cocina de mercado* (fresh market cuisine). La Boqueria even offers cooking classes for the gastronomically inclined, including children.

(Note: All of the market photographs in this book were taken at La Boqueria market in Barcelona.)

Spinach with Raisins and Pine Nuts

Espinacs amb panses i pinyons

[4 servings]

Catalan cooking has a penchant for adding fruits and nuts in the most unlikely of places. The concentrated sugar in the raisins and the soft sweetness of the pine nuts provide a unique flavor contrast to this leafy green vegetable. *Espinacs amb panses i pinyons* is a definitive Catalan dish and disarmingly simple to prepare.

1 pound fresh spinach	½ cup pine nuts
6 large spoonfuls extra virgin olive oil	Coarse salt
½ cup seedless raisins	Freshly ground black pepper

Wash spinach leaves and remove the stems. Tear into small pieces. Drain the spinach and dry thoroughly.

Sauté the raisins and pine nuts in olive oil until the pine nuts are golden brown. Add the spinach leaves and stir for a few minutes until the leaves begin to wilt. Season with salt and pepper. Serve immediately.

Cook's Notes: Swiss chard is also good prepared this way.

Majorcan Vegetable Casserole

Tombet mallorquí

[4 servings]

Typically the vegetables in this casserole are fried individually before baking. Depending on the vegetable, I prefer to use the microwave, oven, or griddle. The vegetables get cooked and their natural flavors are enhanced, but with less oil than you would use if you fried them. A friend of mine prepares a child-friendly variation of this dish. Instead of slicing the vegetables, she dices them and fries them individually in olive oil. After layering them and pouring on the tomato sauce, she then grates cheese over the top.

1 red bell pepper, cored, seeded, and cut in ¼-inch slices

1 green bell pepper, cored, seeded, and cut in ¼-inch slices

Extra virgin olive oil for drizzling

Salt

2 large potatoes, peeled and thinly sliced

1 large zucchini, unpeeled and cut in ¼-inch slices

1 large eggplant, unpeeled and cut in ¼-inch slices

1 large spoonful minced flat-leaf parsley

2 cups tomato sauce (see recipe next page)

Preheat the oven to 400° F. Line a piece of aluminum foil with parchment paper. Arrange the red and green bell pepper slices on the parchment paper, drizzle with olive oil, and season with salt. Fold and seal the aluminum foil to create a pouch. Bake for 30 minutes. Reserve.

Mix the potato slices, some olive oil, and salt together, being sure to coat the potatoes thoroughly with oil. Cover and microwave on high for 10 minutes. Arrange in a greased 13-inch by 9-inch ovenproof baking dish or in individual earthenware ramekins.

Heat a non-stick skillet or griddle over medium-high heat. Drizzle olive oil over the cooking surface. (To avoid soggy vegetables, be sure to use a hot cooking surface and the minimum amount of oil.) Place the zucchini and eggplant slices on the cooking surface. Cook until browned on both sides. Drizzle with a bit of olive oil and salt.

Place a layer of zucchini on top of the potatoes. Place the eggplant on top of the zucchini and arrange the red and green pepper slices on top. Pour the juice from the roasted peppers over the vegetables and cover with tomato sauce. Cover the dish with aluminum foil and bake for 15 minutes. Sprinkle with parsley and serve.

Tomato Sauce

This is my standard recipe for homemade tomato sauce. It makes about 3 cups sauce.

8 ripe tomatoes	2 cloves garlic, minced
Pinch sugar	1 bay leaf
4 large spoonfuls extra virgin olive oil	Salt
1 onion, chopped	

Cut the tomatoes in half and grate them over a strainer to drain off the excess liquid. (If you don't want the seeds, cut them out before grating.) Sprinkle with a pinch of sugar. Reserve.

Heat the olive oil in a skillet over low heat. Gently sauté the onion, garlic, and bay leaf until tender, about 10 minutes. Add the tomatoes and simmer on low for another 30 minutes, stirring occasionally. Remove the bay leaf and blend with an immersion blender. Salt to taste.

Cook's Notes: Eggplant can have a bitter taste, which some people find off-putting. To reduce the bitterness, soak it in salted water or milk for 10 minutes. Drain and dry between paper towels.

Chickpeas, Catalan-Style

Cigrons a la catalana

[4 servings]

These chickpeas incorporate a *picada* (*picar* means "to grind") of almonds, parsley, and saffron. Seasoning foods with finely ground almonds and/or hazelnuts is typical of Catalan cooking.

 BEGIN SOAKING CHICKPEAS 1 DAY IN ADVANCE.

1½ cups dried chickpeas, rinsed	1 large spoonful minced flat-leaf parsley
1 bay leaf	2 large spoonfuls blanched almonds
1 large onion, chopped	Pinch saffron
2 cloves garlic	Salt
4 large spoonfuls extra virgin olive oil	4 hardboiled eggs, sliced
½ cup tomato sauce (page 119)	

Soak the chickpeas in cold water in a large pot overnight.

Add the bay leaf to the pot with the chickpeas (use the same water the chickpeas were soaked in to cook them). Bring to a gentle, rolling boil. Skim the white foam that forms on the surface of the water. Lower the heat, cover, and cook for 2 hours. Drain and discard the bay leaf.

Sauté the onion and garlic in olive oil until tender. Add the tomato sauce. Grind the parsley, almonds, saffron, and salt, using either a mortar and pestle or appropriate kitchen appliance. Add the almond mixture to the onion mixture and stir in the chickpeas. Heat for a few minutes and decorate with egg slices before serving.

Cook's Notes: Legumes require a certain amount of time to cook and a bit of planning ahead. Beans and chickpeas need to be soaked overnight and can take up to two hours to cook. Preparing them in a pressure cooker greatly reduces cooking time.

Spicy Lima Beans

Michirones

[4 servings]

These lima beans are typical of Murcia. They can be served either as a first course or as a tapa.

1 chorizo sausage	1 bay leaf
2 cups frozen lima beans	½ small spoonful *pimentón picante* (piquant
1 ham bone	Spanish paprika)
½ dried red chili pepper, seeds removed	Salt
1 clove garlic, peeled	Freshly ground black pepper

Degrease the chorizo sausage: Prick the sausage with a fork and place in a saucepan with water to cover. Bring to a boil and cook for 5 minutes. Drain and cut into ½-inch slices.

Place the chorizo slices and all the remaining ingredients in a saucepan or earthenware dish and add ½ cup water. Bring to a boil, lower the heat, cover, and cook until tender, about 10 minutes. Remove the ham bone and serve.

Cook's Notes: I've used frozen lima beans (easy to find and available year-round) in this recipe. Many traditional recipes use dried lima beans and, of course, it is also possible to use the freshly shucked version, but fresh lima beans are available only at the end of winter and beginning of spring in Spanish markets. The cooking time in this recipe is for frozen lima beans, so you will need to make adjustments if you use fresh or dried lima beans, and in the case of dried lima beans, they must be soaked overnight.

LA BUENA MESA • CHAPTER 4 The Mediterranean: Catalonia, the Balearic Islands, Valencia, and Murcia

Chicken and Seafood Paella

Paella mixta

[4 servings]

I think it's safe to say that paella lays claim to the title of Most Widely Recognized Spanish Specialty. I would also say that it is the Spanish dish with the most variations. There are paellas with chicken and rabbit, with every kind of shellfish imaginable, and others that add vegetables, legumes, and even snails to the rice base, because paella, like all traditional dishes, is born of ingredients close to home. The paella that I propose here is known as *paella mixta* in Spain, a mixture of chicken and seafood not apt for purists because it mixes surf and turf a bit; however, it is enormously popular. There is nothing intimidating about this rice dish nor does it involve slaying a lobster. While paellas that you order in Spain come with cut-up pieces of chicken that include the bone and shrimp in their shell, I have eliminated bones and shells simply to make the dish a tad neater to eat because, after all, paella is a dish reserved for special occasions and shared with friends and family, though you are certainly free to ignore my neatness tip. One thing you shouldn't ignore, however, is that the rice used in any and all paellas must be short-grain rice. There's no compromising on that point. Any other rice will produce an entirely different dish.

6 large spoonfuls extra virgin olive oil
12 large shrimp, shells removed
½ pound skinless, boneless chicken breast, cut in bite-size pieces
Salt
Freshly ground black pepper
1 onion, chopped
2 cloves garlic, minced
2 thin slices serrano ham, trimmed and minced
2 large spoonfuls minced flat-leaf parsley
1 pimiento, chopped (page xv)

1 ripe tomato, grated
½ cup peas, fresh or frozen
1½ cups short-grain rice
2½ cups chicken broth (page 67)
½ cup dry white wine
Juice of ¼ lemon
1 bay leaf
Good pinch of saffron
½ pound small clams
8 medium mussels, cleaned and debearded
1 lemon, quartered

Heat 1 large spoonful of olive oil in a paella pan with a 13-inch base. Add the shrimp and sauté just until pink on both sides, approximately 1 to 2 minutes. Remove to a platter and reserve.

Salt and pepper the chicken pieces. Add the remaining oil to the paella pan, along with the chicken, onion, and garlic. Sauté until the chicken is golden brown and the onion is tender. Stir in the ham, 1 large spoonful of parsley, the pimiento, and tomato. Cook for a few minutes, and add the peas and rice, being sure to coat the rice thoroughly with the oil. Lightly season with salt. (The dish can be prepared about 2 hours in advance up to this point. Simply cover the paella pan and other ingredients with aluminum foil. Do not refrigerate.)

In a separate pot, bring the chicken broth, wine, lemon juice, bay leaf, and saffron to a full, rolling boil and pour over the rice mixture. Cook uncovered over medium-high heat (the broth should boil rapidly). Avoid stirring the rice. Instead, move the pan from side to side if you need to redistribute the cooking liquid or turn the pan. Ten minutes into cooking, bury the shrimp and clams in the rice. Push the mussels into the rice so that the edge that will open is facing up. Continue cooking for another 8 to 10 minutes. Remove from the heat and let sit for 5 to 10 minutes. To serve, sprinkle with the remaining parsley and decorate with lemon wedges.

Cook's Notes: This is a small paella (only 4 servings) and easy to cook on top of the stove. As paellas become larger, however, one has to be more creative when it comes to cooking them as they no longer fit comfortably on a single burner. A combination of stovetop and oven works well, usually 10 minutes on top of the stove and 15 to 20 in a 325° F oven. There's also the option of taking your paella to the great outdoors, perhaps your grill. In Spain, there are outdoor festivals where paella is prepared for hundreds of people at a time in an extraordinarily large paella pan over an open fire.

Vegetable Paella

Paella huertana de Murcia

[4 servings]

Murcia is known as the vegetable garden of Spain. Like Valencia, it's also rice growing country. Put these two together and you have what was once considered a poor man's dish and today is recognized as a prime example of the healthy, flavorful Mediterranean style of cooking and eating.

1 dried *ñora* pepper, stem and seeds removed
½ small head cauliflower, cut in small flowerets
¼ pound green beans, trimmed and cut in 1-inch pieces
½ cup peas, fresh or frozen
½ cup lima beans, fresh or frozen
6 large spoonfuls extra virgin olive oil
4 artichoke hearts, halved
1 carrot, scraped and chopped

1 onion, chopped
2 cloves garlic, minced
1 pimiento, chopped (page xv)
2 ripe tomatoes, grated
4 large spoonfuls minced flat-leaf parsley
Salt
1½ cups short-grain rice
3 cups chicken broth (page 67)
Good pinch of saffron
1 lemon, quartered

Soak the *ñora* pepper in warm water for an hour. Drain and blot dry with a paper towel. Chop and reserve.

Cook the cauliflower, green beans, peas, and lima beans in salted water until tender but not fully cooked. (You may want to cook them separately due to their different cooking times.) Drain and reserve.

Gently heat 3 large spoonfuls of olive oil in a paella pan with a 13-inch base. Lightly brown the artichokes on all sides. Remove the artichokes and reserve. Add the remaining 3 spoonfuls of olive oil and sauté the carrot, onion, and garlic for 10 minutes. Add the pimiento and tomato and cook for several more minutes. Season the vegetables with the chopped *ñora* pepper, 2 large spoonfuls of parsley, and some salt. Stir in the rice, being sure to coat well with the oil. Add the cooked cauliflower, green beans, peas, lima beans, and artichoke hearts.

In a separate pot, bring the chicken broth and saffron to a full, rolling boil and pour over the rice and vegetables. Cook uncovered over medium-high heat for approximately 15 minutes (the broth should boil rapidly), until almost all of the broth has been absorbed. During the last 5 minutes or so of cooking, as the broth is absorbed, you may need to lower the heat a bit to keep the rice from cooking too fast. Avoid stirring the rice; instead, move the pan from side to side if you need to redistribute the cooking liquid or turn the dish. Remove from the heat and let sit for 5 to 10 minutes. To serve, sprinkle with the remaining parsley and decorate with lemon wedges.

Cook's Notes: If you use the "bomba" variety of short-grain rice, you will need to increase the chicken broth to 4½ cups. "Bomba" rice is especially appropriate for paellas. It absorbs three times its volume in broth, as opposed to the normal two, which makes for a particularly flavorful rice dish. The rice, however, remains intact and is never sticky. This particular variety of rice, which accounts for a small percentage of total rice production in Spain, was brought back from the brink of extinction by Spain's top chefs. It takes longer to produce and requires more care than other varieties, but the effort is well worth it when you taste paella that's been made with "bomba."

Black Rice

Arroz negro

[4 servings]

This paella takes its name from the color the rice takes on when cooked with squid ink. While it may not sound terribly appetizing to eat black rice, I can assure you that this dish is well worth a try and once you've tasted it, you'll go back for more.

1½ pounds squid with tentacles	2 ripe tomatoes, grated
¼ cup dry white wine	1½ cups short-grain rice
4 large spoonfuls extra virgin olive oil	Salt
1 onion, chopped	3 cups fish broth (page 136)
4 cloves garlic, minced	Pinch saffron
1 bay leaf	

To clean the squid, see the recipe for Baby Squid in Ink Sauce, page 50. Cut the squid in ½-inch rings. Dissolve the ink in a cup with the white wine and reserve.

Add the olive oil to a paella pan and sauté the squid, onion, garlic, and bay leaf in the olive oil until the onion is transparent and the squid begins to brown, about 5 minutes. Add the grated tomatoes and reserved ink. Stir in the rice, being sure to coat well with the oil. Lightly season with salt.

In a separate pot, bring the fish broth and saffron to a full, rolling boil. Pour the hot fish broth over the rice mixture. Cook uncovered over medium-high heat for approximately 15 minutes (the broth should boil rapidly) until almost all of the broth has been absorbed. During the last 5 minutes or so of cooking, as the broth is absorbed, you may need to lower the heat a bit to keep the rice from cooking too fast. Avoid stirring the rice; instead, move the pan from side to side if you need to redistribute the cooking liquid or turn the dish. Remove from the heat and let sit for 5 to 10 minutes. If you're a garlic fan, serve with alioli sauce on the side (see page 134).

Cook's Notes: By using frozen squid rings (you'll need 1 pound) and pre-packaged squid ink (two 0.14-ounce packets), you can cut down considerably on the amount of preparation time needed—and enjoy this dish all the more often!

Seafood-Flavored Rice

Arròs a banda

[4 servings]

Though to the naked eye, this dish may look like plain rice with a bit of coloring, it is anything but. There is very little seafood present—just a smattering of shrimp—yet the rice captures all the flavors of the sea. The secret is the strongly flavored fish broth in which the rice cooks. Originally, *arròs a banda* was made without the addition of seafood (*a banda* means "on the side"), but today it is common to find bits of shrimp or squid in the rice. Try serving this seafood-flavored rice with *alioli* (page 134) for yet another taste sensation.

 START PREPARATION SEVERAL HOURS IN ADVANCE.

1 dried *ñora* pepper, stem and seeds removed
6 large spoonfuls extra virgin olive oil
4 cloves garlic, minced
Pinch saffron
1 small spoonful *pimentón dulce* (sweet Spanish paprika)
2 ripe tomatoes, grated
Salt
2 cups short-grain rice

FISH BROTH:
½ pound medium shrimp, in their shells with heads
1 pound whitefish and/or fish heads and bones
½ cup dry white wine
1 carrot, scraped and cut into several pieces
1 onion, quartered
1 sprig flat-leaf parsley
1 bay leaf
6 black peppercorns
Salt

Soak the *ñora* pepper in warm water for an hour. Drain and blot dry with a paper towel. Reserve.

Make the fish broth: Clean and peel the shrimp. Chop the shrimp meat and reserve. Place the shrimp heads, along with the fish, wine, carrot, onion, parsley, bay leaf, peppercorns, some salt, and 4½ cups water in a pot. Bring to a boil and skim the foam off the top. Gently cook for 1½ to 2 hours. Strain the broth and reserve.

(continued on next page)

Seafood-Flavored Rice *(continued from previous page)*

Heat the olive oil in a paella pan or earthenware dish. Gently sauté the garlic and *ñora* pepper until the garlic is golden and the pepper is soft, but not browned. Transfer the garlic and pepper to a mortar (leaving the oil in the pan). Add the saffron and *pimentón* and grind to create a paste (you can use either a mortar and pestle or appropriate kitchen appliance).

Add the chopped shrimp to the paella pan and sauté for a couple of minutes. Stir in the garlic and pepper paste along with the tomatoes and season with some salt. Add the rice, being sure to coat well with the oil.

In a separate pot, bring the fish broth to a full rolling boil and pour 4 cups broth over the rice. Cook uncovered over medium-high heat for approximately 15 minutes (the broth should boil rapidly), until almost all of the broth has been absorbed. During the last 5 minutes or so of cooking, as the broth is absorbed, you may need to lower the heat a bit to keep the rice from cooking too fast. Avoid stirring the rice; instead, move the pan from side to side if you need to redistribute the cooking liquid or turn the dish. Remove from the heat and let sit for 5 to 10 minutes before serving.

Cook's Notes: To make this fish broth, use whitefish or a combination of whitefish, fish heads, and bones. (When buying fish whole, have your fishmonger save the head and bones for fish broth.) Monkfish, including the head, makes a particularly flavorful fish broth. In fact, the fish market where I buy fish sells monkfish heads separately just for fish broth (because I can't imagine why else anyone would want a monkfish head!).

Black Beans and Rice

Moros y cristianos

[4 servings]

The literal translation of this dish is Moors and Christians in reference to the Moorish occupation of Spain which lasted more than 700 years and left deep imprints on the Spanish language, culture, and cuisine.

 START PREPARATION OF BEANS 1 DAY IN ADVANCE.

BEANS:
1 cup dried black beans, rinsed
1 whole onion, peeled; plus 1 onion, chopped
2 whole cloves garlic, peeled; plus 2 cloves
   garlic, minced
1 bay leaf
2 large spoonfuls extra virgin olive oil
1 small spoonful all-purpose flour
Salt

RICE:
1 small onion, chopped
2 large spoonfuls extra virgin olive oil
1 cup short-grain rice
2 chicken broth (page 67)

Place the beans in a pan with cold water to cover and soak them overnight.

Prepare the beans: Add the whole onion, whole garlic cloves, and bay leaf to the beans. The water covering the beans should be about 2 fingers deep. Bring to a gentle, rolling boil. Skim the white foam that forms on the surface of the water. Lower the heat, cover, and cook for 1½ hours. Check periodically to make sure that there's enough water. The beans should have some liquid left when they are finished cooking, but should not be soupy. Remove the onion, garlic cloves, and bay leaf. In a small skillet, sauté the chopped onion and minced garlic in olive oil until tender. Stir in the flour and add to the cooked beans. Season with salt. Continue cooking over low heat for another 30 minutes.

In the meantime, prepare the rice: Sauté the chopped onion in olive oil. Stir in the rice, being sure to coat well with the oil. In a separate pan, heat the chicken broth to a full, rolling boil and pour over the rice. Cook uncovered over medium-high heat

(continued on next page)

LA BUENA MESA • CHAPTER 4 The Mediterranean: Catalonia, the Balearic Islands, Valencia, and Murcia

Black Beans and Rice (continued from previous page)

for approximately 15 minutes (the broth should boil rapidly) until almost all of the broth has been absorbed. During the last 5 minutes or so of cooking, as the broth is absorbed, you may need to lower the heat a bit to keep the rice from cooking too fast. Avoid stirring the rice; instead, move the pan from side to side if you need to redistribute the cooking liquid or turn the dish. Remove from the heat and let sit for 5 to 10 minutes.

To serve, mold the rice by packing it into individual custard cups. Invert the custard cups onto the middle of individual serving plates and gently lift away. Spoon the beans around the molded rice to form a crown.

Cook's Notes: To keep the rice from sticking to the mold, pour water into a bowl and add a bit of oil to the water. Before adding the rice, ladle the "oily" water into the mold and then pour it out. The oil forms a coating on the surface of the mold, which keeps the rice from sticking.

Noodle and Seafood Paella

Fideuà marinera

[4 servings]

Though pasta is an important part of everyday menus in Spain, it is not present in a lot of traditional dishes. When I think of regional pasta dishes, only two come to mind and they are both from the Mediterranean area: *canelons* and *fideuà*. *Fideuà* can best be described as paella with noodles instead of rice. Typically it is served with alioli on the side, which you may mix in with the noodles or not, depending on your love of garlic.

1 small monkfish (approximately 3 pounds), or 1 pound monkfish fillets	4 large spoonfuls extra virgin olive oil
Salt	1 onion, chopped
¾ pound medium shrimp, in their shells with heads	2 cloves garlic, minced
	1 ripe tomato, grated
4 cups fish broth (page 136)	2 cups *fideuà* noodles (available online)
Pinch saffron	¾ pound small clams

When buying the monkfish, ask your fishmonger to fillet it and set the bones and head aside for fish broth. If you're unable to buy the monkfish whole, substitute 2 pounds of whitefish. Using kitchen scissors, cut the monkfish into bite-size pieces and salt lightly. Reserve. Clean and peel the shrimp, reserving the heads. Make the fish broth using the shrimp heads as well.

Preheat the oven to 425° F. Place 4 cups of the fish broth and the saffron in a pot and bring to a boil. Meanwhile heat the olive oil in a metal paella pan with a 13-inch base or an earthenware casserole. Gently sauté the onion and garlic until tender. Add the monkfish and shrimp and continue cooking until the shrimp has turned pink. Stir in the tomato and noodles. Allow the noodles to cook for a few minutes and then add the boiling broth. Cook uncovered until most of the broth has been absorbed, about 15 minutes. Transfer to the oven and bake for 5 minutes. Serve with alioli sauce on the side (see page 134).

Cook's Notes: The lack of bones, the firm flesh, and no fishy taste make monkfish a good choice for people who tend to shy away from fish. This is a very easy fish to handle when it comes to cooking and eating. The flesh is firm, yet light. It's certainly one of my favorites.

Cannelloni with Spinach and Pine Nut Filling

Canelons d'espinacs

[6 servings]

In Catalonia, it is customary to serve *canelons* with a meat filling on December 26, Saint Stephen's Day, a holiday in Catalonia. However, this pasta dish is not just for Christmas nor does the filling necessarily have to be a meat one. During the rest of the year, you'll also find these little pasta squares filled with spinach, tuna, and wild mushrooms. I've opted for the spinach filling, which has all the subtle flavors I find so attractive in Catalan cooking. Nutmeg, pine nuts, serrano ham, and Parmesan cheese blend together magnificently with the fresh spinach to impart a subtle yet distinct flavor to these cannelloni.

24 cannelloni	4 thin slices serrano ham, trimmed and minced
1 pound fresh spinach	Freshly ground black pepper
4 large spoonfuls extra virgin olive oil	½ small spoonful ground nutmeg
4 large spoonfuls pine nuts	6 large spoonfuls grated Parmesan cheese
1 large onion, chopped	Salt
2 cloves garlic, minced	Béchamel Sauce (page 78)

Put a large pot of water on to boil and prepare the pasta according to package directions. Arrange the cooked cannelloni in a single layer on a dish towel. Cover and reserve.

Wash the spinach thoroughly and remove the stems. Coarsely chop the leaves and place them in a microwave-safe bowl. Stir in 1 large spoonful of olive oil. Cover and microwave on high for a minute or two. Drain thoroughly and reserve.

Gently sauté the pine nuts in the remaining olive oil just until they begin to brown. Add the onion and garlic and continue sautéing until tender. Stir in the ham, season with pepper and nutmeg, and continue cooking for another 2 minutes. Remove from the heat and add the cooked spinach along with 2 large spoonfuls of Parmesan cheese and salt to taste.

Place 1 small well-rounded spoonful of filling in the center of each cannelloni square. Roll the pasta so that the fold is on the bottom and place in a greased 13-inch by 9-inch ovenproof baking dish. The cannelloni should fit snugly together.

Preheat the oven to 450° F. Prepare the béchamel sauce using 4 large spoonfuls of flour.* Cover the pasta with the white sauce and sprinkle with the remaining Parmesan cheese. Bake for 10 minutes until bubbly. Run under the broiler to lightly brown.

Cook's Notes: This is a great make-ahead dish and one that freezes well. For a more formal presentation, prepare individual servings using small earthenware ramekins.

The flour measures out to exactly 5 level tablespoons plus 1 level teaspoon.

Sea Bream Baked in Salt with Alioli

Orada a la sal amb allioli

[4 servings]

Anything prepared *a la sal* means that it has been baked in an outer crust of salt. This method of cooking produces a fish that is delicate and tender as the fish bakes in its own juices and, contrary to what you might think, does not produce a salty taste. Sea bream is typically prepared this way along the Mediterranean coast and oftentimes is served with alioli on the side.

The term *alioli* comes from the Catalan *all* (garlic) *i* (and) *oli* (oil) and that's just what this sauce is: garlic and oil! Alioli is served with everything from grilled meat, chicken, and seafood to vegetables, rice, and *fideuà*. According to purists, real alioli has only garlic, olive oil, and a bit of salt. Creating a creamy sauce without using eggs is nothing short of difficult. It means grinding and mixing the garlic and olive oil using a mortar and pestle and maybe, if you're lucky, it will emulsify. Personally, if I want alioli, I head straight for the eggs. That way, I'm sure my sauce will thicken!

---

4 sea bream (about 1 pound each),
    scales and heads on*
8 cups coarse salt (approximately 2 cups
    per fish), preferably sea salt
1 lemon, quartered

ALIOLI:
8 cloves garlic, minced
1 egg
1 large spoonful lemon juice
Salt
1 cup mild extra virgin olive oil

---

*Note: When buying sea bream to prepare in salt, make sure that your fishmonger does not remove the scales or you could end up with dry fish. Simply ask to have the fins trimmed and the intestines removed through the gills so that the fish doesn't have to be opened up.

Preheat the oven to 375° F. Mix together the coarse salt with enough water to create a paste, about 2 large spoonfuls of water per cup of salt. For easier handling, mix 2 cups of salt at a time. Make a layer of salt on the bottom of an ovenproof dish slightly larger than the sea bream. Place the four fish on top of this layer of salt. Mix together more coarse salt and water, and cover the fish completely. Bake for 30 minutes.

Make the alioli: Place the garlic, egg, lemon juice, and some salt in a blender and blend till smooth. Gradually pour in the oil and continue blending until the sauce thickens.

To serve, remove the salt crust that has formed around the fish. Discard the skin and head and carefully bone the fish. Arrange the fillets on individual plates with a lemon wedge and serve with alioli on the side.

Cook's Notes: If you are unable to find coarse sea salt, regular fine table salt also works well. Calculate 4 cups of fine salt per fish, and instead of water, mix the salt with egg white (2 cups of salt per egg white). And so the egg yolks don't go to waste, make a custard dessert that uses only the yolks!

Catalan Fish Stew

Suquet de peix

[4 servings]

Suquet is a dish born on fishing boats, typical of Catalonia, Valencia, and the Balearic Islands. Fishermen prepared fish that had been damaged during handling (and was therefore not apt for sale) in a simple broth that they sopped up with bread; hence the name *suquet* (*suquejar* in Catalan means "to sop up" and suc is "juice"). This traditional fish stew is usually made with two or more types of fish—monkfish, sea bream, and sea bass being the most popular. Shellfish can also be added, as well as potatoes. The stew is seasoned with a *picada* of almonds, garlic, herbs, and spices. The *picada* (from the verb *picar*, which means "to grind") is typical of Catalan cooking and consists of grinding nuts and seasonings using a mortar and pestle to create a paste that is then added to the broth. It's a great invention and adds subtle flavoring to foods.

2 large spoonfuls extra virgin olive oil
1 onion, finely chopped
2 ripe tomatoes, grated
2 potatoes, peeled and cut in ¼-inch slices
1 medium monkfish (approximately 4½ to 5 pounds), cut in serving pieces, or 2½ pounds monkfish steaks
8 large shrimp
12 large clams or small mussels
¼ cup dry white wine
½ cup peas, fresh or frozen

FISH BROTH:
1 monkfish head, cut in several pieces, or 2 pounds whitefish
1 carrot, scraped and cut in several pieces
1 leek, white part only, halved
1 onion, quartered
2 cloves garlic, peeled

1 ripe tomato, halved
1 sprig flat-leaf parsley
1 bay leaf
6 black peppercorns
Salt
½ cup dry white wine

PICADA:
4 large spoonfuls extra virgin olive oil
12 blanched almonds
4 cloves garlic, peeled
4 day-old baguette slices, ½-inch thick
2 large spoonfuls minced flat-leaf parsley
½ small spoonful *pimentón dulce* (sweet Spanish paprika)
Pinch saffron
Salt
Freshly ground black pepper

Note: When buying fish, ask your fishmonger to set the bones and the head aside to make fish broth. If you are unable to buy the fish whole, then simply use some whitefish to make the broth.

Make the broth: Place the fish heads and bones or fish along with the carrot, leek, onion, garlic, tomato, parsley, bay leaf, peppercorns, salt, wine, and 4 cups water in a saucepan. Bring to a boil and skim the foam off the top. Lower the heat, cover, and simmer for 1 hour. Strain the broth. (This is my standard recipe for fish broth and makes approximately 4 cups. Reserve 2 cups for this *suquet* and freeze rest for future use.)

Make the *picada*: Heat the olive oil in an earthenware dish and gently sauté the almonds, garlic, and baguette slices until golden brown. Create a paste by grinding either in a mortar and pestle or appropriate kitchen appliance with the remaining *picada* ingredients. Reserve.

In the same earthenware dish you used to prepare the *picada* (can't let any of those good flavors go to waste!), gently sauté the onion in olive oil until transparent. Stir in the tomatoes and continue cooking for a few minutes. Stir a bit of the 2 cups of fish broth into the *picada* and add that, along with the rest of the fish broth, to the earthenware dish. Add the potato slices. Gradually bring to a boil, lower the heat, and cover. Cook until the potatoes are almost tender, about 30 minutes.

Salt the fish and add it to the dish along with the shrimp, mussels or clams, wine, and peas. Cover and gently cook for an additional 15 minutes. You can either serve the *suquet* in the same earthenware dish or in individual earthenware ramekins.

Cook's Notes: This fish stew is versatile and can be made with different types of fish: hake, cod, sea bass, halibut, tile fish, and sea bream or any combination of the above work well. Monkfish is a common fish along the Mediterranean. It handles very well, and for this reason I've chosen it for this fish stew. It has a delicate flavor, firm flesh, and no fishy taste, making it a good choice for children and people who tend to shy away from fish. The head also makes an excellent fish broth.

Monkfish in Romesco Sauce

Cassola de peix amb romesco

[4 servings]

Romesco sauce is typical of Tarragona, the city where I live. It can be prepared as a sauce, as in this dish, or served as a thick dip that accompanies freshly grilled fish and shellfish. Every September, during the week-long celebration of Santa Tecla, the patron saint of Tarragona, there is a *romesco* contest held in the port area of the city. Local cooks prepare earthenware dishes of fish in *romesco* sauce over gas-fed burners while the general public looks on. If you happen to visit Tarragona, stock up on *romesco* peppers, which are the peppers traditionally used to prepare this dish; otherwise, use dried sweet peppers, but don't even think of omitting the peppers because they are crucial to making a true *romesco* sauce. And while you're there, be sure to visit the city's many Roman ruins, vestiges of an era when Tarragona, known as Tarraco by the Romans, was the capital city of the Roman province Hispania Citerior. Its ruins include an aqueduct located just outside the city, an amphitheater overlooking the sea (those Romans knew where to build!), the remains of a Roman circus, and the Roman wall enclosing parts of the old quarter of the city that date from that period.

1 dried *ñora* pepper, stem and seeds removed
1 dried sweet pepper, stem and seeds removed
1 medium monkfish (approximately 4½ to 5 pounds), cut in serving pieces, or 2½ pounds monkfish steaks
Coarse salt
8 large spoonfuls extra virgin olive oil
8 large shrimp

4 cloves garlic, peeled
24 blanched almonds
24 hazelnuts
4 day-old baguette slices, ½-inch thick
2 ripe tomatoes, grated
¼ cup dry white wine
Salt
2 cups fish broth (page 136)
¼ pound small clams
1 large spoonful minced flat leaf parsley

Soak the dried peppers for the sauce in warm water for an hour. Drain and blot dry with a paper towel. Reserve. Sprinkle the fish with coarse salt on both sides and reserve.

Heat the olive oil in an earthenware dish over medium heat. Add the shrimp and sauté for a minute on each side, just until pink. Remove to a platter (reserving oil) and reserve.

Prepare the Romesco sauce: Add the peppers, garlic, almonds, hazelnuts, and baguette slices to the oil. Sauté until golden brown, except for the dried peppers, which should simply be sautéed until they are soft. Transfer to a blender. (Traditionalists use a mortar and pestle, but a little motorized action goes a long way here.) Add the tomatoes, wine, and some salt. Blend until smooth.

Return the sauce mixture to the earthenware dish and stir in the fish broth. Add the fish and shrimp. Bring to a boil, lower the heat, and simmer uncovered for 10 minutes. Turn the fish halfway through cooking.

While the fish is simmering, prepare the clams by placing them in a saucepan with a bit of water. Bring to a boil. Remove the clams as they open and add them to the fish mixture. Sprinkle with parsley and serve directly in the earthenware dish.

Cook's Notes: Monkfish is a firm-fleshed fish which holds up well when prepared in sauces. Sprinkling the fish with salt and allowing it to sit for a few minutes helps to keep the fish from falling apart during cooking.

LA BUENA MESA • CHAPTER 4 The Mediterranean: Catalonia, the Balearic Islands, Valencia, and Murcia

Chicken with Vegetable Medley

Pollastre amb samfaina

[4 servings]

A classic example of the Mediterranean style of cooking, this dish combines a lean source of protein, in this case, chicken, with a medley of vegetables. The food is cooked over a slow simmer and the only added fat comes from the extra virgin olive oil.

1 chicken (3 to 3½ pounds), cut in serving
   pieces and skinned
Salt
Freshly ground black pepper
4 large spoonfuls extra virgin olive oil
1 onion, thinly sliced
1 clove garlic, minced
1 bay leaf
2 thin slices serrano ham, trimmed
   and minced

1 red bell pepper, seeded and cut in thin
   strips
1 green bell pepper, seeded and cut in
   thin strips
1 eggplant, unpeeled and cut in cubes
1 zucchini, unpeeled and cut in cubes
5 ripe tomatoes, grated, drained, and mixed
   with a pinch of sugar
1 cup dry white wine

Season the chicken pieces with salt and pepper. Heat the olive oil in a large earthenware dish and brown the chicken pieces on both sides. Remove to a platter and reserve.

Add the onion, garlic, and bay leaf to the same oil and sauté until the onion is tender. Stir in the ham, followed by the bell peppers, and continue sautéing for another 10 minutes. Add the eggplant and cook for 5 minutes. Season with salt. Add the zucchini, tomatoes, and wine. Return the chicken pieces to the earthenware dish, spooning some sauce over them. Cover and gently cook for 40 minutes, turning the chicken pieces periodically.

Cook's Notes: This is a dish that is easy to "recycle" if there are any leftovers. Debone the chicken and heat it along with the vegetables. Stir in ½ cup short-grain rice followed by 1 cup boiling water per serving. Cook uncovered for 15 minutes until most of the water has been absorbed. Remove from the heat and let sit for 5 to 10 minutes.

Braised Beef with Wild Mushrooms

Fricandó

[4 servings]

Spaniards are not great consumers of wild mushrooms, with the exception of the Basques and Catalans. Come fall, the marketplace fills up with these much-appreciated fungi in all their variety and glory. That's where I buy my wild mushrooms and where I suggest you buy yours. I would recommend using a meaty variety, such as porcini, but you can certainly experiment with different types of mushrooms or combine them. As is often the case in Catalan cooking, this meat dish is seasoned with cinnamon, which gives *fricandó* its unique flavor.

 START PREPARATION SEVERAL HOURS IN ADVANCE.

Juice of 1 lemon
4 large spoonfuls extra virgin olive oil plus
   additional for frying meat
1¼ pounds lean beef, such as round, thinly
   sliced and trimmed
Salt
Freshly ground pepper
Parsley
Rosemary

Thyme
4 to 6 dashes ground cinnamon
6 to 8 bay leaves
1 onion, chopped
2 ripe tomatoes, grated
All-purpose flour for dusting
8 ounces wild mushrooms, cut in large
   pieces
1 cup dry white wine

Mix the lemon juice and 2 large spoonfuls of olive oil together in a bowl. Place a layer of some of the meat slices in a dish and drizzle some of the lemon juice and olive oil mixture over the top. Season with some salt, pepper, parsley, rosemary, thyme, and cinnamon. Place a couple of bay leaves on top of the meat. Add another layer of meat and repeat the procedure until all the meat is marinated. If possible, allow the meat to marinate in the refrigerator for a few hours; otherwise leave it in the marinade until you're ready to cook it.

(continued on next page)

Braised Beef with Wild Mushrooms *(continued from previous page)*

Gently sauté the onion in the remaining 2 large spoonfuls of olive oil in an earthenware dish until the onion is golden brown. Remove the meat slices from the marinade. Discard all but 2 of the bay leaves and add the marinade to the onion along with the grated tomatoes. Continue cooking for another 10 minutes.

While the tomatoes and onion are cooking, dust the meat slices with flour and fry in olive oil until golden brown on both sides. Remove the meat from the oil and drain on paper towels to get rid of any excess oil. Arrange the meat slices on top of the onion and tomato mixture. Place the mushrooms on top of the meat and add the wine. Cover and cook over low heat for 20 minutes. Serve with a good crusty bread.

Cook's Notes: For really tender meat, use a meat hammer to break down the nerves in the meat and cut any larger nerves you see to keep the meat from rolling up once it starts cooking.

Butifarra Sausage with White Beans

Butifarra amb mongetes

[4 servings]

An emblematic Catalan dish if ever there was one, *butifarra* sausage with white beans is one of the many courses served during a *calçotada*, a sort of "onion fest" that centers around *calçots*, tender onions that bear a striking resemblance to leeks. I've even seen Catalans order *butifarra* sausage with white beans for a hearty, country-style breakfast.

 START PREPARING THE BEANS 1 DAY IN ADVANCE.

1½ cups dried white beans, rinsed
1 onion, peeled
2 whole cloves garlic, peeled; plus 4 cloves garlic, minced
2 carrots, scraped and cut in thirds
1 leek, white part only
1 sprig parsley

1 bay leaf
4 *butifarra* sausages, pricked with a fork in a few places
2 large spoonfuls extra virgin olive oil plus additional for cooking sausages
4 large spoonfuls minced flat-leaf parsley
Coarse salt

Place the beans in a pan with cold water to cover and soak them overnight.

Add the onion, whole garlic cloves, carrots, leek, sprig of parsley, and bay leaf to the beans. The water covering the beans should be about 2 fingers deep. Bring to a gentle, rolling boil. Skim the white foam that forms on the surface of the water. Lower the heat, cover, and cook for 2 hours. Check the beans periodically to make sure that there's enough water and cut the boil with ¼ cup cold water 3 times during cooking to tenderize the beans. Drain and reserve.

Heat a non-stick skillet or griddle over medium-high heat. When the cooking surface is hot, add just enough olive oil to prevent sticking. Place the sausages on the hot surface and cook on all sides. Reserve.

(continued on next page)

Butifarra Sausage with White Beans *(continued from previous page)*

Sauté the minced garlic in the 2 large spoonfuls of olive oil just until it begins to brown. Stir in the beans and minced parsley, and cook until heated through. Season with coarse salt. To serve, arrange the beans on individual plates along with a *butifarra* sausage.

Cook's Notes: Pricking the sausages in several places with a fork before cooking not only keeps them from "exploding," but also allows the sausages to release fat as they cook. For even more flavor, get out the charcoal and grill them.

Mussels in Vinaigrette *Mejillones a la vinagreta*

Green Salad, Spanish Style *Ensalada verde*

Cold Tomato Soup *Gazpacho*

Asturian Bean Stew *Fabada*

Chicken in Saffron-Scented Sherry Sauce with Almonds

Pollo en pepitoria

Vegetable Medley, Rioja Style *Menestra riojana*

a selection of tapas

Sangría

Spanish Omelet *Tortilla española*

Spanish Fritters with Thick Spanish-Style Hot Chocolate
Chocolate a la taza con churros

Caramel Custard *Flan*

the main entrance to
the Boqueria Market
in Barcelona

Both fresh and dried peppers
make their way into a number
of regional Spanish dishes.

An explosion of color in the form of fruits and vegetables is what first catches the visitor's eye upon entering the market.

a *charcutería* where cured ham, sausages, and cold meats are sold

Fish is usually sold whole in Spain and prepared to order.

A variety of shellfish (clockwise beginning in the lower left-hand corner): oysters, langoustines, shrimp, clams, jackknife clams, and scallops

Country Bread

Pa de pagès

[Makes 1 large round loaf]

This hearty country loaf, typical of Catalonia and the Balearic Islands, is the bread of choice for Bread with Tomato and Olive Oil (page 110).

 START PREPARATION SEVERAL DAYS IN ADVANCE TO MAKE THE SPONGE.

¼ cup warm water	1 small spoonful salt*
1 package dry yeast	2½ cups unbleached all-purpose flour
Pinch sugar	1 cup mother sponge (page 19)
2 large spoonfuls extra virgin olive oil*	1 cup cornmeal or breadcrumbs

If you do not already have a mother sponge, then you will need to create one first. To do so, see Galician Rye Bread, page 19.

Dissolve the yeast in warm water, along with a pinch of sugar. Add the olive oil. Mix the salt with 1 cup flour, and using a wooden spoon, add it to the yeast mixture along with the sponge. Gradually stir in the remaining flour until the dough comes together to form a firm ball. Turn onto a floured surface and knead for 5 minutes, adding more flour as needed. Place the dough in a greased bowl, cover, and let rise in a warm place until it doubles in size, about 2 hours.

Punch the dough down and knead for another 5 minutes. Shape the dough into a round loaf. Sprinkle the cornmeal or breadcrumbs on a cookie sheet and place the loaf on top. Place the loaf in a warm place and let rise until it doubles in size, about 1 hour.

Preheat the oven to 400° F. Bake the bread on the middle-upper rack for 30 to 35 minutes. The crust should be brown and the loaf should make a hollow sound when tapped on the bottom. Cool before slicing.

Cook's Notes: This is the perfect bread for toasting. While it is usually toasted in large slices to make Bread with Tomato and Olive Oil, I also like it for breakfast with butter and jam.

*The oil measures out to exactly 2 tablespoons and the salt to 1 level teaspoon.

LA BUENA MESA • CHAPTER 4 The Mediterranean: Catalonia, the Balearic Islands, Valencia, and Murcia

145

Catalan Pizza with Roasted Peppers, Eggplant, and Onion

Coca de recapte

[Makes 1 large or 2 small pizzas]

Coca has a lot in common with pizza. Its base is a bread-like dough, though in the case of *coca*, that dough is given a long oval shape as opposed to pizza's round one. *Coques* are typically found in Catalonia and Valencia. *Recapte* in Catalan comes from the verb *recaptar*, which in this case refers to what one is able to collect from one's vegetable garden. This gives rise to a large number of variations in *coca* toppings, much the same as for pizza. True to its Mediterranean roots though, *coca* is usually made with vegetable toppings, typically *escalivada*. There are savory *coques*, such as this version of *coca de recapte*, and sweet ones, such as *Coca de Sant Joan* (page 152), particularly popular around the feast day of Saint John (June 24).

TOPPING:	BASE DOUGH:
Escalivada (Roasted Eggplant, Red Pepper, and Onion, page 115), with variations	1 packet dry yeast
2 large spoonfuls tomato sauce (page 119)	1 cup warm water
1 large spoonful extra virgin olive oil	1 large spoonful honey
Salt	2 large spoonfuls extra virgin olive oil
8 olive oil-packed anchovy fillets, preferably Spanish	3 cups all-purpose flour
	Good pinch of salt

Follow the recipe for *Escalivada*, but omit the olive oil, lemon juice, salt, and pepper. Drain the vegetables well so that there is no excess liquid (which would make the dough soggy).

Make the dough: Dissolve the yeast in warm water in a bowl, along with the honey and olive oil. Stir in the flour and salt until the dough comes together to form a firm ball. Turn the dough out onto a floured surface and knead for a few minutes. Place in a greased bowl turning once, cover, and let rest in a warm place for 1 hour.

Preheat the oven to 425° F. Punch the dough down and pat or roll out in a long, oval shape, about ½-inch thick. Depending on the size of your oven, you may have to make 2 small pizzas instead of 1 large one. Place the *coca* dough base on a greased cookie sheet. Turn the edges up to create a border just as you would with a pizza. Spread the tomato sauce on the dough. Top with the roasted vegetables. Drizzle with 1 large spoonful of olive oil, sprinkle lightly with salt (remember the anchovies are very salty), and place the anchovies diagonally down the center of the *coca*. Bake for 10 to 12 minutes until the edges begin to brown. Serve either warm or at room temperature.

Cook's Notes: My trick for rolling dough out with a minimum effort and mess is to use parchment paper. Tear off two pieces of parchment paper and grease them with a bit of olive oil. Place the dough between the two sheets of paper and roll it out by placing the rolling pin on top of the parchment paper. Nothing sticks and there's no mess to clean up afterwards. Once the dough is rolled out, remove the top sheet of parchment paper, pick up the bottom sheet and transfer the dough—parchment paper and all—to a cookie sheet.

Murcian Meat Pie

Pastel murciano

[Makes 6 individual pies]

These tasty little meat pies are typically sold in pastry shops in Murcia and consumed as afternoon snacks. They also work well for a light supper, individually or as a large pie. For a particularly appealing presentation, try preparing them in earthenware ramekins.

BASE DOUGH:
2 cups all-purpose flour
Pinch salt
3 large spoonfuls extra virgin olive oil

EASY PUFF PASTRY:
2 cups all-purpose flour
Pinch salt
¼ pound frozen butter
9 to 10 large spoonfuls ice water

FILLING:
2 large spoonfuls extra virgin olive oil
1 onion, chopped
1 clove garlic, minced
1 green bell pepper, chopped
2 chorizo sausages
½ pound veal, diced
Salt
Freshly ground black pepper
¼ pound serrano ham, in a thick slice,
    trimmed and diced
2 ripe tomatoes, grated and drained
1 hardboiled egg, chopped
1 egg, beaten

Make the dough: Mix together the flour and salt. Stir in the olive oil and ½ cup water. Turn onto a floured surface and knead until the dough has a compact consistency. Cover with plastic wrap and let rest for 30 minutes. Roll the dough out ⅛-inch thick on a lightly floured surface and cut out six 6-inch circles.

Make the puff pastry: Mix together the flour and salt. Grate the frozen butter directly over the flour, tossing with a fork so that it's evenly distributed. Add the water and toss lightly with a fork. Turn onto a floured surface and, using your hands, press the dough together until it has a compact consistency. Shape into a ball. Cover with plastic wrap and place in the freezer for 20 minutes. Roll the pastry dough into a rectangle with the long sides running horizontally to you. Lightly dust the surface of the dough with flour. Fold the top third down and the bottom third up as you would a business letter. Lightly dust the dough with flour again. Fold the left edge over so that it meets the right edge. Roll out and fold the dough in the same way two more times. The dough is now ready for use or can be stored in the refrigerator or freezer. To use, roll the dough out ⅛-inch thick on a lightly floured surface and cut out six 6-inch circles and six 1-inch by 6-inch strips of dough.

Make the filling: Sauté the onion, garlic, and pepper in 1 large spoonful of olive oil until tender. Remove the vegetables to a plate and reserve. Degrease the chorizo sausage by pricking with a fork and boiling in water to cover for 5 minutes. Cut in ¼-inch slices. Season the veal with salt and pepper. Add the remaining spoonful of olive oil to the pan, along with the veal. Sauté until the meat begins to brown. Add the chorizo slices and ham, and continue cooking for another minute. Return the vegetables to the pan and add the tomatoes. Reduce the heat and continue cooking for another 5 minutes. Remove from the heat and stir in the chopped hardboiled egg. Drain off any excess liquid before filling the pies.

Assemble pies: Preheat the oven to 425° F. Place the base dough circles on a baking sheet. Spoon some of the filling onto the center of each base dough circle, being sure to leave a margin around the edges. Brush the edges with the beaten egg. Arrange a strip of puff pastry around the edge of each base dough circle, pinching the seams together (this strip acts as the "wall" for the pie). Place the puff pastry circles on top. Seal the edges and brush the top of the puff pastry with the beaten egg. Bake for 20 minutes until the dough is a golden brown color.

Cook's Notes: This is a great make-ahead dish. You can assemble the pies and refrigerate them until ready to bake. If you omit the hardboiled egg, they also freeze well.

Catalan Custard

Crema catalana

[4 servings]

Catalan custard is, without a doubt, the most popular dessert in Catalonia. It is characterized by a crunchy layer of burnt sugar that floats on top of a cool, creamy custard. Like so many Spanish desserts, it begins with lightly infusing milk with the aromas of lemon and cinnamon.

2 cups milk
4 strips lemon peel (approximately ½-inch wide and the length of the lemon)
1 cinnamon stick

4 egg yolks, at room temperature
8 large spoonfuls sugar
2 large spoonfuls cornstarch*

Mix the milk, lemon peel, and cinnamon stick together in a saucepan and gradually bring to a boil. Lower the heat and simmer for 10 minutes.

In a separate bowl, beat together the egg yolks, 4 large spoonfuls of sugar, and the cornstarch with a whisk. Discard the lemon peel and cinnamon stick, and *gradually* stir the warm milk into the egg mixture. Return the egg and milk mixture to the saucepan and continue stirring over low heat until it almost reaches the boiling point. Remove from the heat and continue stirring for another minute before pouring into individual earthenware ramekins. Cool and refrigerate.

Before serving, sprinkle a large spoonful of sugar evenly over each individual custard dish. Caramelize using a mini blowtorch or caramelizing iron. Serve immediately as the sugar will only stay hard for a short time.

Cook's Notes: Crema catalan sets are available online with the earthenware ramekins and caramelizing iron. Another option is to use a mini blowtorch. And if you're not up for specialized equipment, you can also use the bottom of a saucepan that is more or less the same size as the ramekin. Add some oil or water to the saucepan to keep it from burning and wipe it off after each use.

*The cornstarch measures out to exactly 2 level tablespoons plus 2 level teaspoons.

Catalan Almond Pastries

Panellets

[Makes about 35 pastries]

Panellets are traditionally served on the eve of October 31, a holiday known as the *castanyada* (*castanya* is Catalan for chestnut), and again after the main meal on November 1, All Saints' Day. The *castanyada* is traditionally celebrated at home by roasting chestnuts in the fireplace, accompanied by yams. These almond pastries are served for dessert, along with a small glass of sweet Muscatel wine. (Try Málaga, available online.) While they can be rolled in a variety of toppings, the most popular is pine nuts, followed by shredded coconut and almonds.

 START PREPARATION SEVERAL HOURS IN ADVANCE.

DOUGH:
1 large potato or yam
2 cups finely ground almonds (approximately
   ½ pound blanched almonds)
1 cup sugar
Grated peel of 1 lemon

TOPPINGS:
2 cups shredded coconut
1 egg, beaten
1 cup chopped almonds
1 cup pine nuts

Wash the potato or yam and bake until soft. While still warm, peel and mash together with the ground almonds, sugar, and lemon peel. Work the dough with your hands until it has a compact consistency. Divide in half and divide one of the halves in half again.

Take one of the dough quarters and mix it with the shredded coconut. The coconut dough should be stored in a separate container from the rest of the dough as it will be used to make one type of *panellet* and the rest of the dough will be used to make the other two kinds. Refrigerate all of the dough until it has hardened, 2 to 3 hours.

Preheat the oven to 500° F. Take the dough that has been mixed with the coconut and shape it into small balls (approximately 1 small rounded spoonful each). Take ¼ of the plain dough, shape it into small balls, dip the balls in the beaten egg, and roll them in the chopped almonds. *Panellets* made from pine nuts are the most common, and for this reason, I've reserved half the dough for this topping. Shape the dough into small balls, dip the balls in the beaten egg, and roll them in the pine nuts. Place the *panellets* on a non-stick cookie sheet, being sure to leave a space in between, and bake for approximately 8 minutes. Cool before serving.

Cook's Notes: While some people make these almond pastries using a regular potato, I find that a yam produces a richer flavor and adds more color to the "panellets."

Sweet Bread with Sugar and Pine Nut Topping

Coca de Sant Joan

[Makes 1 large coca]

The feast day commemorating the birth of Saint John the Baptist (*Sant Joan* in Catalan) falls on June 24, a few days after the summer solstice. This holiday is of particular relevance along the Mediterranean coast and in Galicia. According to tradition, fire purifies the soul and so it is customary to build large bonfires on the eve of this holiday all along the coast and to spend the better part of the night on the beach with friends and family. Everywhere you go, you are met with the sound of firecrackers going off. Needless to say, no one sleeps much that night. And the traditional dessert for this holiday you might ask? Why, *Coca de Sant Joan*, a sweet bread topped with sugar and pine nuts.

1 package dry yeast
¼ cup warm milk
3¾ cups all-purpose flour
½ cup plus 4 large spoonfuls granulated sugar
1 small spoonful ground coriander
1 small spoonful ground anise seeds
Pinch salt

3 large spoonfuls butter, softened*
3 eggs
¾ cup finely ground almonds (approximately 3 ounces blanched almonds)
¾ cup powdered sugar
Grated peel of 2 lemons
Assorted candied fruits
½ cup pine nuts

Dissolve the yeast in warm milk. Stir in 1 cup of the flour and mix until the dough comes together to form a firm ball. Turn the dough out onto a floured surface and knead until smooth and elastic, about 5 minutes. Cover and let rise for 20 minutes.

While the dough is rising, mix together the remaining flour, ½ cup granulated sugar, coriander, anise, and salt. Mix the butter in with the dry ingredients, either with a pastry cutter or by rubbing the flour and butter between your fingers until crumbly. Stir in the eggs until the dough comes together to form a firm ball. Knead this dough together with the dough that you left rising until smooth and elastic, about 5 minutes. Cover and let rest for 5 minutes.

To make the marzipan, combine the almonds, powdered sugar, and lemon peel together in a bowl. Stir in 4 to 5 large spoonfuls of water, a little at a time, until you have a smooth paste.

Preheat the oven to just warm (minimum setting) and place a bowl of warm water on the lower rack. Turn the dough out onto an oiled surface. Pat or roll out the dough in a long, oval shape, about 1 inch thick. Transfer to a greased cookie sheet. Paint the surface of the *coca* with the marzipan. Decorate with the candied fruit and sprinkle with pine nuts. Place on the center rack in the barely warm oven. Let rise for 20 minutes.

Remove the *coca* from the oven and preheat the oven to 375° F. Sprinkle the *coca* with the 4 large spoonfuls of sugar and bake for 15 to 20 minutes. Serve warm or at room temperature.

Cook's Notes: While coffee cakes are not really a part of Spanish cooking (in fact, as far as I know, the term doesn't even exist in Spanish) this sweet bread works well served alongside coffee for breakfast, American-style.

*The butter measures out to exactly 3½ level tablespoons.

Sweet Spiral-Shaped Yeast Roll

Ensaimadas

[Makes 16 rolls]

Ensaimadas come in various sizes, ranging from small spirals, perfect for breakfast and afternoon snack, to cake-size rolls. The spiral shape and generous dusting of powdered sugar are characteristic of these Majorcan sweet rolls. They take their name from the word *saïm* or lard, which is the fat that was traditionally used to create the separate layers within the roll, much like a croissant, though in this particular recipe, I've used butter.

¼ cup warm milk	Pinch salt
¼ cup warm water	2½ cups unbleached all-purpose flour
1 package dry yeast	1 large spoonful mild extra virgin olive oil
1 egg	2 large spoonfuls butter, melted
4 large spoonfuls sugar	Powdered sugar for dusting

Dissolve the yeast in the warm milk and water. Gradually stir in the egg, sugar, salt, and flour until the dough comes together to form a firm ball. Turn the dough out onto a floured surface and knead, adding more flour as needed, until it is smooth and elastic, approximately 5 minutes. While kneading, gradually work the olive oil into the dough. Wrap in plastic wrap and let rest for 15 minutes.

Divide the dough into 16 pieces. Roll each piece into an approximately 12-inch by 2-inch rectangle. Brush with melted butter and roll each strip as though it were a jelly roll. Curl each rope into a spiral directly onto an ungreased cookie sheet, beginning on the outside of the spiral and working in an inward, upward direction. Cover and let rise in a warm place until the rolls double in size, about 3 hours.

Preheat the oven to 375° F. Brush the rolls with water and generously dust with powdered sugar. Bake for 15 minutes, until lightly browned. Cool for a few minutes and dust again with powdered sugar. Serve warm with coffee, tea or thick Spanish-style hot chocolate (page 244). Reheat any leftovers before serving.

Cook's Notes: A spray bottle also works well for misting the rolls with water.

Catalan Coffee

Cremat

[4 servings]

El meu avi va anar a Cuba a bordo del Català,
el millor barco de guerra de la flota d'ultramar.

My grandfather sailed to Cuba on board the Catalan,
the best warship in the overseas fleet.

So begins one of the most well-known *havaneres*, traditional Catalan songs whose lyrics describe the experiences of fortune-seekers who set out for Cuba during the nineteenth century. They returned home with full pockets, plenty of stories, and a newfound taste for rum, which flavors this coffee drink. *Havaneres* and *cremat* go hand in hand. In the summer, there are outdoor evening concerts of *havaneres* along the Costa Brava, where this music originates. And after the concert, *cremat* is typically served. You don't need an outdoor concert to enjoy *cremat* though. Serve this elegant coffee as the perfect ending to a special meal.

2 cups dark rum
2 large spoonfuls sugar
1 cinnamon stick

Peel of ½ lemon
2 cups strong, hot black coffee, preferably
espresso

Mix the rum, sugar, cinnamon stick, and lemon peel together in an earthenware dish. Slowly heat for 2 to 3 minutes, stirring with a wooden spoon until the sugar is dissolved. Carefully light the rum and let it burn until it is reduced by half, about 5 minutes. When you begin to notice the smell of burnt sugar, then it's time to put out the flames by pouring the hot coffee over the rum. Serve in Irish coffee glasses or mugs.

Cook's Notes: I like to serve "cremat" as one would Irish coffee—with whipped cream. While whipped cream is not a traditional ingredient, it makes for a lovely presentation—and tastes good too!

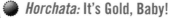

Horchata: It's Gold, Baby!

One can't visit Spain in summer without sampling a glass of refreshing, aromatic *horchata*—not to be confused with its Latin American counterpart made from rice. The taste is hard to describe simply because there is no other drink like it. Really, how many beverages do you know that are made from tiger nuts? In the case of Spanish *horchata*, the complete list of ingredients would also include water, sugar, and cinnamon. While it is available year-round in many supermarkets, the homemade version that is often sold in bars and ice cream parlors comes in with the warm weather and leaves with the first cooling breezes of autumn, making it a seasonal drink.

Horchata's main ingredient, the tiger nut, is a small underground tuber similar to a hazelnut in appearance. The tiger nuts are washed and soaked. They are mashed to create a soft paste. About three parts water is added to one part tiger nuts and the mixture is left to marinate. It is then pressed and strained. Cinnamon and one part sugar are added and the *horchata* is left to chill.

Apart from being a refreshing summer drink, *horchata* is also highly nutritious. It is rich in carbohydrates, unsaturated fats, proteins, and minerals such as magnesium, phosphorus, calcium, and iron. It doesn't contain lactose, gluten, or cholesterol, is low in sodium, and its enzymes aid in digestion. (The only down side is that it is rather high in calories because of the added sugar.)

Tiger nuts were cultivated in the area of Chufi in Sudan (hence the name *chufa* for tiger nut in Spanish) and in ancient Egypt. Excavations have even turned up jars of tiger nuts in the ancient pharaohs' tombs. It was the Arabs who introduced tiger nuts into Spain during the Moorish occupation. The loose sandy soil and warm temperatures of Valencia, specifically the region of L'Horta Nord, offered the optimal conditions for cultivating this crop.

Legend has it that King Jaume I of Catalonia and Aragon was visiting Valencia on a particularly hot day when a young girl offered him a sweet, white liquid which she referred to as tiger nut milk. After tasting this drink, the king exclaimed in Catalan, *"Això no és llet, això és OR, XATA!"* (That's not milk, that's gold, lassie!). When you blend the two words *or* and *xata* together, you get the same sounds that are written in Spanish as *horchata*. Whether the story is true or not, I do not know, but what I am sure of is that *horchata* manages to deliver a pleasing flavor and pack a nutritional punch at the same time! And, like King Jaume, I'd say that's gold, baby!

Chapter 5

When those who have not yet had the pleasure of traveling around Spain imagine what it must be like, they envision a land of passion and romance, of flamenco, bullfighting, and gypsies. The expectant traveler conjures up images of white-washed villages, of courtyards decorated with ceramic tiles, and ancient Moorish palaces. And these images await the visitor to Andalusia.

Located in the south of the Iberian Peninsula, Andalusia is Spain's largest region stretching from the Mediterranean to the Atlantic and north to Córdoba and Jaen. It is a land of varied landscapes: the sea, with coastlines bordering two separate bodies of water, the Sierra Nevada Mountains, home of the highly regarded *jamón de Jabugo*, and the interior, with a climate that is ideal for growing fruits and vegetables.

Andalusian cooking is yet another fine example of a Mediterranean diet with olive oil as its cornerstone. Spain's southern region is one of the largest producers of notable extra virgin olive oils, a key ingredient in many traditional recipes. The silky smoothness of a chilled *gazpacho* would be impossible without the addition of olive oil, and another cold soup, the elegant *ajo blanco*, would simply cease to exist. Other outstanding examples of emblematic Andalusian fare can be found in *fritos* or fried foods, epitomized by heaping platters of freshly caught, batter-fried fish, prepared to perfection. The high temperatures in parts of the south during the summer months call for salads bathed in cooling vinaigrettes made with sherry vinegar, another signature product. Sherry vinegar is made from sherry wine, which can only be produced in a limited area of Andalusia. There is the straw-colored dry *fino* or *manzanilla*, the sweeter amber *amontillado*, and the very sweet mahogany *oloroso*. And one cannot miss the imprint that the Arab cooking of Al-Andalús has left on Spanish food, nowhere more evident than in Andalusia, and present in dishes such as *cordero a la miel* (honey-glazed lamb), *sopa de almendras a la alpujarreña* (almond and pine nut soup), or *pestiños* (honey-glazed fried pastries), to name but a few.

If Spain is famous for its tapas, Andalusia embodies the tapas culture more than any other region. These savory little dishes are meant to be shared and enjoyed in the presence of good company. They are an expression of love for fine food and the enjoyment of life lived to its fullest, something the people of Andalusia know a thing or two about!

APPETIZERS
Tapas
....

Spanish-Style Kebabs *(Pincho moruno)*
Tomato Dipping Sauce *(Salmorejo)*
Marinated Potato Salad *(Patatas aliñadas)*
Batter-Fried Cod Sticks *(Soldaditos de Pavía)*

SALADS
Ensaladas
....

Tomato and Pepper Salad *(Pipirrana)*

SOUPS
Sopas
....

Cold Tomato Soup *(Gazpacho)*
White Almond Gazpacho *(Ajo blanco)*
Almond and Pine Nut Soup *(Sopa de almendras a la alpujarreña)*

VEGETABLES AND LEGUMES
Verduras y Legumbres
....

Poor Man's Potatoes *(Patatas al pobre)*
Chickpeas and Spinach *(Garbanzos con espinacas)*

EGG DISHES
Huevos
....

Baked Eggs with Ham, Chorizo Sausage, and Vegetables *(Huevos a la flamenca)*

FISH AND SHELLFISH
Pescados y Marisco
....

Fried Fish Platter *(Pescaíto frito)*

POULTRY
Aves
....

Rolled Chicken Cutlets *(Flamenquines)*

MEATS

Carnes

Filet Mignon in Sherry Sauce *(Solomillo al vino oloroso)*
Oxtail Stew *(Rabo de toro a la andaluza)*
Honey-Glazed Lamb *(Cordero a la miel)*

DESSERTS AND AFTERNOON COFFEE

Postres y Meriendas

Rich Caramel Custard *(Tocino del cielo)*
Honey-Glazed Fried Pastries *(Pestiños)*

Tapas: Little Dishes with Big Flavors

Tapas are a "little something" to tide you over until the next meal, snacking taken to its highest level. They range from very simple foods like olives, a few slices of dry-cured chorizo sausage or cheese, to elaborate mini versions of complete dishes, such as legumes or even paella. The word *tapa* comes from the verb *tapar*, which means "to cover" in Spanish. It is not customary to drink alcohol in Spain without something to eat and so small dishes of food were placed over the mouth of the wine glass to cover the wine (and keep undesirable flying object from entering), a kind of two-in-one of eating and drinking. It is possible to make a meal out of tapas, either by going from bar to bar and sampling the house specialty—a sophisticated form of grazing, if you will—or by ordering a selection of tapas and having them brought to the table.

There are several theories as to the origins of tapas, two of them involving stories with kings named Alfonso. In the case of Alfonso X (1221–1284), also known as Alfonso the Wise, the story goes that the king became ill and for health reasons had to eat frequent snacks in between meals, accompanied by a bit of wine. (Can you imagine such a doctor's prescription?! Where can I find a doctor like this?) Upon recovering from whatever ailed him, the king ordered that the taverns of Castile should henceforth not serve wine without a little bite to eat to keep the drink from going to the client's head, since not everyone could afford to eat *and* drink or rather drink *and* eat.

The other Alfonso was Alfonso XIII (1886–1941), the current king of Spain's grandfather. It is said that while he was on an official visit to the Andalusian city of Cádiz, he ordered a glass of dry sherry. Just as the waiter went to serve the king, there was a gust of wind and the quick-thinking waiter covered the glass with a slice of serrano ham. Perplexed, the king asked why he had done this and the waiter apologized saying that it was to keep the sand from blowing into the king's wine. Pleased with the explanation, the king ordered another glass of sherry and asked that it be covered in the same way. The rest of the king's entourage followed suit and the tapa was born!

Whether these anecdotes are true or not, no one really knows; however, the tapa no doubt owes its existence to wine, probably sherry. Very dry *fino* sherry and moderately dry *amontillado* are much too strong to serve with meals and are more appropriate served as aperitifs. Owing to their strong nature (over 18% alcohol), you almost *have to* eat something while sipping these wines. It should come as no surprise that Andalusia, where sherry is produced, embodies the tapas culture.

Tapas translate well into the American lifestyle and take appetizers to a whole new level. It is possible to incorporate tapas into a sit-down dinner, by serving a few as appetizers before the meal, or to build a party solely around the tapas themselves. If you serve them as appetizers, be sure that they do not overwhelm the other courses. You can keep them as simple as olives, chorizo, and cheese, which require no preparation whatsoever, or try more elaborate recipes. If you decide to serve tapas exclusively, I would suggest combining the fore-mentioned tapas that require no preparation with ones that can be made ahead of time plus a smattering of dishes that must be prepared on the spot and can be spread out over the course of your gathering. (See page 247 for menu suggestions.)

Be sure to balance cold or marinated tapas with tapas that use sauces or ones that are fried or grilled. Hot tapas with sauces are best served in individual earthenware ramekins. Also keep in mind that toothpicks allow your guests to sample individual tapas without having to use cutlery or their fingers. That's what they do in Spanish bars! To accompany tapas, you can serve beer, wine, *cava*, or for a truly elegant touch, dry sherry (*fino* or *amontillado*). With tapas, you'll soon discover that your guests eat *and* socialize well because good company and good food are at the very heart of the tapas experience. These exquisite little dishes with big flavors are intended to be shared and sampled among friends. Simply put, tapas bring people together.

Spanish-Style Kebabs

Pincho moruno

[Makes 8 kebabs]

The king of hot tapas is, without a doubt, the *pincho moruno*, which owes its spicy flavor to a mixture of seasonings that clearly denote the dish's Arab roots.

 START PREPARATION 1 DAY IN ADVANCE.

1 pound pork loin, cut in bite-size pieces
Salt
Freshly ground black pepper
Ground cumin
½ cup extra virgin olive oil
1 small spoonful *pimentón dulce* (sweet
   Spanish paprika)

½ small spoonful *pimentón picante* (piquant
   Spanish paprika)
1 small spoonful thyme
3 bay leaves, crumbled
24 cherry tomatoes

Sprinkle the meat with salt, pepper, and cumin. In a large bowl, mix together the olive oil, *pimentón dulce*, *pimentón picante*, thyme, and bay leaves. Add the pork and stir to coat well. Cover and refrigerate overnight.

Thread the meat and cherry tomatoes on 8 skewers. Sear on a hot griddle or grill over coals until well browned, basting frequently with the marinade.

Cook's Notes: Marinades are a great way to add flavor and tenderize meat at the same time. The marinades used in Marinated Pork Loin (page 193) and Seasoned Pork Loin (page 229) also work well with these kebabs.

Tomato Dipping Sauce
Salmorejo

[4 servings]

Although *salmorejo* is considered a cold soup, I have included it here as it is also sometimes served as an appetizer. Far more substantial than its lighter cousin *gazpacho*, it works well as a cold dip when served with chilled shrimp or vegetables.

2 cups baguette pieces, crusts removed
4 ripe tomatoes, unpeeled, cut in eighths
Pinch sugar
2 cloves garlic, peeled
½ cup mild extra virgin olive oil
1 large spoonful red wine vinegar

1 hardboiled egg yolk
¼ cup ice water
Salt
2 hardboiled eggs, chopped (optional)
2 thin slices serrano ham, trimmed and cut in strips (optional)

Soak the bread in ice water to cover for a few minutes and then squeeze dry. Add the bread to the tomatoes along with a pinch of sugar, garlic, olive oil, vinegar, egg yolk, and iced water. Blend until smooth (you may have to do this in parts, depending on what tool you use).

Place a strainer over a mixing bowl and press the mixture through the strainer, using the back of a wooden spoon. Salt to taste and chill thoroughly before serving. If you decide to serve *salmorejo* as a first course soup instead of as a dipping sauce, ladle into individual serving bowls and garnish with chopped eggs and strips of ham.

Cook's Notes: Whenever a recipe calls for raw olive oil, it is important to choose a mild, fruity oil. An intensely flavored, bitter oil would overpower the dish and drown out the other flavors. One of my favorite extra virgin olive oils is Nuñez de Prado, a blend of "hojiblanca," "picual," and "picudo" olives. It's smooth with a light, fruity aroma that's good enough to drink straight from the bottle and, like this salmorejo, *it hails from the Andalusian city of Córdoba!*

Marinated Potato Salad

Patatas aliñadas

[4 servings]

The humble little potato is an exceptional flavor sponge and with the addition of an olive oil and sherry vinegar vinaigrette, it becomes a sublime tapa.

---

4 medium potatoes
6 large spoonfuls extra virgin olive oil
3 large spoonfuls sherry vinegar
2 large spoonfuls minced flat-leaf parsley
Salt

1 Spanish onion, chopped
1 (4-ounce) can light tuna, preferably *bonito del norte* tuna
1 hardboiled egg, chopped

Boil the potatoes in their jackets in salted water until tender. When they are cool enough to handle, peel and cut in ¼-inch slices.

Mix together the olive oil, vinegar, parsley, and salt. Arrange the potato slices on a serving platter (you may have to do this in 2 or more layers). Pour the vinaigrette over each of the layers of potatoes, and sprinkle each layer with onion, tuna, and chopped egg. Marinate, either at room temperature or in the refrigerator, for an hour before serving. Serve at room temperature or chilled.

Cook's Notes: Whenever a recipe calls for raw onion, I invariably choose Spanish onions. They are sweeter than other onion varieties and don't leave a strong aftertaste.

Batter-Fried Cod Sticks

Soldaditos de Pavía

[4 servings]

The literal translation of this tapa is "little soldiers of Pavia" in reference to the Spanish troops that occupied this Italian city in the nineteenth century. Apparently the soldiers' uniforms were the same color as the batter on these fish sticks. As if that weren't enough, this tapa is sometimes served with a pimiento strip wrapped around one end of the fish stick to resemble an officer's stripes.

 START SOAKING SALT COD 2 TO 3 DAYS IN ADVANCE.

1 pound thick-cut salt cod fillets	**BATTER:**
Juice of 1 lemon	1½ cups all-purpose flour
Extra virgin olive oil for frying.	1 small spoonful baking powder
1 pimiento, cut in thin strips (page xv)	Pinch salt
	3 large spoonfuls extra virgin olive oil
	2 cups beer

Soak the salt cod 2 to 3 days in advance to remove salt (see salt cod, page xv).

Remove the skin from the cod and cut into strips that are about 2-inches long, 1-inch wide, and ½-inch thick. (I find that simply slicing the cod fillet ½-inch thick works well.) Sprinkle with lemon juice and marinate for an hour.

Make the batter: Mix the flour, baking powder, and salt together in a bowl. Stir in the olive oil and beer and let the batter rest for 15 minutes.

Heat the olive oil over medium-high heat. It should be about 1 finger deep. Dip the fish sticks in the batter and fry until golden on both sides. Drain on paper towels. To decorate, wrap a strip of pimiento around one end of the fish stick before serving.

Cook's Notes: It is also possible to make the batter using still or sparkling water instead of beer.

LA BUENA MESA • CHAPTER 5 The South: Andalusia

Tomato and Pepper Salad

Pipirrana

[4 servings]

In summer, this refreshing salad is a meal in itself. Add thinly sliced serrano ham for the perfect accompaniment.

4 tomatoes, peeled and chopped

1 cucumber, peeled, seeded, and chopped

½ green bell pepper, seeded and cut in julienne strips

½ red bell pepper, seeded and cut in julienne strips

1 (4-ounce) can light tuna, preferably *bonito del norte* tuna

2 thin slices serrano ham, trimmed and cut in strips

2 hardboiled eggs, chopped

4 large spoonfuls extra virgin olive oil

2 large spoonfuls sherry vinegar

1 clove garlic, minced

Salt

Freshly ground black pepper

Mix together the tomatoes, cucumber, peppers, tuna, ham, and eggs. In a separate bowl, mix together the olive oil, vinegar, garlic, and some salt and pepper. Gently fold the vinaigrette into the vegetable mixture. Refrigerate for several hours before serving.

Cook's Notes: Parboiling the tomatoes for 15 seconds makes them easier to peel.

Cold Tomato Soup

Gazpacho

[6 servings]

Gazpacho is one of those dishes that very much reflects the personal taste of the chef. You can vary the proportions or even leave out a particular vegetable altogether and still have *gazpacho*. Everyone has their preference where this cold tomato soup is concerned. Some like the sharpness of the onion and garlic to come through. Others want more or less cucumber. Personally, I prefer my *gazpacho* mild, with just a hint of onion and garlic. In the end, this is a cold tomato soup with tomato being the star. The other ingredients are there to add their aroma to the liquidized tomatoes, but should never overpower the main ingredient. For this reason, I think that the soup is best when the base is delicately flavored. After that, diners can always personalize their *gazpacho* with the vegetable garnish, emphasizing one vegetable over the other to create their own balance, or forgoing the chopped vegetables altogether.

6-inch length of a baguette, crust removed
1 cup ice water
8 ripe juicy tomatoes, unpeeled, cut in eighths
Pinch sugar
1 cucumber, peeled and coarsely chopped
1 green bell pepper, seeded and coarsely chopped

1 small Spanish onion, coarsely chopped
1 clove garlic
2 large spoonfuls sherry vinegar
½ cup mild extra virgin olive oil
Salt

Place the baguette piece in a bowl and add the ice water, followed by the tomatoes and a pinch of sugar. Add the cucumber, green pepper, onion, garlic, vinegar, and olive oil. Using an immersion blender, blend until smooth (or you can use a blender or food processor and blend in batches).

Place a strainer over a mixing bowl and press the mixture through the strainer using the back of a wooden spoon. Salt to taste and chill thoroughly before serving. Whenever *gazpacho* is served, it's customary to prepare small bowls of the individual chopped vegetables so that diners can garnish to taste. Another alternative is to serve the *gazpacho* with croutons.

Cook's Notes: "Gazpacho" is even better the following day after the flavors have had time to blend.

LA BUENA MESA • CHAPTER 5 The South: Andalusia

White Almond Gazpacho

Ajo blanco

[6 servings]

Who says that *gazpacho* has to be red? This white *gazpacho* from Málaga uses almonds instead of tomatoes as its main ingredient. It's refreshingly simple and simply refreshing when the mercury rises, and the fruit and ham garnish adds an elegant touch both for the eyes and taste buds. Just like red *gazpacho*, I find that this almond version is better the next day after the flavors have had time to blend.

Day-old 6-inch length of a baguette, crust
   removed
2 cloves garlic, peeled
4 ounces blanched almonds
3 large spoonfuls sherry vinegar
Salt

4 cups ice water
½ cup mild extra virgin olive oil
36 seedless grapes *or* 36 melon balls
   (Spanish melon or Galia)
2 thin slices serrano ham, trimmed and
   cut in strips

Soak the bread in water. Cut the garlic cloves in halves lengthwise and remove the light green inner part of the cloves. Grind the garlic and almonds in a food processor.

Squeeze the ice water from the bread and add the bread to the almonds and garlic, along with the sherry vinegar, some salt, and ¼ cup of the ice water. Blend to create a paste. Add the olive oil in a thin stream while processing continually until the mixture is well blended.

Transfer the almond mixture to a bowl and beat in the remaining ice water. Adjust the salt and vinegar, if necessary. Chill thoroughly before serving. To serve, garnish with grapes or melon balls and strips of serrano ham.

Cook's Notes: Removing the light green inner part of the clove cuts some of the bite in garlic.

Almond and Pine Nut Soup

Sopa de almendras a la alpujarreña

[4 servings]

With ingredients like almonds, pine nuts, and saffron, this soup clearly reflects the Arab influence on Spanish cuisine. It comes from an area of Andalusia known as La Alpujarra, nestled between the Sierra Nevada Mountains to the north and the Mediterranean Sea to the south, a region of great natural beauty and picturesque "white villages" with startlingly whitewashed houses that contrast with vibrant decorative flower pots in windows and on balconies. In Andalusia, this soup is served year round, while in the rest of Spain, it is primarily a Christmas dish. It is one of my favorites and brings together quintessential Spanish flavors: olive oil, almonds, pine nuts, saffron, garlic, and serrano ham.

---

4 cups chicken broth (page 67)
4 large spoonfuls extra virgin olive oil
Pinch saffron
2 large spoonfuls blanched almonds
2 large spoonfuls pine nuts
6-inch length of a baguette, crust removed

3 cloves garlic, minced
4 thin slices serrano ham, trimmed and
   minced
Oregano
Salt
1 cup heavy cream

Heat the chicken broth in a saucepan until hot.

In a separate saucepan, heat 3 large spoonfuls of olive oil over medium heat. Sauté the saffron, almonds, pine nuts, and bread for a few minutes until the almonds and pine nuts are a toasted color. Remove from the pan and grind to create a paste, either with a mortar and pestle or appropriate kitchen appliance.

Sauté the garlic and ham in the remaining olive oil, just until the garlic begins to brown. Add the almond and pine nut paste to the garlic and ham. Season with oregano and lightly salt (remember the ham is salty). Add the hot chicken broth and cream and simmer for 20 minutes.

Cook's Notes: Saffron is sold in strands and in powder form. I would recommend the strand form of saffron as it's very easy to adulterate powdered saffron. To make your own powdered saffron, simply grind the strands using a mortar and pestle. If you heat the saffron strands in a warm oven for just one minute before placing them in the mortar, you'll find that they're even easier to grind.

Poor Man's Potatoes

Patatas al pobre

[4 servings]

Poor Man's Potatoes form a part of my everyday repertoire of recipes and my 6-year-old son regularly requests them. They get their name from the inexpensive ingredients used because their taste is anything but poor.

4 large spoonfuls extra virgin olive oil	Salt
4 potatoes, peeled and thinly sliced	2 large spoonfuls minced flat-leaf parsley
1 onion, thinly sliced	2 large spoonfuls white wine vinegar
1 clove garlic, minced	

Heat the olive oil in a skillet over medium heat. Add the potatoes, onion, and garlic in layers, salting each layer as you go. Turn the potatoes to coat them with the oil. Lower the heat, cover, and gently cook, stirring frequently until they are tender, about 20 minutes. (Note that these potatoes, unlike fried potatoes, should be tender and not crisp, so for this reason they need to be cooked slowly and at a lower temperature than you would fried potatoes. By covering the potatoes, they steam as well as fry.)

When the potatoes are cooked, add the parsley and vinegar and serve.

Cook's Notes: While extra virgin olive oil is very heat resistant, you still don't want to abuse it by subjecting it to high temperatures and you certainly don't want to heat it to the smoking point. High temperatures cause the oil to break down, destroying many of its health-enhancing properties. When you're sautéing something and it's taking a while, instead of turning up the heat, simply put a lid on the pan!

Chickpeas and Spinach

Garbanzos con espinacas

[4 servings]

These chickpeas are typically served during Lent. Another variation of this recipe involves the use of salt cod. If you decide to add fish, you will need ½ pound salt cod that has been soaked (see page xv). Simply add the cod at the point where you combine the chickpeas, spinach, and sauce.

 START PREPARATION 1 DAY IN ADVANCE.

1½ cups dried chickpeas
1 whole onion, peeled; plus 1 onion, chopped
4 whole cloves garlic, peeled; plus 2 cloves garlic, minced
1 bay leaf
1 pound fresh spinach
4 large spoonfuls extra virgin olive oil

2 baguette slices, ½-inch thick
1 leek, white part only, chopped
1 small spoonful *pimentón dulce* (sweet Spanish paprika)
2 ripe tomatoes, grated
½ cup dry white wine
Salt

Soak the chickpeas in cold water in a large pot overnight. Using the same water they were soaked in, combine the chickpeas with the whole onion, whole cloves garlic, and bay leaf. Bring to a gentle, rolling boil. Skim the white foam that forms on the surface of the water. Lower the heat, cover, and cook for 2 hours. Discard the onion, garlic, and bay leaf. Drain the chickpeas and reserve.

Wash the spinach leaves and remove the stems and middle veins. Tear the leaves into small pieces. Place the wet spinach in a saucepan with a bit of salt. Cover, and gently cook until tender, about 5 minutes. Add the spinach to the chickpeas.

Fry the baguette slices in 2 large spoonfuls of olive oil until brown on both sides. Remove the bread from the oil and reserve. Add the remaining oil to the pan, along with the chopped onion, minced garlic, and leek. Sauté until tender. Remove from the heat and stir in the *pimentón* and grated tomatoes. Add the white wine, season with salt, and cook for 5 minutes. With an immersion blender or other appropriate kitchen appliance, blend the fried bread and onion mixture together to make a sauce. Combine with the chickpeas and spinach. Cover and cook over low heat for 10 minutes before serving.

Cook's Notes: By using canned chickpeas and frozen spinach, you can put this dish together in less than 30 minutes. Add cod and you've got a meal-in-a-pot.

Baked Eggs with Ham, Chorizo Sausage, and Vegetables

Huevos a la flamenca

[4 servings]

Huevos a la flamenca has a long gastronomic tradition within Gypsy cooking and is thought to have originated in Seville. The brightly colored ingredients, artfully arranged and served in Spanish earthenware, make this dish all the more appealing. By adding a few toasted baguette slices, a glass of wine, and fruit for dessert, you have a very satisfying light supper.

1 chorizo sausage, sliced	12 cooked asparagus spears
Extra virgin olive oil for greasing ramekins	1 pimiento, cut in thin strips (page xv)
8 large spoonfuls tomato sauce (page 119)	4 large spoonfuls cooked peas
8 eggs	2 thin slices serrano ham, trimmed and
Salt	quartered
Freshly ground black pepper	

Preheat the oven to 350° F. Heat a skillet over medium-high heat and cook the chorizo slices until they have released most of their grease and are brown on both sides. Remove to a plate and reserve.

Grease 4 individual 6-inch or 8-inch ramekins with some olive oil. Spread 2 large spoonfuls of tomato sauce on the bottom of each ramekin. Crack 2 eggs on top of the tomato sauce. Season with salt and pepper. Arrange the asparagus spears (you may need to trim them so that they fit), pimiento strips, peas, ham, and chorizo around the eggs. (The ingredients should be arranged by group and not mixed together.) Bake for approximately 30 minutes, or less if you prefer your eggs soft-set.

Cook's Notes: Mixing salt and sugar in the cooking water for the asparagus gives them a milder flavor. Fill a pan with enough water to cover the asparagus stalks. Add 1 small spoonful of sugar and another of salt to the water. Heat the water to boiling point. Add the asparagus and gently cook for 8 minutes. Drain and blot dry with paper towels.

Fried Fish Platter

Pescaíto frito

[4 servings]

Platters heaped high with fried fish are common in Andalusia. This fried fish platter requires few ingredients and is seemingly easy to prepare: fresh fish, flour, and extra virgin olive oil. The trick, however, as with any dish that uses so few ingredients is that they must be first-rate. If you eat this fried fish platter in Spain, it is quite possible that the fish on your plate were swimming in the sea just hours earlier. The flour used for dusting the fish is coarse rather than fine, which is why I've used whole wheat flour, and the olive oil is, naturally, extra virgin. Another factor is that the olive oil must be *en su punto*, an ethereal Spanish cooking concept roughly translated as "that moment when conditions are optimal" before adding the dusted fish fillets. How to describe this hard-to-nail-down concept? As the oil slowly heats, it will reach a temperature in which the surface of the oil seems to move, though there are no bubbles and certainly no smoke. When you drop a small piece of bread into the skillet, the oil will bubble up around it and the bread will fry to a golden brown color. It will not lie there in the skillet simply soaking up the oil because the temperature isn't hot enough, nor will it burn to a crisp in a matter of seconds because the oil is too hot. This is *en su punto* as best I can describe it!

The fish used varies according to availability, and of course, different species of fish are found in different parts of the world. The fish that I have suggested are firm-fleshed and stand up well to frying. As much as possible, they reflect the seafood typically served as *pescaíto frito*. While Spaniards would probably not bother to fillet the smelts or sardines, given their small size, fish heads do not generally appeal to American sensibilities, so for this reason, as well as for ease of eating, I suggest filleting the fish.

1½ pounds assorted firm-fleshed fish (for example, any combination of monkfish, whiting, flounder, perch, smelts, sardines, pompano)
8 small squid
8 large shrimp
Juice of 1 lemon

Coarse salt
2 cups whole wheat flour
1 large spoonful baking powder
Extra virgin olive oil for frying
1 large spoonful minced flat-leaf parsley
1 lemon, quartered

(continued on next page)

Fried Fish Platter *(continued from previous page)*

Have your fishmonger fillet the fish. Clean the squid and cut in ½-inch rings, reserving the tentacles (see Baby Squid in Ink Sauce, page 50). Sprinkle the fish, squid, and shrimp with lemon juice and coarse salt.

Mix together the flour and baking powder. Dust the seafood with the flour mixture, shaking off any excess.

To fry the seafood, you will need to heat the oil, which should be about 2 fingers deep, over medium-high heat. It is important that the oil be hot without reaching the smoking point. Fry the seafood until it is a deep golden brown color and drain on paper towels. Arrange on a serving platter and sprinkle with parsley. Decorate with lemon wedges and serve immediately.

Cook's Notes: I happen to love fish and all kinds of seafood, but am aware that many people who are not used to eating fish have an aversion to what they deem a "fishy" smell or taste. If that is your case, I would suggest preparing the fish using a marinade, which, by the way, happens to be a variation of this dish. Mix together 4 large spoonfuls white wine vinegar, the juice of 2 lemons, 1 cup dry white wine, 1 small spoonful sweet Spanish paprika, and 1 small spoonful oregano. Pour the marinade over the fish and refrigerate for at least 30 minutes or overnight. Drain, sprinkle with coarse salt, dust with flour, and fry according to the recipe.

Olive Oil: Liquid Gold

Olive oil (preferably extra virgin) is the cooking oil of choice in Spanish kitchens. Basque chef Karlos Arguiñano refers to it as liquid gold and that's not a bad description when you consider its many health-enhancing properties. Olive oil has been shown to protect against heart disease, cancer, and a host of lesser ills. I think of it as good fat with antioxidants thrown in! It's also one of the pillars of the Mediterranean diet.

The Romans introduced large-scale olive oil production into Spain, and it was Spain, not Italy, that provided the bulk of olive oil to the Roman Empire. To this day, Spain is the world's largest producer of olive oil, particularly the southern region of Andalusia and, to a lesser extent, Catalonia.

Just as wine is not made from one variety of grape, so olive oil is not made from one type of olive. Different olives have different attributes which, alone or blended, give the different brands their distinctive flavors. There are nearly three hundred varieties of olives grown in Spain, but *Hojiblanca*, *Picual*, *Picudo*, and *Arbequina* olives are the most well-known, so much so that many Spanish olive oil producers bottle their extra virgin olive oil according to olive type.

I use nothing but olive oil for cooking and baking, and insist that the olive oil be extra virgin. What this means, according to the International Olive Oil Council, is that the oil has been obtained solely by mechanical or physical means under thermal conditions that do not lead to alterations in the oil and with acidity levels that do not exceed 0.8%. Do not be fooled by the terms "lite" or "light," which refer to the flavor and not the caloric content. "Light" olive oil is refined, which means that chemical processes were involved in extracting the oil. The highest grade of olive oil, the one that tastes the best and is the best for you is extra virgin. Do not settle for anything less. And don't think that olive oil is just for salads. Use it for sautéing, frying, baking, in sauces, drizzled over cooked vegetables or fish—even on toast for breakfast. To preserve the oil's fatty acids and antioxidants, store your container in a cool, dry, dark place, away from heat and light, olive oil's biggest enemies.

Rolled Chicken Cutlets

Flamenquines

[4 servings]

The story goes that *flamenquines* got their name from Flemish settlers in the Andalusian city of Córdoba. The word for *Flemish* in Spanish is *flamenco*, not to be confused with the music or dance. It seems that most of these Flemings were blond, much like the golden breading surrounding these chicken rolls; hence the name *little Flemings* or *flamenquines*.

1 pound boneless chicken cutlets, thinly sliced
4 thin slices serrano ham, trimmed
4 ounces mild *Manchego* cheese, cut in thin sticks (about the length of a toothpick and the width of a pencil)

All-purpose flour for dusting
2 eggs, beaten
1 cup breadcrumbs
Extra virgin olive oil for frying

Place the chicken cutlets between 2 sheets of parchment paper. Use a meat hammer to pound the cutlets. The idea is to make the cutlets as thin as possible without tearing them. Place a slice of ham (the size of the cutlet) on top of each cutlet and a stick of cheese in the middle of each slice of ham. Roll the cutlets and secure with toothpicks.

Dip each *flamenquín* in flour, then in the beaten egg, and finally in the breadcrumbs, being sure to coat well each step of the way. (I don't use salt simply because the ham and cheese are salty.)

Heat the olive oil in a skillet over medium-high heat (or use a deep-fryer). The oil should be about 1 finger deep. Fry the rolls until golden brown on all sides. Drain on paper towels. Serve warm or at room temperature.

Cook's Notes: Apart from chicken, you can also use beef or pork loin to make "flamenquines." These breaded chicken rolls can also be served cut in bite-size pieces and skewered with a toothpick.

Filet Mignon in Sherry Sauce

Solomillo al vino oloroso

[4 servings]

This dish is simple and exquisite at the same time.

4 filets mignons	**SHERRY SAUCE:**
Extra virgin olive oil for drizzling	1 cup sweet sherry (*oloroso*)
Coarse salt	4 large spoonfuls raisins
	1 large spoonful cornstarch
	½ cup beef broth (page 16)
	2 large spoonfuls heavy cream

Make the Sherry Sauce: Mix together the sweet sherry and raisins in a small saucepan and cook over medium heat for 5 minutes until the alcohol has evaporated. Dissolve the cornstarch in the beef broth and add to the sherry, along with the heavy cream. Lower the heat and simmer for 8 to 10 minutes.

Heat a non-stick skillet or a griddle or a grill over medium-high heat. When the cooking surface is hot, add just enough extra virgin olive oil to keep the meat from sticking. Place the filets mignons on the hot surface. Cook on both sides and season with coarse salt. Remove filets to a platter, spoon the sherry sauce over the meat and serve.

Cook's Notes: When grilling meat, it is important to use a cooking surface that has been preheated and is at its optimal (hot) temperature. The heat seals the pores in the meat and keeps the juices from escaping. The reason for salting the meat after it has been cooked is to keep it from drying out.

Oxtail Stew

Rabo de toro a la andaluza

[4 servings]

Where else would this dish come from other than Andalusia, prime bullfighting country? In typical Spanish style, nothing goes to waste and even the bull's tail is eaten. The long, slow cooking process results in exceptionally tender, moist meat.

OXTAIL BROTH:
2 oxtails (3½ to 4 pounds), fat trimmed
    and cut in 2-inch pieces
1 carrot, scraped and cut in several
    pieces
1 onion, quartered
1 sprig flat-leaf parsley
1 bay leaf
2 cloves
6 black peppercorns
Salt

STEW:
4 large spoonfuls extra virgin olive oil
1 onion, chopped
½ red bell pepper, seeded and coarsely
    chopped
½ green bell pepper, seeded and coarsely
    chopped
4 cloves garlic, minced
1 bay leaf
2 large spoonfuls tomato sauce (page 119)
1 cup dry white wine
Salt
Freshly ground black pepper
1 large well-rounded spoonful cornstarch

Prepare oxtail broth: Place the oxtails, carrot, onion, parsley, bay leaf, cloves, peppercorns, and some salt in a saucepan with water to cover. Bring to a boil and skim off the foam that forms on the surface. Lower the heat, cover, and simmer for 3 hours. Remove the oxtails and strain the cooking liquid, reserving 1¼ cups. Degrease the broth.

Prepare stew: Heat the olive oil in a large earthenware dish and sauté the onion, peppers, garlic, and bay leaf until the onion is tender, about 10 minutes. Stir in the tomato sauce and gradually add the white wine and 1 cup of the reserved broth. Cook for a few minutes, stirring continuously, until smooth. Add the oxtails to the sauce and season with salt and pepper. Cover and cook over low heat for 1 hour. Dissolve cornstarch in the remaining beef broth. Add to the stew and cook for a few minutes until the broth thickens.

Cook's Notes: I would suggest making this stew over the course of 2 days. On the first day, make the broth. In this way you can thoroughly degrease it in the refrigerator, as well as break up the long cooking time.

Honey-Glazed Lamb

Cordero a la miel

[4 servings]

This recipe combines meat with honey and dried fruits, as well as contrasting sweet with sour, a clear example of the Arab imprint on Spanish cooking in general and the traditional dishes of Andalusia in particular. The honey, brandy, and sherry blend together to form a dark, thick, sweet glaze that complements the richness of the meat. This Honey-Glazed Lamb, typical of the city of Córdoba, is surprisingly easy to make and perfect for special-occasion meals.

3½- to 4-pound leg of lamb or shank	½ cup honey
Rosemary	½ cup brandy, preferably Spanish
Salt	½ cup sweet sherry (*oloroso*)
Freshly ground black pepper	10 pitted prunes
2 large spoonfuls lard	10 dried apricots

Preheat the oven to 450° F. Season the lamb with rosemary, salt, and pepper. Rub with lard. Roast for 15 minutes.

Coat the lamb with ¼ cup honey. Mix together the brandy and sherry and pour ¼ cup over the lamb. Place the prunes and apricots around the lamb. Reduce the heat to 350° F and continue basting with the remaining honey, brandy, and sherry every 10 minutes until the meat is done, approximately 15 to 20 minutes per pound, depending on desired doneness. (For best results, use a meat thermometer.)

Place the leg of lamb on a meat platter, arrange the prunes and apricots around the meat, and drizzle the glaze over the top.

Cook's Notes: Leg of lamb is probably the most popular cut of lamb; however, for everyday meals, I often use cheaper cuts of lamb, such as shoulder. Unlike a leg of lamb, which you can slice, a shoulder cut doesn't slice well. The meat really needs to be served in individual portions. Simply have your butcher cut through the bone—without cutting through the meat— to mark individual servings. That way you can roast the cut of lamb whole and then finish slicing it right before serving.

Rich Caramel Custard

Tocino del cielo

[6 servings]

The literal translation of this dessert is "pork fat from heaven," not a very appealing name in English, though I like to think that the "fat" refers to the custard's richness. The joke in Spanish goes that if the pork fat tastes this good in heaven, what must the ham be like?

Tocino del cielo originated in the convents of Andalusia. In fact, some of the best desserts in Spain are made by convent nuns. One of the reasons for this phenomenon has to do with wineries. Traditionally wine was clarified using egg whites and vintners were left with the egg yolks, which they donated to local convents. The nuns used the egg yolks to make desserts, which they in turn sold to maintain their convents. Even today it is still possible to buy homemade desserts from some convents.

Imagine *flan* without milk and you've got *tocino del cielo*. For all its richness though, it's not a heavy dessert, and in fact, can be a refreshing ending to a good meal.

---

4 large spoonfuls plus 2 cups sugar
4 strips lemon peel (approximately ½-inch wide and the length of the lemon)

10 egg yolks, at room temperature
2 eggs, at room temperature

Preheat the oven to 350° F.

Make the caramelized sugar: Heat a small skillet until very hot and add the 4 large spoonfuls of sugar, stirring constantly until the sugar turns a golden brown. Immediately pour the caramelized sugar into an 8-inch square or 11-inch by 7-inch rectangular baking pan.

Place the 2 cups sugar and lemon peel in a saucepan along with 1 cup water. Bring to a boil and cook over medium heat, stirring constantly with a wooden spoon until the syrup reaches the string stage (a drop of syrup dropped in cold water stretches into a string), about 20 minutes after it begins to boil. Remove from the heat, discard the lemon peel, and cool for a few minutes.

Beat the egg yolks and eggs together with a wire whisk. Gradually pour in the sugar syrup, beating constantly. Pour the mixture into the caramelized pan. Cover with aluminum foil and place the pan in a water bath. The water should reach halfway up the sides of the baking pan. Transfer to the oven and bake for approximately 40 minutes, until a toothpick inserted in the middle comes out clean. Cool and refrigerate. To serve, loosen the sides of the custard with a knife and invert onto a plate. Cut into individual servings and spoon the caramelized sugar over the top.

Cook's Notes: The trick to making this custard lies in the syrup. It must be the right consistency so that the sugar and water don't separate during the baking process. A couple of pitfalls and what to do if they happen to you: If after you've added the syrup to the egg yolks, you find that there are lumps in the mixture, simply pour the mixture from the bowl through a strainer into the baking pan to remove them. The second problem can come up when you bake the custard. Sometimes a sugar coating will form on the surface. Not to fear because the top of the custard in the baking pan is the bottom of the custard on your dessert plate. Simply lift the crystallized sugar off and invert the custard onto a dessert plate. No one will be the wiser.

Honey-Glazed Fried Pastries

Pestiños

[Makes about 50 pastries]

Dry white wine is not an unusual ingredient in Spanish pastries. It is also common to scent milk with lemon peel and/or cinnamon; however, in the case of these *pestiños*, it is the oil that is infused, flavoring these little honey-glazed pastries with a delicate lemon and anise aroma.

½ cup mild extra virgin olive oil plus
  additional for frying pastries
4 strips lemon peel (approximately ½-inch
  wide and the length of the lemon)
2 large spoonfuls anise seeds

2 to 2¼ cups all-purpose flour
Pinch salt
½ cup dry white wine
½ cup honey
Powdered sugar for dusting

Gently fry the lemon peel in the ½ cup olive oil for a few minutes. Add the anise seeds and remove from the heat. Cool and strain the oil.

Mix the flour, salt, wine, and flavored olive oil together to form a compact ball. Cover with plastic wrap and let rest for 30 minutes. Roll the dough out ⅛-inch thick on a lightly floured surface and cut in 2-inch by 1-inch rectangles.

Heat some olive oil in a frying pan. Fry the dough in the hot oil until golden brown on both sides. Drain on paper towels and drizzle with honey. Arrange on a serving plate, and just before serving, dust with powdered sugar.

Cook's Notes: When frying the pastries, add a few strips of orange and/or lemon peel to the skillet to keep the oil from acquiring a burnt taste.

Chapter 6

If I were to use only one word to describe the cooking of the Canary Islands, Ceuta, and Melilla it would be "fusion." The Canary Islands' unique location off the west coast of Africa has made it a stopping point during centuries for ships en route to other parts of the world, namely the Americas. The cooking on the different islands has borrowed heavily from the Spanish mainland, Africa, and Latin America, blending these different influences with cooking styles native to the islands themselves. The regions of Ceuta and Melilla are actually Spanish cities located on the north coast of Africa within the country of Morocco. Christians, Muslims, Jews, and Hindus live side-by-side in a cultural melting pot, which is well-reflected in local dishes.

The Spanish spent the better part of the fifteenth century conquering *las islas afortunadas* (the fortunate islands), as the Canary Islands are also known. The archipelago is made up of seven islands of volcanic origin: La Palma, El Hierro, La Gomera, Tenerife, Gran Canaria, Fuerteventura, and Lanzarote. Canarian cuisine is straightforward and down-to-earth, using fresh food and simple cooking methods. Some dishes can only be eaten in the Canaries as the ingredients are indigenous to the islands and not available elsewhere. The islands are famous for their *mojos*, dipping sauces typically served with their no-less-famous "wrinkled" potatoes. For those with a sweet tooth, special attention should be paid to the many exceptional desserts that are a characteristic feature of island cookery. This region blends influences from other cultures to create a style that is uniquely its own and offers one of the most innovative regional Spanish cuisines.

The city of Melilla was conquered by the ducal house of Midina Sidonia with the blessings of the Spanish crown in 1496 and Ceuta was ceded to Spain by the Portuguese in 1668, though both cities are a matter of dispute between Spain and neighboring Morocco. The cooking is heavily influenced by the Mediterranean coast of Spain, as well as Andalusia and Morocco. Seafood is king here, which should come as no surprise given that both Ceuta and Melilla are port cities.

Both the Canary Islands and the cities of Ceuta and Melilla use herbs and spices, such as cumin and cilantro, that are practically unheard of in the rest of Spain, at least where traditional cooking is concerned. The food can best be described as a sort of East meets West and, in the case of the Canary Islands, meets Latin America too. These regions offer a new twist on traditional Spanish cooking—a veritable fusion of cultures.

APPETIZERS

Tapas

Spicy Red Dipping Sauce *(Mojo picón)*
Cilantro Dipping Sauce *(Mojo verde de cilantro)*
"Wrinkled" Potatoes *(Papas arrugadas)*

EGG DISHES

Huevos

Colorful Egg and Vegetable Terrine *(Tortilla de colores)*

FISH AND SHELLFISH

Pescados y Marisco

Seafood with Curry Dressing *(Frutos del mar al curry)*

POULTRY

Aves

Chicken Seasoned with Cumin and Cilantro *(Pollo moruno)*

MEATS

Carnes

Marinated Rabbit in Wine and Vinegar Sauce *(Conejo al salmorejo)*
Marinated Pork Loin *(Carne de fiesta)*

DESSERTS AND AFTERNOON COFFEE

Postres y Meriendas

Vanilla Ice Cream with Almond Sauce *(Helado de vainilla con bienmesabe)*
Cream Cookies *(Galletas de nata)*
Turnovers with Sweet Potato Filling *(Truchas)*

Spicy Red Dipping Sauce

Mojo picón

[Makes about 1½ cups]

There are many different types of dipping sauces, *mojo picón* being one of the most popular. As its name implies, it is quite spicy and one should do a small taste test before diving in to avoid any unpleasant surprises, unless you like your food "the hotter, the better." Serve alongside "wrinkled" potatoes (page 188) and you'll know why this dish is a classic in the Canary Islands.

2 dried red chili peppers, seeds removed
1 head garlic, minced
Coarse salt
1 small spoonful *pimentón dulce* (sweet
  Spanish paprika)

½ small spoonful ground cumin
1 cup mild extra virgin olive oil
½ cup red wine vinegar

Soak the chili peppers in warm water for 20 minutes. Drain. Mash the peppers, garlic, and some coarse salt together using a mortar and pestle or appropriate kitchen appliance, until they are the consistency of a fine paste. Stir in the *pimentón* and cumin, and gradually add the olive oil and vinegar in a fine stream, stirring all the while (or with the motor running).

Cook's Notes: Apart from being the perfect accompaniment to "wrinkled" potatoes, this dipping sauce also works well with grilled meat or chicken.

● *Mojos:* Dipping Sauces

Mojos are typical sauces from the Canary Islands that accompany just about anything from meat and fish to vegetables, fruit, and even cheese, though they are usually paired with "wrinkled" potatoes (page 188), tiny spuds that have been cooked in sea water, followed by dry heat, giving them that day-out-in-the-sun look. These dipping sauces have fairly simple, straightforward ingredients: oil, vinegar, garlic, salt, and spices. The seasoning varies depending on the *mojo*, but cumin, paprika, and cilantro are used in abundance. Such is the versatility of *mojos* that they can do double and triple duty as marinades and cooking sauces.

While *mojos* are probably of Portuguese origin, it is interesting that the verb *mojar* in Spanish means "to wet" or even "to dunk," which is why these sauces can best be described as dips. There are *mojos* for all tastes. Two classic dipping sauces, both included in this chapter, are *mojo picón*, which gets its bite from the addition of chili peppers, and *mojo verde*, a green sauce that owes it vibrant green color and distinctive flavor to fresh cilantro.

Cilantro Dipping Sauce

Mojo verde de cilantro

[Makes about 1½ cups]

This mojo verde, like *mojo picón* on page 185 (but without the bite!) is another classic dipping sauce for "wrinkled" potatoes (page 188).

½ green bell pepper, seeded and chopped
6 cloves garlic, minced
1 cup fresh cilantro leaves

Coarse salt
1 cup mild extra virgin olive oil
¼ cup white wine vinegar

Mash the green pepper, garlic, cilantro, and salt together, using either a mortar and pestle or appropriate kitchen appliance, until they are the consistency of a fine paste. Gradually add the olive oil and vinegar in a fine stream, stirring all the while (or with the motor running).

Cook's Notes: Apart from being the perfect accompaniment to "wrinkled" potatoes, this dipping sauce also works well with freshly grilled fish.

"Wrinkled" Potatoes

Papas arrugadas

[4 servings]

These potatoes, some as small as one inch, are cooked in their jackets in large pots of salted water. Contrary to what you might think, they are not salty; rather, the salt draws the water out of the potatoes, creating a wrinkled effect. *Papas arrugadas* are usually served alongside a *mojo* or dipping sauce, but also work well as an accompaniment to grilled meat or fish. And they come complete with their own little rhyme (at least in Spanish)!

Con aceites se disfraza	Oil is used to disguise
Quien dentro no tiene nada,	Those who have nothing inside.
Mejor que una papa frita,	Rather than a fried potato,
Dame una papa arrugada.	Give me a "wrinkled" one.

1 pound new potatoes	1 cup coarse salt, preferably sea salt

Wash the potatoes thoroughly, but do not peel. Place them in a saucepan, along with the salt and water to cover. Stir until the salt is dissolved in the water. Bring to a boil and cook until tender. Drain off the water, leaving the potatoes in the pan. Continue cooking the potatoes over low heat, gently shaking the pan from side to side to ensure that the potatoes don't stick, until they are dry and the skin begins to wrinkle, about 10 minutes.

Cook's Notes: Choose potatoes that are the same size to ensure that they cook evenly.

Colorful Egg and Vegetable Terrine

Tortilla de colores

[4 servings]

This colorful, eye-catching egg dish from Melilla is of Jewish origin.

 START PREPARATION SEVERAL HOURS IN ADVANCE.

6 eggs
2 large spoonfuls mashed potatoes
1 large spoonful baking powder
Salt
Freshly ground black pepper

2 dashes ground nutmeg
2 carrots, scraped, diced, and cooked
2 cups cooked peas
4 hardboiled eggs, chopped

Preheat oven to 350° F. Grease a 6-cup loaf pan with olive oil. Line with parchment paper and grease the parchment paper with olive oil.

Beat the eggs together with the mashed potatoes. Season with salt, pepper, and nutmeg. Fold in the carrots, peas, and chopped eggs.

Pour into the loaf pan and place the loaf pan in a water bath. The water should reach at least halfway up the sides of the loaf pan. Transfer to the oven and bake until set in the middle, about 1¼ hour. Remove from the oven and cool completely. Invert onto a serving plate and slice.

Cook's Notes: Instead of boiling the carrots and peas, try cooking them in the microwave to preserve nutrients.

Seafood with Curry Dressing

Frutos del mar al curry

[4 servings]

This seafood dish is seasoned with curry, a spice that you won't find in traditional Spanish food from the mainland, but that is not unusual in Ceuta.

1 pound whitefish fillets, cooked and cut in
    bite-size pieces
1 pound medium shrimp, cooked and peeled
12 mussels, cooked and shelled
2 tomatoes, cut in bite-size pieces
12 black olives
6 large spoonfuls extra virgin olive oil
1 small Spanish onion, finely chopped

¼ green bell pepper, seeded and finely
    chopped
1 large spoonful minced flat-leaf parsley
½ small spoonful *pimentón dulce* (sweet
    Spanish paprika)
¼ small spoonful curry powder
Salt

Mix the fish, shrimp, mussels, tomatoes, and black olives together and arrange on individual plates. In a small bowl, mix together the olive oil, onion, bell pepper, parsley, *pimentón*, curry, and some salt. Serve the dressing separately in a small pitcher or gravy boat.

Cook's Notes: Instead of boiling the fish, try preparing it "en papillote" to preserve all of the flavors and nutrients. Preheat the oven to 350° F. Grease a sheet of parchment paper with olive oil. Arrange the fish on the parchment paper and drizzle with 1 large spoonful of white wine and 1 large spoonful of olive oil. Lightly salt. Place a bay leaf, a sprig of parsley, and several lemon slices on top of the fish. Wrap tightly in the parchment paper and bake for 15 minutes. Cook the shrimp as you would for Shellfish Vinaigrette, page 216, and the mussels as described on page 3.

Chicken Seasoned with Cumin and Cilantro

Pollo moruno

[4 servings]

Like so many Spanish dishes, this *pollo moruno* from the North African city of Ceuta begins with a little *sofrito*: sauté a bit of onion and garlic in olive oil and add some tomato. However, following the *sofrito*, this chicken dish blends the tastes of Spain with those of neighboring Morocco by adding ground cumin, cilantro, dried fruits, and almonds. The combination is a perfect fusion of flavors that reflects the diversity of cultures in Ceuta.

1 chicken (3 to 3½ pounds), cut in serving
    pieces and skinned
Coarse salt
4 large spoonfuls extra virgin olive oil
1 onion, chopped
2 cloves garlic, minced
3 ripe tomatoes, grated
1 small spoonful ground cumin
6 black peppercorns

1 large spoonful minced fresh cilantro
1 large spoonful minced flat-leaf parsley
1 cup chicken broth (page 67)
8 pitted prunes
4 large spoonfuls raisins
½ cup black olives
½ cup green olives
20 blanched almonds
1 hardboiled egg, chopped

Season the chicken pieces with salt. Heat the olive oil in a large earthenware dish and brown the chicken pieces on both sides. Remove to a platter and reserve.

Add the onion and garlic to the same oil and sauté until the onion is tender. Stir in the tomatoes, cumin, peppercorns, cilantro, and parsley. Continue cooking for another 2 to 3 minutes. Pour in the chicken broth and return the chicken to the earthenware dish, spooning some sauce over the chicken pieces. Cover and cook over low heat for 40 minutes, turning the chicken halfway through cooking.

Add the prunes, raisins, olives, almonds, and egg and serve.

Cook's Notes: Cilantro is not a common herb in Spanish cuisine, with the exception of the Canary Islands, Ceuta, and Melilla. It is usually sold fresh and should be stored in the same way as parsley. Simply rinse the cilantro well with water and store in an airtight container in the refrigerator. It will keep up to a week.

Marinated Rabbit in Wine and Vinegar Sauce

Conejo al salmorejo

[4 servings]

The *pimentón* dressing or *adobo* is the defining characteristic of this dish. In Andalusia, *salmorejo* is a thick version of *gazpacho*, but in the Canary Islands, it refers to a sauce made with heavy doses of vinegar.

 START PREPARATION SEVERAL HOURS IN ADVANCE.

8 cloves garlic, peeled
1 large spoonful minced flat-leaf parsley
1 small spoonful thyme
1 small spoonful oregano
2 bay leaves, crushed
1 small spoonful *pimentón dulce* (sweet Spanish paprika)

Salt
½ cup red wine vinegar
1½ cups dry white wine
½ cup plus 2 large spoonfuls extra virgin olive oil
1 rabbit (2½ to 3 pounds), cut in serving pieces

Use a mortar and pestle to create a paste with the garlic, parsley, thyme, oregano, bay leaves, *pimentón*, and some salt. Add the vinegar. Transfer to a bowl and stir in the white wine and ½ cup olive oil.

Add the rabbit pieces and coat them thoroughly with the marinade. Cover and refrigerate for at least 2 hours.

Remove the rabbit pieces from the marinade and dry with paper towels. Heat 2 large spoonfuls of olive oil in a shallow casserole. Add the rabbit and brown. Place the rabbit on a platter and reserve.

Use paper towels to wipe down the casserole dish and remove the oil from frying. Pour in the marinade and bring to a boil. Add the rabbit, cover, and simmer for 1 hour, turning periodically during cooking. Serve with "Wrinkled" Potatoes (page 188).

Cook's Notes: Rabbit is a very lean meat, which makes it a good choice for people who are watching their cholesterol. And for those who are trying to cut back on salt, it's possible to prepare this dish without any salt at all. Given all the garlic, herbs, vinegar, and wine, this rabbit's got more than its fair share of seasonings!

Marinated Pork Loin

Carne de fiesta

[4 servings]

This traditional dish is often served during local festivals, which would explain its name in Spanish—literally "party meat."

 START PREPARATION SEVERAL HOURS IN ADVANCE OR THE DAY BEFORE.

1 pound pork loin, cut in bite-size pieces
Salt
Freshly ground black pepper
Thyme
Oregano
6 cloves garlic, minced

2 small spoonfuls *pimentón picante* (spicy Spanish paprika)
½ cup extra virgin olive oil
½ cup dry white wine
½ cup red wine vinegar

Season the pork loin with salt, pepper, thyme, and oregano and place in a shallow dish. In a separate bowl, mix together the garlic, *pimentón*, olive oil, wine, and vinegar. Pour over the meat, cover, and refrigerate for several hours or overnight.

Drain the meat, reserving the marinade. Heat a non-stick skillet over medium-high heat. Brown the meat well on all sides. While the meat is cooking, heat the marinade to boiling in a separate saucepan. When the sauce begins to boil, lower the heat, and simmer until the meat is cooked. Pour the marinade over the pork loin and serve.

Cook's Notes: This is a great make-ahead dish that lends itself well to cookouts. The meat can be skewered or sliced, barbecued, and served with the warm marinade sauce.

Vanilla Ice Cream with Almond Sauce

Helado de vainilla con bienmesabe

[4 servings]

This thick custard-like sauce tastes a great deal like *turrón*, probably because it has many of the same ingredients that go into that most classic of Christmas candies. It's also as rich as *turrón*, so a little goes a long way. And then there's the name: *bienmesabe* is three words in one (*bien me sabe*) and literally means "it tastes good to me," which it does!

1 cup finely ground almonds (approximately ¼ pound blanched almonds)
½ cup sugar
1 large spoonful honey
1 cinnamon stick

4 strips lemon peel (approximately ½-inch wide and the length of the lemon)
2 egg yolks, at room temperature

Vanilla ice cream

Mix the ground almonds, sugar, honey, cinnamon stick, lemon peel, and ½ cup water together in a saucepan. Bring to a boil, reduce the heat, and cook uncovered over low heat for approximately 15 minutes.

Beat the egg yolks in a bowl and *gradually* stir in about half of the almond mixture. Return to the saucepan and stir constantly until the sauce begins to boil. Remove from heat and cool, stirring occasionally. (At this point, discard the cinnamon stick and lemon peel.) The sauce should have the consistency of custard.

To serve, spoon approximately 3 large spoonfuls into individual serving dishes and top with a scoop of vanilla ice cream.

Cook's Notes: In Spain, ground almonds are such a common ingredient in recipes that it's possible to buy them already finely ground. To make your own almond meal, grind the almonds a little at a time. I've gotten good results with a vegetable chopper, though a food processor would also do the trick.

Cream Cookies

Galletas de nata

[Makes about 30 cookies]

These cookies originated in simpler times when people had direct access on their farms to butter, cream, and eggs; in fact, I've seen recipes that use nothing more than equal parts heavy cream and sugar and as much flour as this mixture can absorb. While you might expect these cream cookies to taste like sugar cookies, they don't. The use of heavy cream gives them a much smoother texture and contributes its unique flavor. Also, they have less sugar than sugar cookies, which makes them soft rather than moist and crunchy. They are a standard in the Canary Islands and, I find, a nice alternative to sugar cookies.

½ cup butter, softened
½ cup heavy cream
1 egg, at room temperature; plus 1 egg, beaten
½ cup sugar plus additional for sprinkling

Grated peel of 1 lemon
Dash ground cinnamon
1 small spoonful baking powder
2½ cups all-purpose flour

Preheat the oven to 350º F. Blend the butter, cream, and 1 egg together. Stir in the sugar, lemon peel, cinnamon, and baking powder. Gradually add the flour and stir until the dough comes together to form a firm ball.

Roll the dough out on a floured surface. It should be about ½-inch thick. Cut in round shapes with a cookie cutter and place on an ungreased cookie sheet. Brush the cookies with beaten egg and sprinkle with sugar. Bake for 13 to 15 minutes until golden brown around the edges.

Cook's Notes: While these cream cookies have a smoother texture than sugar cookies, the dough handles much the same as sugar cookie dough, which makes them a nice alternative to other rolled cookies.

Turnovers with Sweet Potato Filling

Truchas

[Makes about 12 turnovers]

Truchas are traditionally served at Christmastime. They can be made with a variety of fillings, including a spaghetti squash marmalade known as angel hair (*cabello de angel*) or custard, though the most common is a sweet potato and almond mixture that borders on marzipan. I have yet to figure out where the name for this dessert originates because *trucha* is literally "trout" and these turnovers bear absolutely no resemblance to the fish, nor are trout to be found anywhere in the Canary Islands!

DOUGH:
¼ cup mild extra virgin olive oil
¼ cup dry white wine
3 large spoonfuls butter, softened
Pinch salt
2 cups all-purpose flour

Mild extra virgin olive oil for frying
Cinnamon sugar for dusting

SWEET POTATO FILLING:
1 large sweet potato
1 cup finely ground almonds (approximately
  ¼ pound blanched almonds)
½ cup sugar
Grated peel of 1 lemon
½ small spoonful ground cinnamon
1 egg yolk, at room temperature
1 large spoonful anisette liqueur

Make the dough: Mix the olive oil, wine, butter, and salt together in a bowl. Gradually stir in the flour until the dough comes together to form a firm ball. Turn the dough out onto a floured surface and knead for a few minutes. Cover and let rest for an hour.

Make the filling: Wash the sweet potato and bake until soft. Peel and mash together with the ground almonds, sugar, lemon peel, cinnamon, egg yolk, and anisette liqueur. Cover and let rest for 30 minutes.

Make the turnovers: Roll the dough out ⅛-inch thick on a lightly floured surface and cut into 4-inch circles. Place a large spoonful of the filling in the center of each circle of dough. Fold in half and seal the edges by pressing down with fork tines.

Heat olive oil (about 2 fingers deep) in a skillet. Fry the turnovers until golden on both sides. Drain on paper towels and sprinkle with cinnamon sugar. Serve at room temperature.

Cook's Notes: Roll the dough out a little at a time as it becomes less flexible the more you handle it. Also, when you go to fry the turnovers, add a few strips of orange and/or lemon peel to the skillet to keep the oil from acquiring a burnt taste. And finally, while these turnovers are typically fried, it is possible to bake them if you're trying to use less oil in cooking. Place the turnovers on a cookie sheet and brush them with beaten egg. Bake at 350° F for 15 minutes. Sprinkle with cinnamon sugar and serve.

Denominación de Origen: A Guarantee of High Quality

The denomination of origin or the appellation of origin (from the French *appellation d'origine contrôlée*), as it's also known in English, is the method used in Spain to recognize the quality and origin of a food product, be it ham, legumes, or cheese, to cite but a few examples. The superior quality of these products is a direct consequence of certain defining characteristics related to the area in which they are produced. Nature imparts her own distinctive touch to the grapes that go into making, say a Rioja wine, or the *Arbequina* olives that will be pressed to create a denomination of origin Siurana extra virgin olive oil. Human touch does the rest because the processing and production techniques used are just as important as the raw materials.

Sherry vinegar, for example, is one of only three vinegars in the world to have been granted a denomination of origin. (The other two are *Conde de Huelva*, also from Spain, and *Aceto Balsamico Tradizionale* from Modena and Reggio Emilia, Italy.) Sherry vinegar is produced in the region of Andalusia and can only be made from sherry wines, which in turn must be produced and aged in the "sherry triangle" formed by Sanlúcar de Barrameda in the north and El Puerto de Santa María and Jerez de la Frontera to the west and east respectively. Anything else is simply not true sherry vinegar and cannot bear the denomination of origin seal denoting it as such.

The different denominations of origin are governed by Regulatory Councils which set standards and regulations, as well as make sure that the products sold under their seal meet the necessary requirements. For the consumer, a denomination of origin is a guarantee of high quality and the use of traditional methods; for the manufacturer, a symbol of prestige and credibility. Whenever you see a denomination of origin seal, know that you are in the presence of an artisan product, one that is steeped in tradition and produced with painstaking care.

Chapter 7

THE COMMON DENOMINATOR: SPANISH DISHES FOR ALL TASTES

When I set out to organize recipes for a regional Spanish cookbook, I used geography to define the chapters. This criterion has created some admittedly broad categories; however, it was never my intention to even attempt to compile an all-encompassing cookbook, which in the case of Spanish cooking, would require volumes. What I wanted to do was give the reader a taste for Spain and of Spain.

Though Spanish cuisine is regional, there are certain characteristics that are common to all of Spain. Olive oil is the cooking oil of choice. It's used in sauces, for frying, and is served straight up on anything from salad to *gazpacho* to bread. Onion and garlic is the main seasoning and the base of countless Spanish dishes. Sauté a bit of chopped onion and garlic in olive oil and go from there. Spaniards also eat bread with their meals and can't conceive of a day without a freshly sliced baguette to accompany food. Wine is consumed with meals and Spain produces a wide variety of excellent wines, many of them with a denomination of origin. For every day, fruit or yogurt is the standard dessert. More elaborate desserts are reserved for special occasions, though it is in the area of desserts where the different regions coincide the most.

Not long ago, I listened to a father at my son's school explain that he would be attending a conference in another area of Spain. He asked someone who had recently vacationed in that region if "one eats well there." (Food is a major concern with Spaniards. They *are* devoted eaters.) I thought to myself, "No need to worry; wherever you travel in Spain, you are sure to eat well." The trick is to enjoy the regional specialties that each area has to offer. It's a way of traveling from one pleasant surprise to another. And then there are always the old comfortable standbys that you can find almost anywhere you go in Spain, many of which are to be found in this chapter. You simply can't go wrong with Chicken in Garlic Sauce or Spanish Omelet.

APPETIZERS

Tapas

Marinated Green Olives *(Aceitunas verdes aliñadas)*
Egg Tapa *(Pincho de huevo)*
Stuffed Eggs *(Huevos rellenos)*
Spanish Potato Salad *(Ensaladilla rusa)*
Spicy Potatoes *(Patatas bravas)*
Mushrooms Sautéed in Garlic with Serrano Ham *(Champiñones al ajillo)*
Tuna Turnovers *(Empanadillas de atún)*
Chicken Croquettes *(Croquetas de pollo)*
Garlic Shrimp *(Gambas al ajillo)*
Stuffed Mussels Au Gratin *(Mejillones al gratén)*
Batter-Fried Squid Rings *(Calamares a la romana)*
Mussels in Vinaigrette *(Mejillones a la vinagreta)*
Shellfish Vinaigrette *(Salpicón de marisco)*
Marinated Smelts *(Boquerones en vinagre)*
Pickled Sardines *(Sardinas en escabeche)*

SALADS

Ensaladas

Green Salad, Spanish-Style *(Ensalada verde)*
Melon Slices with Serrano Ham *(Melón con jamón serrano)*

VEGETABLES

Hortalizas

Red Cabbage with Walnuts and Raisins *(Lombarda con nueces y pasas)*

EGG DISHES

Huevos

Spanish Omelet *(Tortilla española)*
Soft-Set Eggs with Mushrooms *(Revuelto de champiñones)*

POULTRY AND GAME

Aves y Caza

Béchamel-Coated Chicken Breasts *(Pollo villeroy)*
Rotisserie Chicken in the Crock Pot *(Pollo asado)*
Chicken in Garlic Sauce *(Pollo al ajillo)*

MEATS

Carnes

Seasoned Pork Loin *(Lomo adobado)*

BREADS
Panes

Spanish Loaf *(Barra de pan)*

DESSERTS AND AFTERNOON COFFEE
Postres y Meriendas

Caramel Custard *(Flan)*
Chocolate Pudding *(Natillas de chocolate)*
Custard with Walnuts *(Natillas con nueces)*
Apple Tart *(Tarta de manzana)*
Yellow Sponge Cake *(Bizcocho)*
Sweet Batter-Fried Toast *(Torrijas)*
Spanish Fritters *(Churros)*
Anise-Flavored Doughnuts *(Rosquillas)*
Epiphany Sweetbread Ring with Marzipan Filling *(Roscón de Reyes)*
Cinnamon-Flavored Ice Milk *(Leche merengada)*

DRINKS
Bebidas

Sangría
Thick Spanish-Style Hot Chocolate *(Chocolate a la taza)*
Cinnamon-Flavored Ice Milk with Iced Coffee *(Blanco y negro)*

Marinated Green Olives

Aceitunas verdes aliñadas

[Makes 2 cups]

Spaniards have a love affair with olives. They snack on them, put them in salads, and use their "juice" for cooking. Just about any Spanish market will have a stand that sells nothing but olives in a myriad of varieties, as well as other pickled vegetables. I've used *Manzanilla* olives in this recipe, which are probably the most common and are found in any supermarket in Spain. If you are serving tapas, a small plate of olives is a must.

 START PREPARATION SEVERAL DAYS IN ADVANCE.

2 cups green *Manzanilla* olives with pits, drained and lightly crushed
½ cup extra virgin olive oil
1 large spoonful sherry vinegar

6 cloves garlic, peeled and lightly crushed
2 bay leaves
Several dashes oregano

Combine the olives, olive oil, vinegar, garlic, bay leaves, and oregano in a glass jar. (If the olives come in a jar, you can even use that container. If the olives have been packed in extra virgin olive oil, take advantage of that oil too and omit the olive oil in this recipe.) Cover the jar tightly and refrigerate for several days. Give the jar a little shake from time to time whenever you open your refrigerator door. Serve the olives at room temperature.

Cook's Notes: Also try this recipe using Arbequinas, *small greenish brown olives that are grown in Aragon and Catalonia and available in the United States.*

Egg Tapa
Pincho de huevo

[Makes 2 appetizers]

The word *pincho* comes from the verb *pinchar* meaning "to prick," which is just what happens with these appetizers as they are served with a toothpick speared through the center. This *pincho* in particular is open to a lot of variations. Olives, tuna, anchovies, pimiento, and shrimp are all ingredients that in one combination or another work well together. You could even assemble an assortment of egg tapas by varying the ingredients slightly on each egg.

1 hardboiled egg, cut in half lengthwise
2 small spoonfuls mayonnaise (page 204)
2 bite-size chunks tuna

2 pimiento strips, rolled
2 anchovy-stuffed olives

Place 1 small spoonful of mayonnaise on top of each egg half. Skewer a chunk of tuna, a pimiento, and an olive with a toothpick and insert in the egg so that the olive is on top.

Cook's Notes: Boil the eggs in salted water to which you've added a good squirt of vinegar. This will cut short any "leaks" should the eggs crack slightly during boiling.

LA BUENA MESA • CHAPTER 7 The Common Denominator: Spanish Dishes for All Tastes

Stuffed Eggs

Huevos rellenos

[4 servings]

Topped with béchamel, these eggs make a wonderful light supper. If you are serving them as an appetizer, I would recommend using mayonnaise unless you are planning to serve the eggs right away as béchamel tends to harden a bit once it has cooled. I've included recipes for both.

Béchamel is a delicately-scented white sauce that works well with a variety of savory foods and is widely used in Spanish cooking. Most people use butter when making it, but I prefer the lighter, healthier olive oil. Of course, you are always free to substitute butter for olive oil, if you wish.

Mayonnaise is one of those everyday sauces we take for granted; however, you should know that this universal spread both originates and takes its name from the city of Mahón on the Balearic Island of Menorca. (Well, at least according to the Spanish; the French would beg to differ.) It's very easy to make, though given that it contains raw egg, care should be taken when serving homemade mayonnaise in summer and it should be consumed within a short time of being made.

8 hardboiled eggs
1 (4-ounce) can light tuna, preferably *bonito del norte* tuna
4 large spoonfuls tomato sauce (page 119)
Béchamel sauce (recipe on page 78 with variation below) or homemade mayonnaise
2 large spoonfuls minced flat-leaf parsley

MAYONNAISE:
1 egg
1 egg yolk
1 large spoonful lemon juice
Salt
½ cup mild extra virgin olive oil
½ cup vegetable oil

Cut the hardboiled eggs in halves lengthwise. Remove the egg yolks. Crumble half of the yolks and reserve. Mix the other half of the yolks in a bowl with the tuna and tomato sauce. Spoon the tuna mixture back into the eggs (approximately 1 well-rounded small spoonful) and arrange them on a plate with the flat filled side of the egg facing downward. Top with the béchamel sauce or some mayonnaise and sprinkle with the crumbled egg yolks and parsley.

Make the béchamel sauce: Double the recipe for béchamel sauce on page 78, but use only 4 large spoonfuls of all-purpose flour, instead of 6.

Make the mayonnaise: Place the egg, egg yolk, lemon juice, and salt in a blender and blend. Gradually add the oil in a thin stream and continue blending until the mayonnaise thickens.

Cook's Notes: It pains me to have to use anything other than extra virgin olive oil, but I find that mayonnaise that's been made using only olive oil has too strong a flavor. Taste does matter and it matters a lot, so I combine olive oil with another vegetable oil.

Spanish Potato Salad

Ensaladilla rusa

[6 servings]

The literal translation of this potato salad's name is "Russian salad." It is the descendent of a rather elaborate cold salad invented by Lucien Olivier, the chef of the now defunct Hermitage restaurant in Moscow, in the late nineteenth century. The original salad was made using rare, expensive ingredients, such as grouse, veal tongue, crayfish tails, and caviar. Olivier's sous-chef attempted to steal the recipe and ended up publishing his version of what later became known as an Olivier Salad. The recipe became popularized and made its way into other cuisines, including Spanish cooking. Many of the original ingredients were replaced by cheaper, more readily available foodstuffs and today this "Russian salad" is found in tapas bars all over Spain.

 START PREPARATION SEVERAL HOURS IN ADVANCE.

4 potatoes
2 carrots, scraped
½ cup cooked peas
1 (4-ounce) can light tuna, preferably *bonito del norte* tuna
2 hardboiled eggs, chopped
2 large spoonfuls extra virgin olive oil

1 large spoonful sherry vinegar
1 large spoonful minced flat-leaf parsley
1 clove garlic, minced
Salt
¾ cup mayonnaise (page 204)
1 pimiento, cut in strips (page xv)

Place the unpeeled potatoes in a large pan with water to cover. Bring to a boil and gently cook for 45 minutes. During the last half hour of boiling, add the carrots. Once cooked, remove the potatoes and carrots from the water and cool. Peel the potatoes and cut them into cubes. Dice the carrots.

Using a wooden spoon, gently mix the potatoes and carrots with the peas, tuna, and eggs. In a separate bowl, mix the olive oil, sherry vinegar, parsley, garlic, and some salt. Fold the vinaigrette into the potato mixture. Refrigerate for a few hours. Gently fold the mayonnaise into the potato salad. Decorate with the pimiento strips and refrigerate until ready to serve.

Cook's Notes: Ensaladilla rusa is traditionally made using mayonnaise, but I prefer a lighter olive oil and vinegar combination. Simply eliminate the mayonnaise and increase the olive oil from 2 large spoonfuls to 6 and the sherry vinegar from 1 to 3 large spoonfuls.

Spicy Potatoes

Patatas bravas

[4 servings]

This is a classic among Spanish tapas and one of only a few "spicy" dishes in all of Spanish cooking, though "piquant" would be a better term.

---

3 potatoes, peeled and cut in bite-size
  pieces
1 large spoonful extra virgin olive oil plus
  additional for frying
Salt
1 small spoonful *pimentón picante* (piquant
  Spanish paprika)

1 dried red chili pepper, seeds removed and
  crumbled
2 large spoonfuls red wine vinegar
Dash Tabasco
½ cup tomato sauce (page 119)

Fry the potatoes in abundant hot oil until golden brown. Drain on paper towels and sprinkle with salt. Reserve.

In a small skillet, mix the 1 spoonful olive oil, *pimentón*, and chili pepper. Stir in the vinegar and Tabasco, followed by the tomato sauce. Simmer on low for a few minutes until warm. Fold in the potatoes, coating them thoroughly with the sauce. Serve warm or at room temperature with toothpicks inserted in the potatoes.

Cook's Notes: While these spicy potatoes are usually served as a tapa, they also make a nice accompaniment to a simple pan-seared chicken breast, fish fillet, or beef cutlet.

Mushrooms Sautéed in Garlic with Serrano Ham

Champiñones al ajillo

[4 servings]

Al ajillo is a common term in Spanish cooking and refers to a dish where garlic is used as the main seasoning.

---

4 large spoonfuls extra virgin olive oil
1 pound white button mushrooms, stems trimmed and sliced
4 cloves garlic, minced
4 thin slices serrano ham, trimmed and minced

2 large spoonfuls minced flat-leaf parsley
1 large spoonful dry white wine
Coarse salt

Heat the olive oil in a skillet and sauté the mushrooms, garlic, ham, and parsley over medium heat until the mushrooms are tender and lightly browned. Stir in the white wine and continue cooking for a few minutes until most of the liquid has evaporated. Season with salt.

Cook's Notes: While this recipe is usually made with white button mushrooms, it's just as easy to try other types of mushrooms, especially in the fall when they're in season.

Tuna Turnovers

Empanadillas de atún

[Makes about 16 turnovers]

These little turnovers are a well-loved tapa and light dinner. Spanish grocery stores cannot begin to compare to American supermarkets in terms of the amount of prepared foods available and yet it is possible to buy both frozen *empanadillas* and the pre-cut circles of dough necessary to make them in almost any Spanish supermarket.

DOUGH:
¼ cup dry white wine
3 large spoonfuls extra virgin olive oil
1 egg
Good pinch of salt
2 cups unbleached all-purpose flour

FILLING:
1 large spoonful extra virgin olive oil plus
  additional for frying
1 small onion, finely chopped
1 pimiento, chopped (page xv)
1 (4-ounce) can light tuna, preferably *bonito del norte* tuna
1 hardboiled egg, chopped
4 large spoonfuls tomato sauce (page 119)

Make the dough: Mix together the wine, olive oil, egg, salt, and ¼ cup water in a bowl. Gradually stir in the flour until the dough comes together to form a firm ball. Turn the dough out onto a floured surface and knead for a few minutes. Cover and let rest for 30 minutes. Roll the dough out as thinly as possible on a lightly floured surface and cut into 4-inch circles.

Make the filling: Gently sauté the onion in 1 spoonful olive oil until tender. Add the pimiento and cook for another minute. Remove from the heat and stir in the tuna, hardboiled egg, and tomato sauce. Place a large spoonful of filling in the center of each circle of dough. Fold in half and seal the edges by pressing down with fork tines. Fry in abundant hot oil (about 2 fingers deep) until golden on both sides. Drain on paper towels. Serve immediately.

Cook's Notes: While these turnovers are typically fried and, to be quite honest, taste better when prepared this way, it is possible to bake them if you're trying to use less oil in cooking. Place the turnovers on a cookie sheet and brush them with beaten egg. Bake at 350° F for 15 minutes.

Chicken Croquettes

Croquetas de pollo

[Makes about 24 croquettes]

If you make chicken croquettes from start to finish, they are rather labor-intensive. However, if you break the process down and do a little at a time, then they don't really take that long, and on top of it, they're easy to freeze. For me this process begins with leftover chicken and broth whenever I make Rotisserie Chicken in the Crock Pot (page 227). I degrease the juices by refrigerating them and am left with a concentrated version of chicken stock and no fat. Of course, you can use regular chicken broth, but this particular stock is heavily flavored with sherry, onion, garlic, thyme, and bay leaf. With leftovers, all that remains to be done is make a béchamel sauce, add the chicken pieces to the sauce, and refrigerate for a few hours or overnight until it's time to put the croquettes together. When I shape the croquettes, I either fry them right away or freeze them for later use. (If you decide to freeze the croquettes, remove them from the freezer and allow to thaw for 10 minutes before frying.) They're great as appetizers or as a second course. They're also real kid pleasers. My son regularly requests them.

 START PREPARATION SEVERAL HOURS IN ADVANCE.

4 large spoonfuls mild extra virgin olive oil plus additional for frying	Salt
	Freshly ground black pepper
5 large well-rounded spoonfuls all-purpose flour plus additional for dusting	Several generous dashes ground nutmeg
	2 cups shredded cooked chicken
¾ cup milk	2 eggs, beaten
¾ cup chicken broth (see above)	1½ cups breadcrumbs

Mix the olive oil and flour together in a saucepan to make a smooth paste. Gradually add the milk and chicken broth, stirring constantly to avoid lumps. Season with salt, pepper, and nutmeg. Stir over medium heat until the sauce begins to thicken and reaches boiling point. Remove from the heat and stir in the shredded chicken. Spread the mixture on a plate and cool. Refrigerate for several hours until the sauce hardens.

Place the flour for dusting in one small bowl, the beaten eggs in another, and the breadcrumbs in another. Heat some olive oil in a skillet over medium-high heat (the oil should be about 2 fingers deep). Use 2 small spoons to shape the chicken mixture into croquettes. Dip the croquettes in flour, then in egg, and finally in breadcrumbs, making sure to coat them well each step of the way. Fry until golden brown. Drain on paper towels and serve.

Cook's Notes: Apart from chicken, in Spain croquettes are also made using tuna, cod, serrano ham, meat, and cheese. They're a great way to use up leftovers.

Garlic Shrimp

Gambas al ajillo

[4 servings]

This is a classic tapa that never fails to please. It's also quite easy to turn this appetizer into a main course for a light supper. Simply crack a couple of eggs per person over the cooked shrimp and stir until the eggs are soft-set.

4 large spoonfuls extra virgin olive oil	**2 large spoonfuls dry sherry** *(fino)*
1 pound medium shrimp, peeled	**Coarse salt**
4 cloves garlic, minced	

Sauté the shrimp in olive oil over medium-high heat until pink. Reduce the heat and add the minced garlic. Pour in the dry sherry and cook for a few more minutes until most of the sherry has evaporated. Season with coarse salt and serve immediately.

Cook's Notes: If you use frozen shrimp, it's very important to thaw the shrimp according to package directions and to make sure that they are thoroughly thawed before cooking; otherwise, you could find yourself with "soupy" shrimp. To prevent this from happening, place the thawed shrimp between paper towels so that the towels absorb the excess moisture.

Stuffed Mussels Au Gratin

Mejillones al gratén

[Makes about 24 mussel half shells]

A great make-ahead appetizer for a tapas party or a formal dinner. These little stuffed mussels practically serve themselves on the half shell.

2 pounds medium mussels	4 cloves garlic, minced
1 lemon, sliced	4 tomatoes, grated and drained
4 bay leaves	2 large spoonfuls breadcrumbs
2 large spoonfuls dry white wine	2 large spoonfuls minced flat-leaf parsley
2 large spoonfuls extra virgin olive oil	Salt
1 onion, chopped	½ cup grated mild *Manchego* cheese

Prepare the mussels as you would for Steamed Mussels (page 3), using the lemon, bay leaves, and wine listed above. Cool and remove the mussel meat from the shells. Chop the meat and reserve. Set aside half of the shells.

Gently sauté the onion and garlic in olive oil until the onion is golden brown. Add the chopped mussels, grated tomatoes, breadcrumbs, parsley, and some salt. Continue cooking over low heat for another 5 minutes. Spoon the mussel mixture into the empty mussel shells, sprinkle with the grated cheese and place under the broiler until the cheese begins to brown. (To avoid a messy clean-up, line the tray with parchment paper.) Serve immediately.

Cook's Notes: Prepare these mussels ahead of time on the day you plan to serve them and refrigerate. When it's time to roll out the appetizers, simply pop them under the broiler.

Batter-Fried Squid Rings

Calamares a la romana

[4 servings]

Batter-fried squid rings are quite common in Spanish cooking, so much so that they make it into the pre-cooked frozen-food section of almost any Spanish grocery store. In Madrid, there is even a famous sandwich made with these batter-fried squid rings.

1 pound small squid	2 eggs, beaten
1 cup all-purpose flour	Coarse salt
1 small spoonful baking powder	1 lemon, quartered
Extra virgin olive oil for frying	

To clean the squid, see Baby Squid in Ink Sauce on page 50. Cut the squid in ½-inch rings.

Mix the flour and baking powder together in a plastic bag or a container with a cover. Heat the olive oil in a skillet over medium-high heat (the oil should be about 2 fingers deep). Add the squid rings to the flour and shake to coat them well. Shake off the excess flour, dip the rings in the beaten egg, and fry them in the hot olive oil until golden brown. Drain the rings on paper towels. Sprinkle with coarse salt and serve immediately with lemon wedges.

Cook's Notes: Before flouring the rings, use paper towels to absorb most of the moisture. This will prevent spattering during frying.

Mussels in Vinaigrette

Mejillones a la vinagreta

[Makes 24 mussels on the half shell]

These colorful mussels on the half shell are wonderful make-ahead appetizers. The shell serves as its own "plate" and eating utensil in one.

 START PREPARATION 1 DAY IN ADVANCE.

24 medium mussels
1 lemon, sliced
4 bay leaves
2 large spoonfuls dry white wine
2 large spoonfuls extra virgin olive oil
1 large spoonful red wine vinegar
2 large spoonfuls finely chopped pimiento
(page xv)

1 large spoonful finely chopped Spanish
onion
1 small spoonful small capers
1 large spoonful minced flat-leaf parsley
Salt
Freshly ground black pepper

Prepare the mussels as you would for Steamed Mussels, page 3, using the lemon, bay leaves, and wine. Cool and remove the mussel meat from the shells. Reserve. Place half of the mussel shells in a covered container and refrigerate until ready to use.

Mix together the olive oil, vinegar, pimiento, onion, capers, parsley, and some salt and pepper. Fold in the mussel meat. Cover and refrigerate overnight.

To serve, spoon the mussels along with a bit of marinade into the shells.

Cook's Notes: The marinade in this recipe is open to a lot of variations. Some recipes call for finely chopped tomato, others for chopped hardboiled egg, and still others for minced red and green bell pepper. By all means, experiment with your own combinations.

Shellfish Vinaigrette

Salpicón de marisco

[4 servings]

A versatile tapa if ever there was one, *salpicón de marisco* also works well as a first course. You can serve this appetizer as a salad on a bed of lettuce or over tomatoes that have been sliced instead of chopped. A sprinkling of chopped hardboiled egg or minced parsley rounds out the presentation. Shrimp is the classic shellfish used, but you can also add mussels and whitefish to this dish, and if you're feeling really splendid, lobster and crabmeat.

2 pounds medium or large shrimp, in their shells	1 Spanish onion, chopped
½ green bell pepper, seeded and chopped	4 large spoonfuls extra virgin olive oil
2 tomatoes, chopped	2 large spoonfuls sherry vinegar
	Salt

Put a large pot of salted water on to boil. When the water reaches the boiling point, add the shrimp. When the water starts to boil again, remove the shrimp and plunge them into icy cold salted water for 2 to 3 minutes. Drain and peel the shrimp; cut in ½-inch slices.

Mix together the shrimp and vegetables. In a separate bowl, combine the olive oil, vinegar, and some salt. Fold into the shrimp and vegetable mixture, and chill until ready to serve.

Cook's Notes: Dishes involving vinaigrettes and marinades require only the best extra virgin olive oil. For a smooth, fruity flavor, try 100% Arbequina olive oil.

Marinated Smelts

Boquerones en vinagre

[4 servings]

This tapa, found in bars all over Spain, has a long history and is most likely of Sephardic origins. It's a great make-ahead dish if you're planning a dinner involving tapas.

 START PREPARATION 5 DAYS IN ADVANCE.

¾ pound smelts, filleted	1 large spoonful extra virgin olive oil
4 small spoonfuls coarse salt	2 cloves garlic, minced
1 cup white wine vinegar	1 large spoonful minced flat-leaf parsley

To fillet the fish, begin by cutting the head off and, using your thumb, gently push the belly open so that the fish is lying flat with the backbone in the center. Peel the backbone off towards the tail and as you reach the tail, you'll find that it will come off as well. Split the smelts in half so that you have 2 fillets per fish. Rinse the fillets under cold running water and dry them thoroughly between paper towels. (As you're doing all of this, remember how healthy they are and how good they're going to taste.) Lay a single layer of the fillets side by side on paper towels that you've placed in a covered container. Layer the remaining smelts, placing a paper towel between each layer. Freeze the fish for no less than 48 hours.

Thaw the smelts completely (or the paper towels will stick to the fish) and place the smelts in a glass, plastic, or ceramic container (no metal) in a single layer, skin side up. Sprinkle with salt and pour vinegar over the top. Cover and refrigerate for 2 days.

Remove the smelts from the vinegar mixture and arrange them skin side down on a serving platter. Drizzle the olive oil over the fillets and sprinkle with garlic and parsley. Cover with plastic wrap and refrigerate for 1 day before serving.

Cook's Notes: Given that the fish in this recipe is uncooked, it is very important to freeze the fillets for no less than 48 hours to kill any possible Anisakis parasites.

Pickled Sardines

Sardinas en escabeche

[4 servings]

Escabeche is a classic Spanish marinade involving heavy doses of oil, vinegar, garlic, and aromatic herbs. These sardines *en escabeche* are one of the ways Spanish cooks traditionally took advantage of low prices at the marketplace given that meat or fish prepared in *escabeche* keeps for up to a week in the refrigerator. Today, it is possible to buy these pickled sardines already canned at any local grocery store in Spain, but the homemade version is better and not at all difficult to make.

 START PREPARATION 1 DAY IN ADVANCE.

16 fresh sardine fillets	1 sprig dried thyme
Salt	3 black peppercorns
All-purpose flour for dusting	1 small spoonful *pimentón dulce* (sweet
½ cup extra virgin olive oil plus additional	Spanish paprika)
for frying	½ cup dry white wine
4 cloves garlic, peeled	½ cup red wine vinegar
1 bay leaf	

Sprinkle the sardine fillets with salt and dust with flour. Fry in olive oil until golden on both sides. Drain on paper towels and reserve.

Heat the ½ cup olive oil in a separate skillet over medium-low heat. Add the garlic and bay leaf and gently fry until the garlic begins to brown. Add the thyme and peppercorns and continue cooking for another 2 to 3 minutes. Remove the skillet from the heat and stir in the *pimentón* and wine. Gradually heat to boiling. When the mixture begins to boil, add the vinegar and season with salt. Gradually heat to boiling again, lower the heat, and simmer for 5 minutes.

Arrange the sardines in an earthenware, glass, or ceramic dish (no metal). Pour the marinade over the fish and cool. Refrigerate overnight. Drain and serve.

Cook's Notes: To clean and fillet sardines, see Cook's Notes on page 42.

Green Salad, Spanish-Style

Ensalada verde

[4 servings]

This is a typical, everyday salad found all over Spain. It is either served on individual plates as a first course or as an accompaniment to the main course, in which case the salad is prepared on a large platter and placed in the middle of the table. The salad becomes communal and everyone eats from the platter while enjoying their entrées.

½ head romaine lettuce
2 tomatoes, cut in wedges
1 small Spanish onion, thinly sliced
½ cup green olives
1 (4-ounce) can light tuna, preferably *bonito del norte* tuna

6 to 8 white asparagus spears
8 large spoonfuls extra virgin olive oil
4 large spoonfuls red wine or sherry vinegar
Salt

Wash and tear the lettuce leaves and arrange them on a platter or in individual bowls. Add the tomatoes, onion slices, olives, and tuna. Arrange the asparagus spears on top of the salad. Mix together the olive oil, vinegar, and some salt. Drizzle over the top of the salad.

Cook's Notes: To make a creamy vinaigrette, put equal parts salt and sugar in a bowl. (The sugar helps cut the acidity of the vinegar.) Add the vinegar and extra virgin olive oil and mix together with a whisk.

Melon with Serrano Ham

Melón con jamón serrano

[4 servings]

Spanish melons, also known as *Piel De Sapo* (toad skin), have a green rind and are elongated. When they're at their peak, they're juicy and sweet, the perfect accompaniment to serrano ham.

1 Spanish melon	**16 thin slices serrano ham**

Cut the melon in half lengthwise and scoop out the seeds. Slice into 8 wedges and arrange 2 wedges on 4 individual plates. Top each wedge of melon with 2 slices of serrano ham.

Cook's Notes: If you're unable to find Spanish melon, try cranshaw, casaba, or honeydew.

Red Cabbage with Walnuts and Raisins

Lombarda con nueces y pasas

[8 servings]

In Spain, the family Christmas meal is either celebrated on Christmas Eve, followed by midnight mass, or at midday on the 25th, depending on what region you live in. Along with the turkey, lamb, or fish which is served as the main course, you're likely to find this red cabbage dish seasoned with contrasting sweet and savory flavors.

1 red cabbage, outer leaves and center stem removed, coarsely chopped	1 cup diced pancetta
Salt	4 cloves garlic, minced
½ cup vinegar	½ cup seedless raisins
4 large spoonfuls extra virgin olive oil	1 cup walnut pieces

Put a large pot of salted water and vinegar on to boil. When the water reaches the boiling point, add the cabbage. Gently cook for 1¼ hours. Drain and reserve.

Sauté the pancetta in olive oil until browned. Stir in the garlic, raisins, and walnut pieces. Cook for a minute until the garlic begins to brown. Stir in the drained cabbage, season with salt, and cook for a few minutes until heated through.

Cook's Notes: Adding vinegar to the cooking water helps the cabbage retain its bright reddish purple color, as does rinsing in cold water just after it's been chopped.

Spanish Omelet

Tortilla española

[4 servings]

When I was a child, one of the few Spanish dishes my mother made was *tortilla española*, a potato and onion omelet that we referred to as "potato cake." This omelet is made by slowly frying the potato and onion slices in olive oil until tender. This takes a certain amount of practice until you get just the right texture and consistency with the potatoes and onion. The potatoes aren't fried to a crisp; rather they are cooked slowly until they start to fall apart. When I first moved to Spain, I remember making this omelet over and over again until my Spanish roommate finally pronounced it "just right."

Extra virgin olive oil for frying
4 medium potatoes, peeled and thinly sliced
1 large onion, thinly sliced

Salt
6 eggs
4 large spoonfuls milk

Heat the oil over medium to medium-high heat in a large skillet. Add a layer of potato slices to the hot oil. Add some onion slices and sprinkle with salt. Continue adding layers of potato slices and the onion slices and sprinkling each layer with salt. Stir to coat the potatoes with the oil and lower the heat. Lift and turn the potatoes occasionally until they are tender, but not brown, about 30 minutes. Remove the potatoes from the skillet and drain them. Empty the oil out of the skillet, reserving 2 large spoonfuls.

Beat the eggs in a bowl with the milk and some salt. Fold in the potatoes and onion. Allow to sit for 10 minutes.

Heat approximately 1 large spoonful of the reserved olive oil over medium-high heat in a non-stick skillet. When the oil is hot, pour the egg and potato mixture into the skillet and lower the heat to medium. It will take approximately 5 minutes for the omelet to cook on this side. During that time, turn the skillet frequently so that the omelet cooks evenly, and using a wooden spoon or spatula, loosen the omelet from the sides of the skillet.

Now comes the tricky part. Take a plate that is larger than the skillet and place it over the top. Flip the omelet onto the plate. (I usually do this over the sink, just in case.) Add the other large spoonful of oil to the skillet and gently slide the omelet back in so that it continues cooking on the other side, another 2 to 3 minutes. When the omelet is ready, place a plate over the skillet and invert the omelet onto the plate. Allow at least a few minutes for the omelet to set or, better yet, cool it to room temperature, cut into wedges, and serve. This omelet can also be served as an appetizer by cutting it into small 1-inch squares and placing a toothpick in each square.

Cook's Notes: Ferran Adrià, one of Spain's foremost chefs (imagine Salvador Dalí in the kitchen) describes a novel way to make this traditional omelet in his book "Cocinar en Casa." I should point out that this is a cookbook he did in conjunction with a local chain of supermarkets; in other words, everyday cooking with a flare. What he suggests is crunching up a bag of potato chips (cooked in olive oil, of course) and substituting them for the potatoes and onion.

Soft-Set Eggs with Mushrooms

Revuelto de champiñones

[4 servings]

These soft-set eggs are perfect for a light supper and can be whipped up in a matter of minutes. They're fast food that doesn't compromise flavor or nutrition.

---

4 large spoonfuls extra virgin olive oil
2 cups sliced white button mushrooms
2 cloves garlic, minced
1 large spoonful minced flat-leaf parsley

8 eggs
4 large spoonfuls milk
Salt

Heat the olive oil in a skillet over medium heat. Sauté the mushrooms until tender, approximately 3 to 5 minutes. When the mushrooms are almost cooked, add the garlic and parsley and stir for another minute until the garlic is cooked.

Beat together the eggs, milk, and some salt. Add to the mushrooms, stirring until the eggs are almost set but still soft. Serve immediately.

Cook's Notes: In the fall when they're in season, I often substitute wild mushrooms (that I buy at the market) for the white button mushrooms.

Béchamel-Coated Chicken Breasts

Pollo villeroy

[4 servings]

I have never met anyone who has tried these chicken breasts who didn't like them. This is everyday home cooking that your grandmother would make if she were Spanish.

2 skinless, boneless chicken breasts, butterflied and halved
1 carrot, scraped and cut in several pieces
1 celery rib, cut in several pieces with a few leaves remaining
1 onion, quartered
1 sprig flat-leaf parsley
1 bay leaf
Thyme
Salt
Freshly ground black pepper
All-purpose flour for dusting

2 eggs, beaten
1 cup breadcrumbs
Extra virgin olive oil for frying

BÉCHAMEL SAUCE:
4 large spoonfuls extra virgin olive oil
5 large well-rounded spoonfuls all-purpose flour*
¾ cup milk
Salt
Freshly ground black pepper
Several generous dashes ground nutmeg

Place the chicken breasts in a saucepan, along with the carrot, celery, onion, parsley, bay leaf, and some thyme, salt, and pepper. Cover with water and cook for 15 minutes. Remove the chicken and boil the broth down for a more concentrated flavor. Reserve ¾ cup of the broth for the béchamel sauce. Allow the chicken to cool and refrigerate.

Make the béchamel sauce: Mix the olive oil and flour together in a saucepan over medium heat to make a smooth paste. Gradually add the milk and the ¾ cup reserved chicken broth, stirring constantly to avoid lumps. Season with salt, pepper, and nutmeg. Stir over medium heat until the sauce begins to thicken and reaches the boiling point. Cool.

(continued on next page)

Béchamel-Coated Chicken Breasts *(continued from previous page)*

Dip—and spread, because the sauce is quite thick—the cold chicken pieces in the cooled béchamel sauce, being sure to coat well on both sides. Refrigerate the béchamel-coated chicken until the sauce hardens, about an hour.

Heat the olive oil in a skillet over medium-high heat (the oil should be about 1 finger deep). Place the flour, eggs, and breadcrumbs on individual plates. Dip the chicken breasts in the flour, then in the eggs, and finally in the breadcrumbs, making sure to coat the cutlets well each step of the way. Fry in olive oil until golden brown on both sides. Drain on paper towels and serve.

Cook's Notes: The trick to making this dish lies in refrigerating the chicken once it's been coated in the béchamel sauce. This is a great make-ahead recipe and given the steps involved, one that you practically have to prepare ahead of time.

*The flour measures out exactly to 6 level tablespoons plus 2 level teaspoons.

Rotisserie Chicken in the Crock Pot

Pollo asado

[4 servings]

Rotisserie chicken is a common takeout food in Spain and it's not difficult to find a shop that sells chicken prepared in this way. In the village of L'Argilaga, which is half an hour's drive from where I live, there is a place that sells what is probably the best rotisserie chicken I've ever eaten. I could walk around the corner to buy chicken on a spit, but the drive is well worth it. Unfortunately, I had never been able to duplicate that wonderful combination of moistness and flavor when I roasted chicken at home, albeit in the oven, until I tried "roasting" it in my trusty American crock pot. The result is a very moist, juicy chicken that's loaded with the flavors of garlic, bay leaf, pepper, and thyme. The meat just falls away from the bone it's so tender.

1 chicken (3 to 3½ pounds)
Salt
Freshly ground black pepper
Thyme
1 lemon, quartered

2 large spoonfuls dry sherry (*fino*)
1 large spoonful extra virgin olive oil
1 small onion, coarsely chopped
6 cloves garlic, halved
2 bay leaves, crumbled

Rinse the chicken and remove any excess fat. Season the outside of the chicken, as well as the interior cavity, with salt, pepper, and thyme and place in a crock pot. Squeeze the juice from the lemon wedges and mix together with the sherry and olive oil. Coarsely chop the lemon quarters and combine with the onion, garlic, and bay leaves. Stuff this mixture into the cavity. Pour the lemon juice mixture into the cavity. Cover and cook on low for 8 to 10 hours or on high for 4 to 5. (Please note that cooking times can vary from one manufacturer to another.)

Cook's Notes: When you "roast" the chicken in a crock pot, you'll find that it gives off a lot of juice. I degrease the juice by allowing it to cool and then refrigerating it. What's left is something akin to a natural bouillon cube. If I'm not planning on using the broth right away, rather than letting all of that flavor go to waste, I freeze it in an ice-cube tray. Later on when I'm cooking something that might benefit from a bouillon cube, I've got a homemade version already made up in my freezer.

Chicken in Garlic Sauce

Pollo al ajillo

[4 servings]

This dish manages to be both simple and sublime. You simply can't go wrong with a chicken cooked in garlic sauce. It's a classic of Spanish cooking.

---

1 chicken (3 to 3½ pounds), skinned and cut
   in small serving pieces
4 large spoonfuls extra virgin olive oil
Freshly ground black pepper

8 cloves garlic, minced
¼ cup dry white wine
1 large spoonful minced flat-leaf parsley
Coarse salt

The butcher at my local supermarket cuts the chicken up in the following way when I tell him that I'm making Chicken in Garlic Sauce: Cut the chicken into quarters. Remove skin. Remove the bony tip of the legs and wings. Cut the whole breasts into 5 pieces each and the wings in half. Cut the thighs into 5 pieces each and the drumsticks in half.

Heat the olive oil in a large earthenware dish or skillet and brown the chicken pieces on both sides. Season with pepper and add the garlic. Pour the white wine over the chicken. Sprinkle with parsley. Cover and cook over low heat for 10 minutes, turning the chicken after 5 minutes. Season with coarse salt and serve.

Cook's Notes: Instead of white wine, try using Spanish brandy.

Seasoned Pork Loin

Lomo adobado

[4 servings]

Adobo almost always denotes the presence of Spanish paprika or *pimentón*. *Lomo adobado* is a standard at the butcher's counter in any supermarket in Spain and even comes sliced and pre-packaged along with the other trays of meat. When you're in a hurry and don't know what to make, this seasoned pork is an easy option in Spanish kitchens. Someone else has already marinated the meat for you, the butcher slices it, and all that's left to do is sauté it in a bit of olive oil.

Marinades allow you to prepare dishes ahead of time. The other big advantage is that the meat will keep for up to a week because of the seasonings. Enjoy *lomo adobado* as a main course or as a tapa on slices of bread.

 START PREPARATION 2 DAYS IN ADVANCE.

6 cloves garlic	Salt
1 large spoonful *pimentón dulce* (sweet Spanish paprika)	3 large spoonfuls extra virgin olive oil plus additional for sautéing
2 bay leaves, crushed	Juice of ½ lemon
½ small spoonful oregano	1½ pounds boned pork loin roast

Mix the garlic, *pimentón*, bay leaves, oregano, and some salt together using a mortar and pestle. Stir in the olive oil and lemon juice. Coat the meat on all sides with this mixture. Place in a non-metal container and cover. Allow the meat to marinate for at least 2 days.

To cook, cut the meat in thin slices and sauté in a bit of olive oil.

Cook's Notes: This marinade also lends itself well to making pinchos morunos. *Simply cut the meat in bite-size chunks and rub well with the marinade. The meat can then be put on a kebab skewer and grilled.*

Spanish Loaf

Barra de pan

[Makes 2 baguettes]

Homemade bread (and by that, I don't mean bread that is made from scratch, but rather at home) is not common in Spain and once you've been to a Spanish bakery, you'll know why. Fresh bread is considered a necessity and when everything else is closed, you will still find a bakery open, if only for a few hours in the morning. Most Spaniards can't conceive of a meal without a basket of fresh bread on the table. This Spanish loaf is the standard baguette found all over Spain.

1 cup warm water
1 package dry yeast
Pinch sugar
1 small spoonful salt*

2½ cups unbleached all-purpose flour
1 cup cornmeal or breadcrumbs
1 egg white

Dissolve the yeast in warm water along with a pinch of sugar. Mix the salt with 1 cup flour, and using a wooden spoon, blend it with the yeast. Gradually stir in the remaining flour until the dough comes together to form a firm ball. Turn onto a floured surface and knead for 5 minutes, adding more flour as needed. Place the dough in a greased bowl, cover, and let rise until it doubles in size, about 2 hours. (The dough is ready when you press it with a finger and the indent doesn't bounce back.)

Punch the dough down and knead for another 5 minutes. Divide in half. Using your hands, roll each half back and forth to make 2 long, thin loaves (about the length of the cookie sheet and the diameter of your fist). Sprinkle the cornmeal or breadcrumbs on a cookie sheet and place the loaves on top. Dip a sharp knife in cold water and cut several diagonal slits in the top of each loaf. Place the dough in a warm place and let rise for another hour.

Preheat the oven to 450° F. Bake the bread on the middle-upper rack for 10 minutes. Lightly brush the loaves with egg white and continue baking for another 20 minutes. The crust should be brown and the loaf should make a hollow sound when tapped on the bottom.

Cook's Notes: Be sure to concentrate most of the cornmeal or breadcrumbs directly below the loaves. This layer keeps the bottoms of the loaves from burning by absorbing the excess heat.

*The salt measures out exactly to 1 level teaspoon.

Caramel Custard

Flan

[6 servings]

This Spanish dessert is a classic and needs no translation.

9 large spoonfuls sugar
1½ cups milk
1 cinnamon stick

4 strips lemon peel (approximately ½-inch wide and the length of the lemon)
4 eggs, at room temperature

Preheat the oven to 350° F.

To make the caramelized sugar, heat a small skillet over high heat and add 5 large spoonfuls sugar, stirring constantly until it turns a golden brown. Immediately pour the caramelized sugar into 6 (½-cup) ovenproof custard cups or flan molds (available online).

Place the milk, cinnamon stick, and lemon peel in a saucepan and gradually bring to a boil. Lower the heat and simmer for 10 minutes. In a separate bowl, beat together the eggs and remaining 4 spoonfuls sugar with a whisk. Discard the lemon peel and cinnamon stick, and *gradually* stir the warm milk into the egg mixture. (I say *gradually* because if you don't, you could end up with scrambled eggs!)

Pour the milk mixture into the caramelized cups and place the cups in a water bath in a pan. The water should reach at least halfway up the sides of the cups. Transfer to the oven and bake until set, about 30 minutes. Cool and refrigerate. To serve, loosen the sides of the *flan* with a knife and invert onto a dessert plate.

Cook's Notes: While flan is usually prepared using smooth or fluted semi-conical flan molds, it can also be served as a loaf. Simply double the recipe and pour into a 6-cup loaf pan. Bake as above until set in the center, about 1 hour.

LA BUENA MESA • CHAPTER 7 The Common Denominator: Spanish Dishes for All Tastes

Chocolate Pudding

Natillas de chocolate

[4 servings]

There are several traditional pudding desserts that are so popular in Spain that they make it into the dairy case alongside the yogurt and cheese. This chocolate pudding is one of those desserts. (In case you're wondering what the others are, they are *flan, tocino del cielo,* and *arroz con leche.*) However, as is usually the case, the store-bought version can't begin to compare with the homemade version. Given that this chocolate pudding is easy to make, whip up a batch, and enjoy it as often as you like.

4 large spoonfuls sugar
2 large spoonfuls cornstarch*
2 well-rounded large spoonfuls cocoa
Pinch salt

2 cups milk
2 egg yolks, at room temperature
1 small spoonful vanilla extract
4 large spoonfuls slivered almonds (optional)

Mix the sugar, cornstarch, cocoa, and salt in a saucepan. Gradually stir in the milk and cook over medium heat, stirring constantly until the mixture begins to boil. Remove from heat.

In a separate bowl, mix the egg yolks and vanilla extract. Gradually stir the hot milk mixture into the egg yolks. Return the mixture to the saucepan and boil 1 minute, stirring constantly. Pour into individual dessert dishes and sprinkle each dish with a large spoonful of almonds. Cool and refrigerate.

Cook's Notes: Don't discard the egg whites. Use them to make an omelet!

*The cornstarch measures out exactly to 2 level tablespoons plus 2 level teaspoons.

Custard with Walnuts

Natillas con nueces

[4 servings]

This is the non-chocolate version of the preceding recipe. I find that both of these puddings are enhanced by the addition of nuts: almonds in the previous recipe and walnuts with this custard.

2 cups milk
4 strips lemon peel (approximately ½-inch wide and the length of the lemon)
4 large spoonfuls sugar

2 large spoonfuls cornstarch*
3 egg yolks, at room temperature
20 to 24 walnut pieces

In a medium saucepan, heat the milk with the lemon peel slowly until it reaches the boiling point. Lower the heat and simmer for 10 minutes.

In a separate bowl, beat the sugar, cornstarch, and egg yolks with a whisk until creamy. Discard the lemon peel and *slowly* add the hot milk to the egg mixture, stirring constantly to keep the eggs from curdling. Return the egg and milk mixture to the saucepan and continue stirring over low heat until it almost reaches the boiling point. Remove from the heat and stir for a minute before pouring into individual dessert dishes. Cool and refrigerate. Place 4 to 5 walnuts pieces on top of each individual custard before serving.

Cook's Notes: When using lemon peel, be sure to use the yellow part only as the white part tends to be bitter.

*The cornstarch measures out exactly to 2 level tablespoons plus 2 level teaspoons.

Apple Tart

Tarta de manzana

[Makes a 9-inch tart]

Walk into any pastry shop in Spain and you're sure to see this apple tart. It's rich and delicious, perfect for those of us with a sweet tooth.

DOUGH:
1½ cups all-purpose flour
2 large spoonfuls sugar
Pinch salt
¼ pound butter
1 egg

TOPPING:
2 apples, peeled, cored, quartered, and
thinly sliced
½ cup apricot jam

FILLING:
2 cups milk
1 cinnamon stick
2 strips lemon peel (approximately ½-inch
wide and the length of the lemon)
2 strips orange peel (approximately ½-inch
wide and the length of the orange)
1 apple, peeled, cored, and cut in bite-size
pieces
3 egg yolks, at room temperature
½ cup sugar
2 large spoonfuls flour

Make the dough: Preheat the oven to 350° F. Combine the flour, sugar, and salt in a bowl. Cut in the butter until it resembles fine crumbs. Add the egg and mix together until the dough forms a firm ball. (You may need to use your hands.) Refrigerate for 10 minutes. Roll the dough out and place in a loose-bottom 9-inch tart pan. Trim the edges. Bake for 10 minutes (see note) and remove from the oven.

Make the filling: Mix the milk, cinnamon stick, citrus peels, and apple together in a saucepan. Gradually bring to a boil, lower the heat, and simmer for 10 minutes. In a separate bowl, beat the egg yolks, sugar, and flour with a whisk until creamy. Discard the cinnamon stick and fruit peels, and slowly add the hot milk to the egg mixture, stirring constantly to prevent curdling. Blend until smooth. Return the mixture to the saucepan and continue stirring until it almost reaches the boiling point. Spread the filling over the dough.

Arrange the apple slices going around the tart so that each slice overlaps the next one. Use a brush to paint half the jam on the apples. Bake for 30 minutes. Remove the tart from the oven and brush the apples with the other half of the jam. Cool. To serve, simply remove the sides of the tart pan and slice. Serve at room temperature or chilled.

Cook's Notes: To keep the dough from rising when you bake it on its own, place a sheet of aluminum foil over the dough and fill with dried chickpeas or beans.

Yellow Sponge Cake

Bizcocho

[Makes a 13 x 9 inch cake]

This cake is wonderful served with coffee on those occasions when friends drop by. In Spain, it also makes its way to school when children celebrate their birthdays with classmates.

2 cups all-purpose flour
1 cup sugar
1 large spoonful baking powder*
Pinch salt
Grated peel of 2 lemons

1 cup milk
½ cup mild extra virgin olive oil
3 eggs
Powdered sugar for dusting

Preheat the oven to 350° F and grease a 13-inch x 9-inch rectangular baking pan or 2 round 9-inch pans.

Mix the dry ingredients and lemon peel together in a bowl. Using a whisk or electric mixer, add the wet ingredients and mix.

Pour the batter into the prepared pan(s) and bake until a wooden toothpick comes out clean (approximately 30 to 35 minutes if you use the rectangular pan and 20 to 25 minutes if you use two round ones). Sprinkle with powdered sugar immediately before serving.

Cook's Notes: If you pour the batter for Yellow Sponge Cake into cupcake liners instead of baking pans, you will have yet another typical Spanish pastry, "magdalenas" (small Spanish muffins), typically served for breakfast or afternoon snack. Spanish muffins are smaller than their American counterpart and are usually the same size as a cupcake. Fill the cupcake liners two-thirds full and bake for 20 minutes. (Makes 24 muffins)

*The baking powder measures out exactly to 4 level teaspoons.

Sweet Batter-Fried Toast

Torrijas

[4 servings]

A *torrija* is the Spanish version of French toast. This simple yet rich and satisfying dessert dates from the Middle Ages, where it was prepared in convents as a way of using up bread that had turned stale. Though they are served year round, *torrijas* are especially popular during Holy Week.

 START PREPARATION 2 DAYS IN ADVANCE.

1 cup milk
2 large spoonfuls sugar
1 large spoonful honey
4 strips lemon peel (approximately ½-inch wide and the length of the lemon)
4 strips orange peel (approximately ½-inch wide and the length of the orange)

1 cinnamon stick
8 day-old baguette slices, 1-inch thick
Mild extra virgin olive oil for frying
1 egg, beaten
Powdered sugar for dusting
Ground cinnamon for dusting

Mix together the milk, sugar, honey, citrus peels, and cinnamon stick in a saucepan and gradually bring to a boil. Lower the heat and simmer for 10 minutes.

Arrange the bread slices in a single layer in a baking dish. Remove the fruit peels and cinnamon stick from the milk. Pour the milk over the bread and allow the bread to absorb the milk for a minute. Turn the bread over so that it absorbs the milk evenly on both sides. Place a colander on a plate. Remove the bread from the milk mixture (most of the milk will have been absorbed by the bread) and arrange the slices around the colander so that any excess liquid drains off. Allow the bread to dry for approximately 2 hours.

Heat the oil in a skillet over medium to medium-high heat (the oil should be about 1 finger deep). Dip the bread in the beaten egg and fry until golden brown on both sides. Drain on paper towels. Sprinkle with powdered sugar and ground cinnamon and serve immediately.

Cook's Notes: When slicing lemon or orange peel, it's important to slice only the top layers of the fruit. You don't want to have any traces of pulp on the peel or you could end up with curdled milk.

Spanish Fritters

Churros

[Makes about 15 fritters]

Churros are typically served with cups of thick, Spanish-style hot chocolate for breakfast, as an afternoon snack, or as the perfect ending to a night out on the town when you've shut everything down and the *churrerías* or fritter stands are just opening up. These long slender fritters (straight or looped) are also standard street carnival fare and no local *fiesta* would be complete without them. The fritters are fried in large vats of oil, served in paper cones, and sprinkled with copious amounts of sugar. They're a little calorie intensive, but oh-so-good!

1 large spoonful mild extra virgin olive oil
   plus additional for frying
Pinch salt

2 cups all-purpose flour
Sugar for dusting

Bring 2 cups water to a boil. Lower the heat and add the spoonful of oil, salt, and flour. Stir constantly with a wooden spoon until the dough forms a firm ball. Remove from the heat and allow the dough to cool for a few minutes.

Use a *churro* pastry maker or a pastry bag that has been fitted with a fluted tube to press the dough into 8-inch-long strips. You can either shape the strips into loops or leave them straight.

Heat the olive oil in a skillet over medium-high heat (the oil should be about 1 finger deep). Fry 3 or 4 *churros* at a time until they are a golden color. Turn them over and repeat on the other side. Remove from the oil and drain on paper towels.

Sprinkle the *churros* with sugar and serve with Thick Spanish-Style Hot Chocolate (page 244). *Churros* do not keep well and must be eaten immediately (not to worry because there won't be any left).

Cook's Notes: Churro pastry makers are available online. It is important to use a fluted attachment when making the fritters. Without the ridges, they will turn out doughy instead of crisp.

Anise-Flavored Doughnuts

Rosquillas

[Makes about 30 small doughnuts]

In Pedro Almodovar's film *Volver*, I couldn't help but notice the perfect flan that emerged from the everyday gray pan, or the *rosquillas*, small anise-flavored doughnuts that "magically" appeared in one character's kitchen. In fact, after seeing the movie, I was so inspired that I went home and made a batch of these little doughnuts! They make a wonderful mid-morning or mid-afternoon snack with coffee.

1 egg
4 large spoonfuls milk
2 large spoonfuls mild extra virgin olive oil
   plus additional for frying
1 large spoonful anisette liqueur
½ cup sugar

Grated peel of 1 lemon
1 large spoonful baking powder
2 cups all-purpose flour
Powdered sugar for dusting
Ground cinnamon for dusting

Beat the egg, milk, olive oil, and anisette liqueur together in a bowl. Add the sugar, lemon peel, and baking powder and continue mixing. Gradually stir in the flour until the dough comes together to form a firm ball. Turn the dough out onto a floured surface.

Pinch off pieces of dough and roll them into ½-inch by 6-inch ropes. Shape into rings pressing the ends together. Heat some olive oil in a skillet over medium-high heat (the oil should be about 1 finger deep). Fry the doughnuts until golden brown on both sides. Drain on paper towels. Dust with powdered sugar and ground cinnamon on both sides.

Cook's Notes: Adding a few strips of orange and/or lemon peel to the oil will keep it from acquiring a burnt taste.

Epiphany Sweetbread Ring with Marzipan Filling

Roscón de Reyes

[Makes 1 large sweetbread ring]

January 6 is *El Día de los Reyes Magos* or simply *Reyes*, the Day of the Three Kings, in reference to the magi, a much-awaited day by the youngest members of the family as this is when Spanish children traditionally receive their gifts. The arrival of "their majesties" is televised and splashed across the front page of major newspapers, and wherever they go, they are met by local authorities and paraded through the streets on floats in what is known as *la cabalgata de los reyes magos* (the parade of the magi). Children and adults alike pour into the streets in droves on this most magical of nights to greet the kings and then run home to place their shoes in nice neat rows so that Melchior, Gaspar, and Balthasar will leave them gifts. Those who have behaved badly during the year receive a lump of coal in their shoes and it is even possible to buy candied "coal" at this time of year. It is also traditional to leave a bit of *turrón* and sweet wine as a snack for the kings, as well as carrots and water for their camels. Children typically write letters to the Three Wise Men, which they leave with their royal pages, who are sent as emissaries in the weeks preceding January 6 to collect their young subjects' wish lists. On the morning of the 6th, children awake to their gifts and then enjoy a large family meal at midday. The dessert, served only on this day, is *Roscón de Reyes*. Buried deep within the *roscón* is a fava bean and a small ceramic king. Whoever finds the fava bean has to pay for the sweetbread ring and the ceramic figure is said to bring good luck for the year to its finder. If you buy the *roscón* in a bakery, it also comes complete with its own gold cardboard crown.

MARZIPAN FILLING:
1 cup finely ground almonds (approximately
  ¼ pound blanched almonds)
1 cup sugar
1 egg white

SWEETBREAD RING:
1 package dry yeast
½ cup warm milk
4 cups unbleached all-purpose flour
3 eggs, at room temperature
¼ pound butter, melted

½ cup sugar
Pinch salt
1 large spoonful orange flower water
  (*agua de azahar*)
1 large spoonful dark rum
Grated peel of 1 lemon
Grated peel of 1 orange
1 egg, beaten
Assorted candied fruit slices
1 large spoonful sugar (preferably coarse)
  for dusting

Make the marzipan: Mix the ground almonds and sugar together. Stir in the egg white and mix well. Use your hands to form a compact paste. Refrigerate for several hours until well chilled for easier handling.

Make the sweetbread: Dissolve the yeast in warm milk. Stir in 1 cup flour. Cover and let rise in a warm place for 1 hour.

In a separate bowl, mix together the eggs, butter, sugar, salt, orange flower water, rum, and grated citrus peels. Stir in the remaining flour. Turn onto a floured surface and knead for 5 minutes, adding more flour as needed. Add the yeast dough and knead for another 5 minutes, until smooth and elastic. Place the dough in a greased bowl, turning once, cover, and let rise in a warm place until double in size, about 2 hours.

Punch the dough down and roll it out into a rectangle (about the size of a cookie sheet). Shape the marzipan into a cylinder that is slightly shorter in length than the rectangle and place it on one side of the dough. (If desired, insert a small ovenproof ceramic figure and large dried bean in the marzipan after first wrapping them in aluminum foil.) Roll the dough around the marzipan. Place the roll on a greased cookie sheet. Curl the ends around into a ring shape, inserting one end into the other. Pinch the ends together with your fingers to seal. (I find it useful to place a greased round metal mold in the middle to prevent the ring from "baking together" in the center.) Cover and let rise in a warm place for 2 hours.

Preheat the oven to 350° F. Brush the sweetbread ring with beaten egg, decorate with candied fruit, and sprinkle with sugar. Bake for 40 to 45 minutes on the lower rack (to prevent burning) until golden brown.

Cook's Notes: This Epiphany sweetbread is also available without any type of filling. If you would prefer your roscón plain, simply omit the marzipan. To create the ring, shape the dough into a ball. Make a small hole in the center of the mound and push the dough outward to form a ring.

Cinnamon-Flavored Ice Milk

Leche merengada

[6 servings]

Leche merengada, like *horchata* (page 156), is a seasonal treat that is available in bars and ice cream parlors only in summer. Fortunately, it's easy to make, which means that you can enjoy this ice milk year-round.

3 cups milk	2 cinnamon sticks
1 cup heavy cream	4 egg whites
¾ cup sugar	2 large spoonfuls powdered sugar
Peel of 1 lemon	Ground cinnamon for dusting

Mix the milk, cream, sugar, lemon peel, and cinnamon sticks together in a saucepan. Gradually bring to a boil, lower the heat, and simmer for 30 minutes. Cool and refrigerate until cold.

Remove the lemon peel and cinnamon sticks. Place the milk mixture in the freezer until well chilled but not frozen.

Beat the egg whites and powdered sugar together until they form soft peeks. Gradually beat in the chilled milk mixture. If you have an ice cream maker, follow the manufacturer's instructions. If not, pour the mixture into a stainless steel or glass dish and place it in the freezer. When the mixture begins to harden, remove it from the freezer and stir until silky. Repeat several times. To serve, sprinkle with ground cinnamon.

Cook's Notes: There is a liquid version of leche merengada *that is bottled and sold in supermarkets and makes a refreshing summer drink. Use 4 cups milk and omit the cream and egg whites. And instead of placing the cooled milk in the freezer, simply store it in the refrigerator.*

Sangría

[Makes about 4 cups]

I can't think of a better accompaniment to paella in summer than a glass of icy cold *sangría*.

1 cup freshly squeezed orange juice
½ cup freshly squeezed lemon juice
2 large spoonfuls sugar
2 large spoonfuls brandy, preferably Spanish
1 peach, peeled and cut in wedges

1 orange, quartered and sliced
½ lemon, halved and sliced
1 cinnamon stick
Peel of 1 lemon, cut in a spiral shape
1 bottle dry, full-bodied red wine

Use a wooden spoon to mix together the fruit juices and sugar in a large glass or earthenware pitcher. Stir in the brandy, peach wedges, orange and lemon slices, cinnamon stick, and lemon peel. Pour the wine into the fruit mixture and stir. Cover and refrigerate several hours or overnight. Serve chilled in balloon-shaped wine glasses or in Spanish earthenware mugs (without handles).

Cook's Notes: If you like, substitute an orange liqueur such as Grand Marnier or Cointreau for the brandy, and for a different touch, make ice cubes using freshly squeezed fruit juices (peach, apple, orange, kiwi), grenadine, and/or blue Curaçao.

LA BUENA MESA • CHAPTER 7 The Common Denominator: Spanish Dishes for All Tastes

Thick Spanish-Style Hot Chocolate

Chocolate a la taza

[4 servings]

You will notice that this thick, rich hot chocolate uses neither flour nor cornstarch as thickeners. That's because the milk and chocolate are boiled and cooled *four* times creating an unusually creamy cup of hot chocolate. Serve with Spanish fritters, known as *churros* (page 238), for an irresistible combination.

5 cups milk
8 ounces dark chocolate, broken in pieces

1 large spoonful sugar or to taste

Heat the milk until it almost reaches the boiling point. Remove from the heat, add the chocolate and sugar and stir until the chocolate has melted. Return to the heat and heat the chocolate milk to the boiling point stirring constantly. Once the milk begins to boil, remove from the heat and cool for a few minutes. Repeat this process 3 more times.

Cook's Notes: My Spanish grandmother used to add vanilla to her hot chocolate. Other flavors to try include cinnamon and star anise. Simply add a pod of vanilla, a stick of cinnamon, or a couple of pieces of star anise to the milk before warming it. Heat to boiling and simmer for 10 minutes. Discard the flavoring before adding the chocolate.

Cinnamon-Flavored Ice Milk with Iced Coffee

Blanco y negro

[6 servings]

Blanco y negro or "white and black" is a favorite summer menu item in ice cream parlors and outdoor cafés, an elegant dessert and coffee in one.

1½ cups strong black coffee, preferably espresso, chilled
Cinnamon-flavored ice milk (*leche merengada*, page 242)

Ground cinnamon for dusting

Pour ¼ cup chilled coffee into each individual parfait glass. Add scoops of *leche merengada* and sprinkle with cinnamon. Serve immediately, along with a straw and long spoon.

Cook's Notes: This iced coffee drink is dessert and coffee in one. It's perfect for entertaining as it can be made in advance and makes an elegant ending to a summertime meal.

● Spanish Food Presentation: *La comida entra por los ojos*

La comida entra por los ojos ("food enters by way of the eyes") is a popular saying in Spanish. Roughly translated, it means that one's first impression of a dish is based on appearance and that when the presentation looks appealing, it's as though you could eat the food with your eyes alone. The point here is that eating is a sensory experience and it doesn't take a lot of effort to present food in an attractive way. Spanish cooks are masters at presentation from the everyday mom-and-pop bar on the corner to the most sophisticated restaurant.

I recently arrived early for an appointment and decided to treat myself to an *almuerzo* (that would be breakfast #2) while I waited. I went into the nearest bar, ordered a *café con leche* and a small sandwich to go with it. As I live in Catalonia, I ordered *pa amb tomàquet* (bread with tomato and olive oil), which is how sandwiches are typically prepared here, and a few slices of serrano ham. As I said, there was nothing spectacular about this bar, but when the lady in the kitchen making sandwiches brought mine out, it was garnished with various kinds of olives arranged on a skewer. In seconds, my sandwich went from mundane to "my, how nice!"

When serving individual pieces of food, be they sandwiches, prime cuts of grilled meat, or perfectly pan-seared fresh fish, think of a little something to accompany the entrée on the plate. In Spanish, the term is *guarnición*, but the literal translation, "garnish," doesn't quite do the word justice because I'm not talking about a smattering of parsley leaves here. A *guarnición* can be a few olives artfully arranged, as in the case of my sandwich, or perhaps some roasted tomatoes or glazed onions for that lone piece of meat. Individual dishes get their decoration too. For example, in the case of soup, the cook might add a few lines of heavy cream, croutons, minced parsley, or an herbal sprig. A nice table setting, food that has been artfully arranged rather than plopped onto a plate, a couple of mint leaves, some lemon slices . . . these are all nice touches that turn eating into dining. *¡Que aproveche!*

Whenever possible, I like menus in which the bulk of the work can be done ahead of time. The point of having friends and family over to eat is to enjoy their company in the presence of good food and that's hard to do if the hosts are sequestered in the kitchen. So plan ahead, cook ahead, and when everyone arrives, join the party, and savor the fruits of your labor!

A Tapas Party

No-prep tapas: a selection of dry-cured Spanish sausages, such as chorizo, *lomo*, and *salchichón* (available online); thin slices of serrano ham; a cheese board with assorted Spanish cheeses; *Largueta* almonds (available online); a bread basket with baguette slices

Tapas that can be made ahead of time: Marinated Green Olives (page 202); Shellfish Vinaigrette (page 216); Spanish Omelet (page 222); Egg Tapa (page 203)

Tapas with some last-minute preparation: Chicken Croquettes (page 210); Spicy Potatoes (page 207)

Tapas that must be prepared on the spot: Clams in White Wine Sauce (page 29); Batter-Fried Squid Rings (page 214)

Choose from an assortment of drinks, such as beer, *cava*, dry sherry (*fino*), red and white wines, and/or mineral water.

A Paella Dinner

Start by setting out a variety of tapas (all make-ahead), including thin slices of serrano ham, *Manchego* cheese, *Manzanilla* and *Arbequina* olives, Mussels in Vinaigrette (page 215), and Spanish Omelet (page 222). For drinks, serve dry sherry (*fino*), beer, and mineral water on ice, which guests can help themselves to. For dinner, chilled *gazpacho* (page 167), Chicken and Seafood Paella (page 122) washed down with icy cold *sangría* (page 243), and to finish the meal, dessert and coffee in one, *blanco y negro* (page 245).

A Buffet-Style Cookout with Spanish Flavors

Set up a tub of ice with drinks that guests can serve themselves, including beer, mineral water, dry white wine, and soft drinks. A few tapas to get things started: the no-prep variety, such as olives, a cheeseboard with a selection of Spanish cheeses, potato chips (fried in olive oil, of course), slices of chorizo sausage, and a Tuna Pie (page 17), cut in small squares. Arrange a selection of salads; for example, Marinated Cod and Lobster Salad (page 33), Melon with Serrano Ham (page 220), and Spanish Potato Salad (page 206). Fire up the barbecue and grill some *butifarra* sausages and Spanish-Style Kebabs (page 162). For dessert, Cheese Custard (page 54) and Cream Cookies (page 195).

A Brunch Menu

For appetizers serve *Marcona* almonds (available online), Bread with Tomato and Olive Oil (page 110) with thin slices of serrano ham, Ham-Stuffed Mushroom Caps (page 65), and Chorizo Sausages in Cider (page 28). Once guests are seated, serve Tomato and Pepper Salad (page 166), Stuffed Eggs with Béchamel Sauce (page 204), and Sweetbread with Sugar and Pine Nut Topping (page 152). To drink, serve *cava*.

A Seafood Dinner with the Flavors of the Mediterranean

Seafood-Flavored Rice (page 127) with Green Salad, Spanish-Style (page 219)
Sea Bream Baked in Salt with Alioli (page 134)
Catalan Custard (page 150)

A Meat Dinner with the Flavors of Andalusia

Almond and Pine Nut Soup (page 169)
Honey-Glazed Lamb (page 179)
Rich Caramel Custard (page 180)

A Chicken Dinner with the Flavors of Castile

Garlic Soup (page 68)
Chicken in Saffron-Scented Sherry Sauce with Almonds (page 89)
Fresh Cheese with Walnuts and Honey (page 101)

A Hearty Winter Dinner with the Flavors of Asturias

Green Salad, Spanish-Style (page 219)
Asturian Bean Stew (page 37)
Rice Pudding (page 56)

INDEX

Argentina Cooks! *Expanded Edition*
Shirley Lomax Brooks

Argentine cuisine is one of the world's best-kept culinary secrets. As a result, a great variety of foods are available—lamb, an incredible assortment of fish and seafood, exotic fruits, and prime quality beef. Inside are sophisticated culinary offerings like *Pavita Relleno a la Criolla* (Roast Turkey with Persimmon, Sausage, and Jalapeño Stuffing) and *Gaspado de Cazador* (Game Stew with Wild Rabbit, Partridges, Quail, and Gin), as well as home-style favorites like *Gazpacho de Mesopotamia* (Raw Vegetables in Chicken Broth and Fresh Lime Juice). The 190 recipes are all adapted for the North American kitchen. Complete with black-and-white photographs and illustrations.

ISBN 0-7818-0997-5 · $24.95

Brazil: A Culinary Journey
Cherie Hamilton

The largest nation in South America, Brazil is home to vast rain forests, pristine tropical beaches, the Amazon River, and one of the region's most interesting cuisines. The recipes presented in *Brazil: A Culinary Journey* provide a glimpse into the surprisingly diverse repertoire of Brazilian cooking, from the heavily African-influenced cuisine of the Northeast to the Southern cookery. More than 130 recipes range from *Feijoada*, Brazil's national dish of beans, rice, and various meats (in its many regional variations), to lesser-known dishes, such as Shrimp and Bread Pudding, Crab Soup, and Banana Brittle. With more than 130 recipes, this cookbook is features black-and-white illustrations, photographs, and maps.

ISBN 0-7818-1080-9 · $24.95

Aprovecho: A Mexican-American Border Cookbook
Teresa Cordero-Cordell and Robert Cordell

This book will entertain and enlighten readers about life along the Border. In addition to more than 250 recipes, *Aprovecho* includes special sections that relate popular legends such as "La Llorona and the Chupacabra," explain how tequila is made, and provide instructions for making your own festive piñatas. Also included are a glossary of chiles and cooking terms, and a Mexican pantry list so you'll always be prepared for a fiesta! Complete with black-and-white photographs.

ISBN 978-0-7818-1206-1 · $16.95pb

My Mother's Bolivian Kitchen
José Sánchez-H.

More than a cookbook, *My Mother's Bolivian Kitchen* is a memoir of a Bolivian childhood. Along with recipes for everything from *salteñas* (Meat-Filled Pastries) and quinoa soup to *picante de pollo* (Spicy Chicken), Sánchez-H. shares many poignant childhood memories. Come to Aunt Nazaria's sixty-ninth birthday party to feast on *picante de pato con chuño* (Spicy Duck with Freeze-Dried Potatoes); to observe El Día de Todos Santos (All Saints' Day), when traditional shaped breads are baked in honor of the deceased; and camping in the mountains, where the memory of his mother's food leads him home. Complete with black-and white photographs, illustrations, and maps.

ISBN 0-7818-1056-6 · $24.95

Tasting Chile: A Celebration of Authentic Chilean Foods and Wines
Daniel Joelson

Tasting Chile puts the native cuisine into context by describing staple ingredients and the influences other countries and cultures have had upon it. These exotic ingredients are described and substitutes are provided so that every recipe may be prepared in an American kitchen. The book includes a section on Chilean wines, and wine recommendations appear throughout. *Tasting Chile* contains more than 140 traditional recipes from this fascinating nation, spanning a variety of dishes that range from spicy salsas and hearty soups to the ubiquitous empanada and *manjar*-based (Carmel Cream) desserts. Complete with black-and-white photographs.

ISBN 0-7818-1028-0 · $24.95

Secrets of Colombian Cooking
Patricia McCausland-Gallo

Secrets of Colombian Cooking provides a window into the diverse cuisine of this little-known South American nation. Author Patricia McCausland-Gallo, a native Colombian, traveled throughout the many regions of Colombia to gather the most authentic dishes. *Secrets of Colombian Cooking* presents the wide spectrum of Colombian cuisine to home cooks in more than 175 inviting recipes from simple, hearty sancochos (soups and stews prepared differently in every region) to more exotic fare such as Langosta al Coco (Lobster in Coconut Sauce) and Ají de Uchuvas (Yellow Gooseberry Sauce). Complete with black-and-white photographs.

ISBN 0-7818-1025-6 · $24.95

Corsican Cuisine
Arthur L. Meyer

Corsican cuisine draws on French, Italian, Spanish, and North African influences while remaining fiercely distinct. Using fresh ingredients to create complex flavors, these 100 authentic recipes make simple and satisfying fare. Try your hand at traditional staples like garlic soup, ragout of game hen with myrtle, and wild boar meatballs with roasted red peppers. Or satisfy your sweet tooth with Chestnut Beignets and sweet cheese-filled turnovers. Also included are a 16 page color photo insert, and a glossary of Corsican foods and culinary terms.

ISBN 978-0-7818-1248-1 · $35.00

Old Havana Cookbook (Bilingual)

Havana is one of the oldest and most picturesque cities of the western hemisphere. It was a popular winter destination for North American tourists in the 1950s, and this cookbook recaptures the spirit of Old Havana—*Habana la vieja*—and its celebrated culinary traditions. Cuban cuisine, though derived from its mother country, Spain, has been modified and refined by locally available foods like pork, rice, corn, beans and sugar, and the requirements of a tropical climate. Fine Gulf Stream fish, crabs, lobsters, tropical fruits also have their places on the traditional Cuban table.

ISBN 0-7818-0767-0 · $14.95

Cuisines of Portuguese Encounters, *Expanded Edition*
Cherie Hamilton

From famous dishes like spicy pork vindaloo from Goa, the classic bacalhau of Portugal, and all varieties of feijoada, to lesser-known treats like Guinean oyster stew and coconut pudding from East Timor, this cookbook has something for every adventurous gastronome. The 8-page section of color photographs brings the recipes to life! Menus for religious holidays and festive occasions, a glossary of terms, a section on mail-order resources, and a bilingual index will assist the home chef in celebrating the rich, diverse, and delicious culinary legacy of this old empire.

ISBN 978-0-7818-1181-1 · $29.95

Mastering Spanish with 2 Audio CDs, Second Edition
ISBN 0-7818-1064-7 · $24.95pb

Spanish-English/English-Spanish Pocket Legal Dictionary
ISBN 978-0-7818-1214-6 · $19.95pb

Spanish-English/English-Spanish Children's Picture Dictionary
625 entries · ISBN 0-7818-1130-9 · $14.95pb

Chilenismos-English/English-Chilenismos Dictionary & Phrasebook
1,500 entries · ISBN 0-7818-1062-0 · $13.95pb

Emergency Spanish Phrasebook
ISBN 0-7818-0977-0 · $5.95pb

Hippocrene Children's Illustrated Spanish Dictionary
500 entries · ISBN 978-0-7818-0889-7 ·$14.95pb

Spanish-English/English-Spanish (Latin American) Compact Dictionary
3,800 entries · ISBN 0-7818-1041-3 · $9.95pb

Spanish-English/English-Spanish (Latin American) Concise Dictionary
8,000 entries · ISBN 0-7818-0261-X · $12.95pb

Spanish-English/English-Spanish Practical Dictionary
35,000 entries · ISBN 0-7818-0179-6 · $12.95pb

Spanish False Friends
ISBN 0-7818-11783 · $19.95pb

Spanish Learner's Dictionary: Spanish-English/English –Spanish
14,000 entries · ISBN 0-7818-0937-1 · $14.95pb

Beginner's Basque with 2 Audio CDs
ISBN 978-0-7818-1227-6 · $26.95
Book only: ISBN 978-0-7818-0933-9 · $14.95

Basque-English/English-Basque Dictionary & Phrasebook
4,000 entries · ISBN 0-7818-0622-4 · $11.95pb

Catalan-English/English-Catalan Dictionary & Phrasebook
Available Spring 2011
4,000 entries · ISBN 978-0-7818-1258-0 · $13.95pb

Ladino-English/English-Ladino (Judeo-Spanish) Concise Encyclopedic Dictionary
ISBN 0-7818-0658-5 · $29.95pb

Beginner's Ladino with 2 Audio CDs
ISBN 978-0-7818-1225-2 · $29.95pb

Prices subject to change without prior notice. **To purchase Hippocrene Books** contact your local bookstore, visit www.hippocrenebooks.com, call (212) 685-4373, or write to: HIPPOCRENE BOOKS, 171 Madison Avenue, New York, NY 10016.